Reviewing the Covenant

SUNY Series in Jewish Philosophy

Kenneth Seeskin, Editor

Reviewing the Covenant

Eugene B. Borowitz and the Postmodern Renewal of Jewish Theology

Peter Ochs, editor,
with Eugene B. Borowitz

Including responses by:
Yudit Kornberg Greenberg
Susan Handelman
David Novak
Thomas Ogletree
Norbert Samuelson
Edith Wyschogrod

State University of New York Press

Published by
State University of New York Press, Albany

© 2000 State University of New York

For information, address State University of New York Press,
State University Plaza, Albany, N.Y., 12246

Production by Michael Haggett
Marketing by Anne M. Valentine

Library of Congress Cataloging-in-Publication Data
Reviewing the covenant : Eugene B. Borowitz and the postmodern revival of
    Jewish theology / edited by Peter Ochs with Eugene Borowitz.
        p.   cm. — (SUNY series in Jewish philosophy)
    Includes bibliographical references and index.
    ISBN 0–7914–4533-X (hc. : alk. paper). — ISBN 0–7914–4534–8 (pb. :
alk. paper)
    1. Borowitz, Eugene B. Renewing the covenant.   2. Judaism—20th
century.   3. Commandments (Judaism)—History of doctrines—20th
century   4. Covenants—Religious aspects—Judaism—History of
doctrines—20th century.   5.   Postmodernism—Religious aspects—
Judaism.   I. Ochs, Peter, 1950–   .   II. Borowitz, Eugene B.
III. Series.
BM601.B623R48   2000
296.3—dc21   99–37866
                                                                 CIP

10 9 8 7 6 5 4 3 2 1

Contents

Readings of the Readings

Postmodern Theological Renewal: A Meditation

Preface

For decades, Eugene B. Borowitz has served as rabbi for America's liberal Jewish congregations, philosophic theologian for its liberal rabbis, and philosopher-rabbi for its Jewish intellectuals. His is one of the few voices heard and loved among all genres of Jewish life, from congregants to philanthropic institutional workers, to rabbis, to academics. It is also one of the few voices that speak across temporal bounds, as well as institutional ones. Known for so many years as a philosophic and rabbinic spokesperson for the ideals of modern Judaism, Rabbi Borowitz has, in the past decade and a half, begun to speak as well to American Judaism in what he calls its "postmodern condition." In *Renewing the Covenant: A Theology for the Postmodern Jew*, he declares an end to the epoch of modern Jewry's efforts to identify its norms with enlightened reason's search for humanity's universal ideals. Disillusioned with that search, he says "and still in the shadow of Holocaust, we turn again to Judaism's classical traditions and texts and beliefs," not to turn our backs on the redeeming aspects of modernity, but to re-commit that modernity to the Covenant from which it had lost its way. A bold turn, indeed, and one which has already helped recenter discussions of theology and religious conduct throughout the Reform movement. New questions are now on the agenda of liberal Jewish inquiry: Who is a postmodern Jew? How does she differ from the modern Jew and the traditional Jew? What does it mean to speak today of "Jewish theology"? What happens to reason when we speak of renewing the Covenant? How can it be renewed after Shoa?

These are pressing questions for everyday Jewish practice. But they are also heated questions for the Jewish academy. The new visions of Gene Borowitz the Rabbi-theologian are also the new arguments of Gene

Borowitz the philosopher-Jew, and these are arguments that make his work of urgent significance for contemporary Jewish academics, as well as their Christian peers.

In this volume, Rabbi Borowitz' fellow academics receive his recent work in the academics' privileged language of love, which is a language of intense intellectual analysis, challenge, response, and dialogue. Here are leading Jewish scholars—and a Christian scholar—who are also driven to reconsider the relation of reason and religion in a postmodern age. Seeking, on the side of the university, to challenge Western academic presumptions about the dividing line between disciplined reason and religious / communal life, these scholars are warmed by Prof. Borowitz' complementary efforts to maintain the religious community's engagements with reason as well as tradition. And they are prepared to meet the challenge of his claims about just what "postmodernity" may mean to the practicing Jew. So they engage him here, in shared argument, and analysis, and care, and study. General readers may need to brace themselves here and there, since the academics gathered here have been stimulated to bursts of rather abstract thinking, but more rigid academics may need to brace themselves as well; for the abstract is wedded on these pages to the concrete, the philosophic to the empirical, the conceptual to the moment of faith. The style of religious philosophy on the pages may also be surprising; for Gene Borowitz has stimulated his colleagues to interactive, friendly, and dialogic expressions of their rigorous habits of reasoning.

In these meetings of academy and community, modernity and rabbinic covenant, rabbi and philosopher, we may very well see a glimpse of a new approach for the academy as well as a new discipline for everyday Jewish religion.

Before proceeding to the conversation, perhaps some of you may like to hear first a little more formally about the conversation leader. David Ellenson has recently written a biographical tribute to Gene Borowitz and, with the biographer's indulgence, we'll excerpt form his tribute the following, brief biographical sketch:

Eugene Borowitz received his B.A. from Ohio State University; was ordained rabbi in 1948 by Hebrew Union College in Cincinnati, which also awarded him the degree of Doctor of Hebrew Letters in 1950. He also received the Ed.D in 1962 from Columbia University. During the 1950s, Professor Borowitz served as founding rabbi of The Community

Synagogue in Port Washington, Long Island. After serving as Director of Religious Education for the Union of American Hebrew Congregations, he joined the faculty of the Hebrew Union College-Jewish Institute of Religion in 1962. He remains there as Sigmund L. Falk Distinguished Professor of Jewish Education and Religious Thought. Gaining national reputation through the 1960s through his many journal articles, as well as his emerging role as theologian of the Reform Movement, he introduced his systematic statement of an existentialist theology of Judaism through three books in 1968–69: *A New Jewish Theology in the Making, A Layman's Guide to Religious Existentialism,* and *How Can a Jew Speak of Faith Today?* Some ten books later, the "postmodern" phase of Borowitz' theological project began to appear explicitly, in the early 1990s, in chapters of *Exploring Jewish Ethics* and in the second edition of *Choices in Modern Jewish Thought.* (See David Ellenson, "Eugene B. Borowitz: A Tribute On the Occasion of His 70th Birthday, *Jewish Book Annual,* Vol. 51 [1993–94]: 125–136.)

In closing, we are grateful to Gene Borowitz himself for sitting for this academic portrait. With his customary grace, he consented to contribute his own energies to a project that should simply have been done for him. We are grateful to the editor of this State University of New York series, Kenneth Seeskin, for giving encouragement and insightful counsel on this project beyond the call of any editor's duty. Prof. Seeskin's editorial commentary led to significant improvements in the intellectual clarity and reader-friendliness of the book. Our thanks to James Peltz of State University of New York Press, for caring editorial oversight. Our thanks to Lara Covington for her persistently insightful work as editorial assistant to the entire book project. Our thanks to Gerald Ochs, of SCMC/Editorial Services, for preparing the final text for publication, and to Suzanne Esterson, for preparing the index. And our gratitude for underwriting assistance from a research fund of the UAHC.

Introductory

1

The Emergence of Postmodern Jewish Theology and Philosophy

PETER OCHS

In *Renewing the Covenant: A Theology for the Postmodern Jew* (JPS 1991), the renowned Jewish theologian, Eugene B. Borowitz, offers a history of his intellectual and spiritual calling to serve as philosophical pastor to Jews in a postmodern world. He has been so influential and representative a modern Jewish thinker that this personal odyssey illustrates the emergence of postmodern Judaism in general: from its complaints against the religious authorities of the past, through its disillusionments with modernity's secular vision of the future, to its efforts now to renew the present by re-reading the past.[1] Jewish modernists may have sought to abandon traditional teachings about Torah, God, and Israel. Rather than abandon Jewish modernism, Borowitz rereads it in terms of these teachings, introducing Jewish postmodernism as the relational life—or covenant—that binds Jewish modernity to the traditions of its past, rather than as an alternative to either.

If Borowitz' narrative is to be read in this way, then its theory of renewal is a theory of rereading, and its own virtues will be displayed through the ways in which it is reread, rather than through any single attempt to portray its intrinsic meaning. In only three years after its publication (when this book was conceived), Borowitz' work already attracted a family of readings; it has been the subject of two conference sessions and

ten journal reviews. This means that it was soon possible to read Borowitz'
book through its effects rather than just its words: simultaneously reading
the book and re-reading its initial *readings*—to read it *along with* a community of fellow readers, rather than reading it alone. This, in fact, is the
subject of this volume: a study of the *reception* of Borowitz' book by the
community of postmodern Jewish theologians who, gathered around and
alongside Borowitz, have begun the task of both reviewing and renewing
the Jewish covenant in a postmodern world.

    *Reviewing the Covenant: Eugene Borowitz and the Postmodern Renewal
of Jewish Theology* is postmodern in both its subject matter and method.
The authors participate in an emergent community of thinkers, first gathered in 1991 as members of the *Postmodern Jewish Philosophy Network:* an
electronic dialogue network and quarterly journal devoted to articulating
the varieties of Jewish philosophy that have emerged after the demise of
the dominant modern paradigms of Kantian or transcendental Jewish
thought—including their existentialist, phenomenological, and analytic
expressions. In this book, the postmodern thinkers reason about Borowitz'
way of renewing the classic Jewish themes of Torah, Covenant, God,
Commandment, the people Israel, and Evil. They reason through their
own manner of renewing the classic Jewish methods of commentary, response, interpretation, and redacted dialogue. And they reason in light of
postmodern concerns with Holocaust, conceptual imperialism, deconstruction, feminism, pluralism, and life-after-disillusionment.

    Since this is a book that re-reads Borowitz, some readers may want to
have a first look at *Renewing the Covenant* before proceeding. Other readers, however, may enjoy these re-readings as an introduction to Borowitz'
project: reading from effects back to cause, the way traditional students
might read rabbinic commentaries before the biblical text, or the way
Franz Rosenzweig says he reads books from their concluding chapters
back to their beginnings. In this case, such reading back will be both clarified, enriched, and complicated (or "doubly coded," to anticipate Edith
Wyschogrod's words) by the ways Borowitz' readers both teach his basic
claims, celebrate his overall project, and also raise questions about this or
that element of it.

    There is some drama behind these questions. Here is the great theolo-
gian and moralist of liberal Judaism, known for his Kantian-like concern
for universal ethics and later for his Jewish existentialism—a scholar of

modern Jewish philosophy, but always attentive as well to everyday life in the American Jewish communities—a social commentator, pastoral teacher, and rabbi to Reform rabbis. What is he doing in the company of, at times, highly specialized academic postmodernists, denizens of deconstruction and suspicion—albeit within the context of religious studies, Jewish thought, and also Christian theology? And what is their interest in him? Can Reform Judaism really participate in the postmodern critique of religious rationalism and of universalizing ethics? Can liberal Judaism more broadly take part in the specifically Jewish postmodern and post-Holocaust turn toward ethnic and religious particularity and communalism? Can academic postmodernists, on the other hand, really share in an effort to renew theology, and a Jewish-Covenantal theology at that?

These questions animate all of the chapters to follow, as leading thinkers on religion and postmodernism enter into a lively dialogue with Borowitz' book and as Borowitz responds to them. In the second chapter of this introductory section, Gene Borowitz offers an opening account of the terms he brings to the dialogue: what Jewish postmodernism and Jewish theology mean to him. In this first chapter, I offer an opening thesis: not to anticipate or prejudge the debates to follow, but perhaps to raise the stakes. My thesis is that this volume exhibits the complementary challenges faced today by both liberal Judaism (and liberal religion) on the one hand and academic, postmodern Judaism (and postmodern religion) on the other hand. Liberal Judaism's challenge is to recover text- and tradition- and community-based religiosity while maintaining its respect for the dignity of the individual person, for Jewish moral obligations to the non-Jew, and for standards of rational discourse among communities and traditions. This is a difficult challenge, because Jewish communalism appears to conflict with liberal doctrines of individual rights and of universal ethics, and text-based religiosity appears to conflict with liberal standards for rational discourse. Postmodern Judaism's challenge is to maintain its disciplined criticisms of modernism while also recovering bases for individual moral agency, for trans-national or trans-communal standards of reason and of ethics, and for referring to love of (and relationship or obedience to) God as a legitimate element of public discourse. While leaving detailed analyses for the chapters to follow, I will say a little more here about these postmodern challenges; the terminologies are so abstruse and controversial that readers would most likely welcome some preliminary definitions. Readers must bear in mind that, in the postmodern context, to offer a definition is also to make a choice among possible meanings and, therefore, to assert some thesis: the definitions I propose here, or that I borrow from Borowitz' work, may be modified or even controverted by other authors in this volume!

Modernism: We might start by using the term to refer to a complex of values and behaviors that have accompanied the world hegemony of Western (and to some extent northern) European civilization in the seventeenth through the twentieth century. This complex includes the emergence of mercantilism, capitalism, the search for worldwide economic resources and markets, the Industrial Revolution, the nation-state and its variously parliamentary, autocratic, or totalitarian governments; the liberal ideals of individual autonomy, individual and universal rights, and democracy; as well as the various socialist ideals that emerged from and came to oppose the liberal ideals. When academic postmodernists refer critically to "modernism," they are usually referring to some set of anachronistic, inflexible, and now demonstrably harmful societal values and behaviors that have emerged from this complex and that continue to be reinforced through patterns of political, economic, and *academic* behavior as well. Different postmodernists characterize the harmful elements of modernism in different ways and offer different remedies for them. Among the more typical targets of opprobrium are:

Epistemological Foundationalism: This refers, first, to what the pragmatist John Dewey called "the quest for certainty": the desire of individual modern thinkers to achieve personal certainty about the universe they inhabit and what they are to do in it. It is associated, next, with what the philosopher Richard Bernstein has dubbed "the Cartesian Anxiety": a fear that we will, ultimately, find no order to this universe at all unless we, as clear-visioned individual thinkers, can see for ourselves what is true and what is false and, therefore, have our own indisputable criterion for distinguishing between them. Bernstein's insight is that this hyperbolic need to know is associated, not with the human condition, but with a particular psychosocial condition in the modern West: associated with the absence of strong social bonds and functional traditions and, thus, with the compensatory desire to salve the individual consciousness with rational certainty as substitute for relationship, behavioral purpose, and love. Bernstein's analysis is influenced, in part, by what may be the first, postmodern-like critique of Cartesian efforts to discover an Archimedean point on which all knowledge could be based. This is the American philosopher Charles Peirce's critique of what he called the "Cartesian tendency" in modern science and logic and ethics, which is to believe that knowledge is grounded in individual intuitions that are self-legitimating: such as the naive realist's belief that "I see what I see and it must be so," or the idealist philosopher's belief that "with my disciplined powers, I see clearly and distinctly certain universal propositions of logic," or with the biblical literalist's belief that "the text means just what it says, and I know directly what it plainly says." Ludwig Wittgenstein and his students have since given postmodernists the terminology of "foundationalism" per se and of the studies that correct it, particularly of natural languages and their inherent vaguenesses of meaning.

Individualism, Atomism, and Egoism: Beginning with Peirce, the early postmodernists also criticized the individualist theories of ethics, metaphysics, and psychology that are inseparable from the foundationalist theory of knowledge. Peirce and Dewey offered Aristotelian-like arguments about the social character of human beings. Wittgenstein criticized the illusory character of doctrines of private knowledge and private language. The early Jewish postmodernists, from Martin Buber through Emmanuel Levinas, directed much of their criticism against the egocentric ethics and metaphysics of modernism.

Self-presence: Just as Peirce criticized the modernist notion of self-legitimating intuition, so Jacques Derrida has criticized the myth of self-presence that is implicit in modern metaphysics: the belief that the real makes itself known to its observer and, thus, that knowledge is a function of self-disclosure. For Derrida, this belief displays the effort of Western metaphysicians, classic through modern, to identify signs with their objects and, thus, appropriate the sign's deferred presence: as if the object could be possessed, wholly, now; or as if, in the terms of Martin Buber's related criticism, we could possess the things we know, as "Its" captured by our "I's." The postmodern critique of self-presence necessarily leads to some theory of signs, or semiotic: if things do not simply make themselves known to us, then we must come to know them by interpreting the signs of which they are objects. Knowing entails interpreting. Languages are not the only sign systems we know (there is knowledge without language), but they are the ones we know best. For this reason, postmodern studies of knowledge tend to begin, and sometimes end, with studies of language. While languages are both oral and written, written languages illustrate more readily the distance between signs and their absent objects, and oral discourse illustrates more readily the give-and-take that is part of the activity of receiving and interpreting signs. For these reasons, perhaps, postmodern theorists tend to adopt the model of written language to illustrate their theories of interpretation in place of self-presence, and they tend to adopt the model of oral speech to illustrate their dialogic, rather than static, theories of how interpretation works. In either case, postmodern theorists are also attentive to the multidimensionality of any activity of interpretation. For one, there is enough distance between sign and object that the signs may point to it in more than one way; for two, a given sign may point to, or reflect the influences of, more than one object; for three, we who read the sign may bring to our reading more than one interest, or more than one habit or rule of interpretation.

Universalism: A recurrent postmodern theme is that modernist thinkers attribute "objectivity" and "universality" to their own subjective interpretations of the world around them, thereby overgeneralizing the domain of their own knowledge and veiling its dependence on some finite context of knowledge and interpretation. One theory is that this reflects the modernists' "Cartesian anxiety": overly suspicious of their own traditions of knowledge and relation, modernists seek hyperbolic reassurance that what they believe must be *the* truth. A related theory is that the modernists' individualism *and* foundationalism both lead them to believe that knowledge must be unreliable if it is not ultimately self-evident and, if self-evident, it must be so for all observers universally. The various postmodern alternatives tend to emphasize the probabilistic, social and context-related character of human knowing; from this perspective, the polarities "universal *vs.* individual" represent abstract ideals of little use in understanding how we actually know the world or know others.

Master Narratives: François Lyotard has introduced the term "master narratives" to refer to the West's efforts to privilege certain models for human behavior, as if these models were self-evidently necessary or good for all humans. His critique, adopted by many recent postmodern theorists, is that, by way of such narratives, ruling classes or dominant subcultures insert self-promoting world views into Western societies without offering those views, overtly, for inspection or argument. The critique here is not necessarily of the content of such narratives, but of their use as means of covert social control. Lyotard is calling for them to be subject to self-conscious disclosure and examination. Unexamined, such narratives function for an entire subculture the way self-legitimating intuitions function for the modernist individual: reinforcing assumptions uncritically, but under the guise of some description or account of the world. In Edith Wyschogrod's terms (from a previous essay), the postmodernist complains that modern philosophy's

> thought constellations are concealed narratives that lay claim to . . . being all-encompassing frameworks into which the contingencies of aberrant experience and social and linguistic context are stretched to fit and must be interpreted as such.[2]

Colonialism and Imperialism: According to postmodern critics, modernist epistemology and ethics have tended to generate, or at least accompany, hyperbolic political and social agendas. Some examples are the need to solve a social problem by overturning, rather than reforming, a particular social system, followed by a need to advertise, share, and then perhaps impose the same method of revolution on all neighboring societies as well. In general, the political and ethical criticisms of modern Western colonialism complement the previous epistemological criticisms: the problem, once again, is located in efforts to objectify and universalize the perceptions, beliefs, or, in this case, communal or national policies of some social entity—individual, group, or institution—that is not merely finite, but also individuated, or separated from relation to other such entities.

Postmodernists: There are many different claimants to the title "postmodernist." In her chapter, Wyschogrod alludes to the origins of the term in turn of the century architecture and the dominant, contemporary use of the term to refer to the work of certain French thinkers (Derrida, Lyotard, and Michel Foucault prominent among them), to genres of literary criticism associated with them, and with related cultural critics on the Continent and, more recently, in the United States. Self-described "postmodern" Jewish *and* Christian religious thinkers are not, however, necessarily loyal to the dominant academic uses of the term. In our case, I find it helpful to distinguish among several, different claimants to the title "postmodern" and to imagine their being arrayed in something like the following continuum of movements: what I will label secular academic postmodernists placed arbitrarily on the left, neo-Orthodox somewhat anti-academic post- or anti-moderns on the right, and other variants, including postmodern Jewish theology somewhere in-between. Over the past eight years, members of the Society for Textual Reasoning have, to varying degrees, adopted all of these movements as conversation partners. I provide somewhat more detail for the latter movements on this list, because readers may be less accustomed to identifying them as "postmodernists" *and* because their postmodernism may prove to be closest, in the end, to Borowitz'.

French or Continental: Secular academic postmodernists. Derrida, Lyotard, and Foucault are the most quoted, with influences from Franco-German critical philosophy, Marxism, phenomenology, existentialism, and Ferdinand de Saussure's linguistic distinction between sign *(signe)* and signified *(signifié)*. Emphasizing the disclosure of covert power relations, totalizing assumptions, and also layers of conflicting, "double-coded" meanings behind the West's dominant narratives, including those expressed in the form of philosophic argument or scientific analysis. In his contributions to this volume, Borowitz will clarify which aspects of postmodern criticism he shares with the French school and which aspects he does not share.

Varieties of Literary Criticism: Secular academic postmodernists, in the United States and Europe, who adopt the French theories as bases for deconstructing modern literature, as well as for identifying various forms of modern expression, including philosophy, *as* literature. Includes critics who emphasize psychology, Julia Kristeva, feminist theory, Luce Irigaray, and semiotics, Gilles Deleuze.

American Neopragmatists: Academic postmodernists, for the most part secular, primarily in the United States. These are philosophically trained social critics, such as Richard Rorty, Jeffrey Stout, and Cornell West, who re-read the pragmatists William James and, especially, John Dewey, as precursors to the French postmodernists. They tend to rewrite modern philosophy into a form of literary criticism, but applied to the broadest set of cultural forms, especially political discourse.

American Pragmatists: Academic philosophers with postmodern tendencies, mostly secular, but including religious philosophers (such as the Jewish thinkers Mordecai Kaplan and Max Kadushin, and the Christian thinkers Reinhold Neibuhr and John E. Smith). Like the neo-pragmatists, they reinvoke the classical pragmatists, including Charles Peirce, but do not interpret the pragmatists' critique of modern philosophy to signal the end of philosophy, ethics, or metaphysics as legitimate disciplines. They believe it is possible to place these rational disciplines in the service of so-cial criticism and reform, without risking foundationalism, false universal-ism, or philosophic individualism. In their logic of problem-solving, prag-matists tend today to make use of a form of sign-theory, or semiotics, that is unlike the Continental model, because it is based on a three-part dis-tinction of sign/meaning/context-of-interpretation, rather than de Saussure's two-part distinction of sign/signification. This approach draws the pragmatists close to Wittgenstein, who replaces logic with grammars of natural language, and to Rosenzweig, who replaces logic with what seems to be the grammatical/semiotic study of "speech thinking" *(Sprach-denken)*. By way of illustration, I believe that the kind of postmodernism Borowitz envisions is compatible with a religious pragmatism.

American Process Theologians: Academic, religious philosophers with post-modern tendencies, who base their critique of modern philosophy and modern culture on the work of Alfred North Whitehead, or later Charles Harteshorne. Most are Christian, but there are significant Jewish thinkers as well (such as Norbert M. Samuelson), who associate the work of Mor-decai Kaplan (and to some degree Max Kadushin) as much with process thought as with pragmatism. Like the pragmatists, process thinkers com-bine their critique of modern philosophic foundationalism, individual-ism, and totalism with a persistent trust in the usefulness of philosophic disciplines to solve problems of ethics and social life. Like the pragmatists, they make use of a logic that emphasizes relations over atoms or individu-als. Many pragmatists, however, tend to criticize the process thinkers' metaphysical system-building as overly general, or universalistic in the modern fashion. Borowitz would share in this criticism, as well as in a cri-tique of the process thinkers' naturalistic understanding of God. Nonethe-less, some aspects of Borowitz' vision may remain compatible with some aspects of Jewish process thought.

Christian Postliberal Theologians: Academic theologians whose work and influence extends outside academe to clergy and congregants. The most well-known post-liberals are sometimes labeled the "Yale school." These are colleagues and students of the Yale professors, Hans Frei and George Lindbeck, who derive from Karl Barth and other sources, including Wittgenstein and the anthropologist Clifford Geertz, an argument for a postmodern renewal of the theological programs of Martin Luther and John Calvin as well as of the early Church. Frei invokes deconstruction's "immanent subversion" of modern totalism and foundationalism. He argues, however, that such subversion is misapplied to classical Christian *or* rabbinic hermeneutics. Postmodern criticism should apply only to the West's efforts to universalize, or over-extend, finite conceptual constructions, but biblical religion lends authority to traditions of interpreting texts whose meanings cannot be limited to any finite conceptual constructions. Lindbeck criticizes efforts *within* the Christian biblical tradition to identify the meaning of Scripture with either propositional statements (such as "God is *x* or *y*") or with expressions of experience (such as claims that God is known through experiences of the "numinous"); such meaning inheres only in what he calls "cultural-linguistic" traditions of practice, or of living according to the Bible as a rule of life. Borowitz' postmodern approach to Judaism may correspond in many ways to this postliberal approach to Christianity.

What then, of *Jewish postmodernism*? Within that, what of the *postmodern Jewish philosophy* of most of this book's respondents? And what, finally, of Borowitz' *postmodern Jewish theology*? I hope that this expanded list of self-described "postmodern" options may already have suggested to the reader additional ways of answering the questions raised earlier about Borowitz' relation to the postmodern movement. The rest of this chapter will serve as an introduction to the specifically *Jewish* view of modernism that Borowitz offers. Since this Jewish view is not identical to the *general academic* view described above, it may offer readers an even more expanded context for interpreting this volume's dialogue among different kinds of biblical and of Jewish postmodern inquiry.

A JEWISH VIEW OF MODERNISM

One subject of this volume is Borowitz' *movement* from a modernist to a postmodernist approach to theology. Even in his earlier work, however, Borowitz rejected the thoroughgoing *constructivism* of the modern West:

that is, the effort to build theological, philosophic, and ethical systems *de nouveau*, directly out of the creative faculty of the human mind. The alternative is to enlist human reason, hermeneutically, as critic, commentator, and editor of received knowledge. While Borowitz has joined his theology to the contemporary hermeneutics of rabbinic texts and of Scripture, his prior and still significant focus has been on a hermeneutics of history and of social practice. As I read him, he has not turned from a liberal conceptualist (adopting certain philosophic principles as privileged rules for interpreting the meaning and norms of Jewish tradition) to some post-liberal textualist for whom the words of Bible or Talmud replace the first principles of reason. I would say, instead, that he began as and remains a liberal Jewish theologian whose first principles are defined by the way *clal yisrael*, in its historical situation, can best live its Covenant with God, and, more specifically, about how American Jews can best live a non-Orthodox, religious life. From this perspective, his postmodern turn concerns his judgment about the interpretive tools that the community of Israel uses in its efforts to understand Torah and God's will. He has always been "post-modern" in the sense of interpreting Torah from within the historical context of Israel's life, rather than from out of certain privileged principles. In his early work, however, he respected the significant role of several conceptualized principles of interpretation *within* the community of American, liberal Jews. In the last decade or two, he has observed this community's loss of faith in such principles; he now reassures the community that it can maintain its covenantal religiosity *and* its non-Orthodoxy by replacing those principles with the family of interpretive practices that he discusses in his book and which we review in this book. As in this sense a theological servant of his community of Israel, Borowitz' theological argument evolves with the historical evolution of his community. To understand his most recent evolution, it may be best to ask how he believes liberal religious Jews have previously lived their modernism and, then, how he believes they now seek something beyond it.

Modernism as Emancipation and Enlightenment

In Borowitz' history of Judaism, Jewish modernism is, first, a sociopolitical condition, and only consequently a source of certain epistemological and ethical claims. This modernism is initiated by the Emancipation:

After more than a millenium of ostracism and persecution, European Jews were astounded when the French Revolution signaled a turn to political equality in Europe, including even Jews. . . . Slowly, often begrudgingly, states granted Jews civil and social equality—a process not fully realized today even in the United States, the freest of modern nations. Regardless, Emancipation revolutionized Jewish spirituality, for whenever Jews were permitted to modernize, they did so avidly, and uncomplainingly accepted its accompanying secularization.

The startling effects of this fundamental shift of cultural context cannot be overemphasized. Freedom from segregated existence brought on a transition from a life oriented by revelation, tradition, and a sense of the holy to one in which religion became privatized if not irrelevant or obsolete. This had the advantage of making a Jew's religion no longer a public handicap. It also meant that as the realm of religiously neutral activity expanded, the twin questions of Jewish identity and continuity became increasingly troublesome. Jews began to ask, "What does it mean to be a Jew today? Why should one undertake its special responsibilities?" Modern Jewish thought arose as Jews sought to respond to these questions in ways that would be culturally credible and Jewishly persuasive.[3]

Masses of Jews sought to escape, readily, not only from the ghettoes imposed on them, but also from age-old practices of self-segregation: from life in autonomous Jewish communities, governed by Jewish communal authorities, Jewish social customs, and by practices of biblical-rabbinic education, study, and law *(halakhah)*. By what criteria would they now choose which aspects of their Jewishness to retain and which to discard?

According to Borowitz, modern Jews chose criteria offered by Western, Enlightenment sources rather than traditional, rabbinic sources: sharply separating private and public spheres; relegating religion to the private sphere; and adopting, for the public sphere, the rules of scientific reason, modern statehood, individual rights, and universal ethics.[4] The modern nation state was the agent of Jewish emancipation, an expression of the state's movement toward democracy. Both citizenship in the state and democracy brought with them the substitution of individual for communal enfranchisement and rights:

To European Jews, [this enfranchisement] seemed nearly miraculous, for political equality was given to everyone. . . . The intellectual-ethical roots of the emancipation were rationalistic. Citizenship was to be universal. . . .

Living largely among gentiles created a conflict with what the rabbinate taught was the necessary form and tone of Jewish life. To some extent the Torah directly mandated a good measure of Jewish separatism; more critically the recent centuries of segregation and persecution had heightened the desire for self-isolation. . . . In response, many Jews simply did what modernity had taught them: they made up their own minds about what they ought to do. . . . In all [the] new modes of Jewish existence, the modern concept of ethics was essential, providing Jews with their essential view of being human and staying Jewish.[5]

Basically a "Greek way of looking at duty [as]. . . derived from reason,"[6] ethics offered modern Jews a way of continuing the Jewish value of caring within the terms of modern Europe's liberal rationalism. In a statement that could almost have been drafted as a manifesto for liberal modernist Judaism, Jürgen Habermas explains:

The project of modernity formulated in the eighteenth century by the philosophers of the Enlightenment consisted in their efforts to develop objective science, universal morality and law, and autonomous art according to their inner logic.[7]

Wyschogrod explains:

the leitmotif of liberal modern Jewish theology has been what is perhaps the grandest of Enlightenment modernity's metanarratives, that of Kantian and post-Kantian philosophy. Moses Mendelssohn, Kant's contemporary, offered a Jewish theological version of this narrative . . . when he argued that Judaism's belief in God's existence and just governance of the world are in conformity with the requirements of reason and as such, available to all rational beings.[8]

For both Wyschogrod and Borowitz, Hermann Cohen articulated the overlapping interests of Kantian moral philosophy and the liberal Jewish theology of Emancipation. For Cohen's "ethical monotheism, [h]umankind is engaged in an infinite task of self-betterment," whose vehicle is scientific reason, but only as completed by the infinite idea of God.[9] This God is the God of Israel, but only as studied in the university by Jewish thinkers, who later brought Cohen's philosophy of ethical monotheism with them to the United States, initiating American professors of Jewish studies into the Continent's traditions of ethical universalism.[10] This does not mean that Cohen should be defined strictly as "Jewish modernist," but only that his writing served the needs of Jewish modernists. From Borowitz' perspective, however, "Jewish modernism" will also contain the seeds of self-criticism or even self-negation, since it represents an historically particular condition of social assimilation that cannot over time adequately represent, or serve, the people Israel's covenantal norms of community and traditional religious law. Cohen's writing would also serve the needs of those seeking to recover such norms in the midst of modernity. The same can be said of Borowitz' early work which, in dialectical fashion, not only served the liberal Jewish community in its modernist condition, but also serves the current, postmodern turn.

Borowitz first came to broad public attention as a Reform Jewish thinker who offered religion and theology for Jews living in the modernist context.[11] In his many journal essays, as well as his first major books in the late 1960s, however, his message was already complex. He wrote, at once, as Jewish philosopher, as pastoral rabbi to the liberal religious Jewish community, and as theologian and teacher of the Reform movement. He thus spoke to and for liberal Judaism's vision of the individual Jew's personal autonomy, and against the *halakhic* and ideological authority of the traditional rabbinate. He spoke of the Jew's moral and *halakhic* "choice" rather than "inheritance." But he already wrote of this choice as "an act of faith," and he described a liberal's faith as paradoxical:

> One does not arrive at the content of Judaism without faith, but liberals also believe they cannot affirm everything to which believing Jews in the past centuries have been committed. That is why they seek to limit their faith in Judaism by some sort of regulating principle. Only now it is clear that no self-justifying, autonomous principle exists, but all the possibilities themselves involve a prior act of faith. Thus, one can delimit Jewish faith only by acknowledging that one has a prior faith in whose name he is willing to alter and revise traditional Judaism. . . . Thus the structure of Jewish theology is tripartite and its work is dialectical. It begins in faith and this makes possible the work of reason which, in turn, ends with faith—from this point on, it is always faith followed by reason followed by faith in infinite, better messianic development.[12]

This leaves open the question, still, "in which approach shall liberals today put their faith?" Borowitz' answer, already in 1968, was:

Theologians in the past century have acted as if they knew a truth superior to Judaism. But I do not know a body of knowledge or a system of understanding God and man and history superior to Judaism. I do not have a faith more basic to my existence than my Judaism.13

This existentialist conclusion also displayed its own dialectic: between personal existence—that situation into which Borowitz the individual is thrown—and the historical situatedness of one's community of Israel: call it a covenantal existentialism. Borowitz already invoked a doctrine of Covenant in his 1957–58 Ed.D. dissertation. In short, his Jewish modernism was multileveled and dialectical from the start: a doctrine of personal autonomy tied to an anti-rationalist search for Covenant, a critique of the rabbinate's and the rabbinic tradition's authority over the Jewish person's everyday life tied to a critique of modern Jewish secularism, antinomianism, and individualism. While arguing in 1969, for example, for a personalist albeit religious Jewish sexual ethic, Borowitz added:

What I have tried to do in this analysis is to comprehend the problem in its contemporary setting and speak to those it concerns in their own language. Many of the most thoughtful things college students themselves say about sex ethics are put in terms of what it means to be a person. I imagine they think of that as a purely secular value. For me it is a matter of religious belief. . . . I do not see how secularism alone might validate such a fundamental faith in persons—all persons—today. . . . Had I not believed in what Judaism has taught me about what it means to be a person, I could not have written as I have. I spoke to a universal problem in universal terms in order to be understood. But that universal is based on a quite particularly Jewish faith.14

Borowitz continues his explanation by writing about the Jews' Covenant with a God who "is not neutral, but Holy," and about the role of the Jewish person in that Covenant.

Jewish Disillusionment with Modernity

Borowitz made no effort to cover over the dialectical tensions inherent in his Jewish modernism. The Jewish Covenant accompanies Jews in their modern movement to Emancipation and assimilation, but it allows this movement to go just so far. Well before the Shoah, two world wars, and the dehumanizing excesses of industrialism, nationalism, colonialism, and commercialism bred a growing Jewish disillusionment with the seductions of modernity:

> For most of two centuries almost all Jews who could modernize did so. They knew that modernity was good for them, that the great gains that equality and opportunity brought made the problems connected with modernization acceptable. But as the twentieth century waned, doubts about modernity's beneficence arose throughout Western civilization. People were profoundly disturbed by the deterioration of the quality of life. A great deal of their unhappiness was disappointment. The Enlightenment, the intellectual credo of modernity, had promised that replacing tradition with rational skepticism, hierarchy with democracy, and custom with freedom would bring messianic benefit—and certainly it hasn't. . . . On a much deeper level, this loss of confidence in Enlightenment values has come from the collapse of its philosophical foundations. All the certainties about mind and self and human nature that once powered the bold move into greater freedom now seem dubious.[15]

Borowitz notes how this disillusionment with Enlightenment has been experienced, specifically by American Jews since the 1960s:

> This remarkable amalgam of social experience, self-interest, and moral intuition [in the Jewish liberal movement through the early 1960s] then began to fall apart as each of its components came under increasing challenge. As a result, the meanings popularly associated with the terms *Jewish, ethics* and *Jewish ethics* were thrown into doubt.
>
> To begin with the social context . . . American democracy, with surprising quickness, lost much of its moral stature. A strong civil-rights law did not lead to full equality for blacks, and as numerous other minority groups learned the politics of confrontation and protest, the limits of American tolerance became clear. The Vietnam War made suspicion rather than respect the common attitude toward government. . . . In the Jewish community, the general misery had pointed focus in the special pain of the Holocaust. Modern culture, even democracy, did not prevent such ineffable evil. It took American Jews nearly twenty years to face this horror—one intimately connected, I am convinced, not with the death of a biblical God that a largely agnostic community no longer affirmed, but with the loss of its operative faith in Western culture and human competence. . . . The depth of anti-Semitism in Western culture seemed immeasurable . . .
>
> Intellectually, too, the vision of humankind as rational and rationality

itself implying a Kant-like ethics lost its old compelling power, perhaps mostly as a result of the incredible carnage of World War I. What remained of Kantian ethics faded as psychoanalysis from within and anthropology and Marxism from without demonstrated that, realistically, "conscience" mostly meant the introjected parent or group interest . . .

The postmodern situation begins with the recognition that ethics has lost its old certainty and priority. . . . It should come as no surprise, then, that the familiar identification of Jewish ethics with liberal politics also has been rejected. . . . The needs of the State of Israel also militated against identifying Jewish ethics with liberal politics.16

At the same time, Borowitz also notes that the disillusionment of liberal Jews with their modern, secular ideals led very few to anti-modern orthodoxies:

Most Jews, despite their disillusionment with modernity, have refused to give up its teaching about ethics. [Among the reasons are] a revulsion at the extremism and fanaticism that an unmodernized religious traditionalism can readily engender. . . . Modernists also reject Orthodoxy as a therapy for our society's moral ailments, because they find its social vision more inner-directed than they believe right in our democratic situation. . . . This issue becomes particularly upsetting when some Jews insist that the Holocaust proves people cannot be expected to act ethically towards Jews so we have good reason to concentrate on taking care of ourselves. . . . Third, feminism has provided a dramatic, specific focus for the limit to the modernist's embrace of the Jewish tradition.17

Borowitz concludes that the result of these disillusionments and resistances is an uncertain, ambivalent, and even cynical liberal American Jewry. While their optimism about humanity and reason has faded, liberal Jews remain compulsively resistant to God and to rabbinic tradition.17

In *Renewing the Covenant*, Borowitz offers a personal—and personalist's—history of how such a loss of confidence led him and fellow liberal Jews to a spiritual and intellectual crisis. "Modernity betrayed our faith," he writes, referring to faith in "the one 'god' in whom [all] moderns had avidly trusted—ourselves, humankind."18 It was humankind that failed: its universal visions bred also imperialisms, colonialisms, and, ultimately, totalitarianisms; its critical rationality bred also moral disarray and anomie; its scientific and technological discovery and ingenuity brought the worst as well as the best human designs to fruition—and the worst have defined our memories of this century: civilizational miseries of many sorts, most vividly, unspeakable wars and Holocaust.[19] Jewish disillusionment with modern humanity has had many sources, but all are sealed by reflections on the Holocaust as ultimate expression of the dangers of modern European civilization. Borowitz cites Elie Wiesel's observation that "the death camps, rather than shattering the faith of the traditionalists, most fully undid the worldview of the [modern] intellectuals and liberals."[20]

What then? To speak of unadorned disillusionment with modernity is not yet to speak of any alternative vision: this is postmodernism's early point of negation and that is all.

POSTMODERN RESPONSES TO LIBERAL JEWISH DISILLUSIONMENT

Without putting it in these exact terms, Borowitz' postmodern writings allow for a distinction between a strictly "anti-modern" and a "non-modern" response to liberal disillusionments with modernity. The anti-modern response is to seek some way of cutting off all explicitly modern rules of behavior or ways of thinking: out of the ashes of a modern past, in other words, to build a world unfettered by modernism. According to the non-modernist, such revolutionary anti-modernism would, in fact, replay the logic of modernist criticism: judging one's (modern) practices to be wrong and *therefore* wholly wrong and unusable as a source of guidelines for correct (non-modern) behavior in the future. To avoid replaying this sort of over-generalized criticism, the non-modernist would envision a messier future: seeking, over a long period of time, to strengthen dimensions of contemporary Jewish thought and practice that are not subservient to modernist rules and ideals but that remain, instead, vehicles of a more deep-seated, reliable, and enduring Covenant. Such a Covenant is not anti-modern, nor even thoroughly non-modern, but simply irreducible to the terms of any single period of Jewish life and thereby pertinent to each period.

Borowitz identifies both secular and religious expressions of anti-modernism. The secular expression would include the sorts of non-religious, academic postmodernisms that were outlined earlier in this chapter, for example, Continental philosophic and literary critics of modern master narratives, universalisms, or rationalisms. The religious expression would include neo-Orthodox or traditionalist thinkers who criticize all *secular* master narratives, universalisms and rationalisms and who replace them with selective arguments on behalf of *certain* communal traditions and their master narratives and recognized teachers. Various twentieth-century fundamentalisms illustrate a type of religious anti-modernism; for example, efforts among the Christian Right in the 1990s to draw sharp contrasts between the evils of liberal individualism and the good of Christian faith, generalized as a vehicle for better government in the United States. Another illustration is the increasing militancy of Jewish ultra-Orthodoxy in the 1990s in both the United States and Israel: displayed, for example, in ultra-orthodox efforts to identify as "not Jewish" both the liberal governments of Yitzhak Rabin, *z"l*, and Shimon Peres, and the liberal religious movements of Reform or Conservative Jewry. In the latter case, "not Jewish" would be equivalent to "expressing merely human and therefore localized interests," or "not worthy contributors to any master narrative."

In *Renewing the Covenant* and other recent writings, Borowitz is as much a critic of anti-modernism as he is a critic of modernism. He argues, on the one hand, that secular anti-modernists search for an absolute to substitute for the modernism they had once adopted, in turn, as substitute for rabbinic religion:

> The postmodern search for a substitute absolute began as it became clear that modernity had betrayed our faith. Repelled by the social disarray and moral anarchy around us, we are attracted by systems which provide clear cut authoritative direction . . . that is, a strong absolute.[21]

One direction has been a flight to ethnicity, another to Zionism, yet another to Holocaust study. But, for Borowitz, these all remain false absolutes: appropriate subjects of concern, but not of absolute and exclusive concern. They are attempts to replace an absolutized modernism, altogether, with one of its imagined contraries. Borowitz argues, on the other hand, that religious anti-modernism is no more legitimate than the secular variety. Orthodox Jews today offer legitimate criticisms of the failings of modernist humanism, from its permissivism to its imperialistic universalisms, but they use the very logic of modernism to promote a contrary ideal: a Judaism without humanism, permissiveness, or universality.

Had orthodox religions not behaved so badly when they had effective power, liberal religion would most likely not have come into being. . . . Liberals reject Orthodoxy not because, given the power, orthodoxies *will* [necessarily] be intolerant, but because their basic faith can generate extremism, zealotry, and fanaticism—something they have often done in the past and still do today. These, simple human experience has taught us, desecrate God's name while claiming to exalt it and therefore are among the foulest of human sins.

Among the particular areas of Orthodoxy inimical to what Borowitz considers enduring concerns of Judaism are democracy and some manner of appealing to a supra-legal conscience, to supra-ethnic loyalties, to supra-communal obligations.

Orthodoxies have a principled problem with democracy . . . [and pluralism, even though, within themselves,] orthodoxies often disagree as to what constitutes God's own will. . . . The general discomfort of orthodoxies with sinners and evildoers creates another of its problematic manifestations: the limited moral horizon we call ethnocentrism. . . . [E]ven in less self-ghettoized settings the orthodox appreciation of the universal can highly constrict, and charity, most broadly construed, not only begins at home but tends to stay there. . . . All [such] unhappy consequences of orthodox theories of revelation come to a climax in the orthodoxies' necessary subordination of persons to text, interpretation, structure, and precedent. God stands behind just these words and no others . . .22

Borowitz argues that these orthodox positions are not to be identified, however, with the demands of Torah, as if a liberal Judaism was a compromise with the non-Jewish world, rather than a means of heightening dimensions of Judaism that are selectively suppressed in orthodox reactions to the modern world. For Borowitz, postmodernism does not, therefore, preclude the possibility of liberal Judaism. Modernism may have provided Reform Judaism with powerful instruments for separating Judaism from what Reform leaders considered oppressive forms of medieval rabbinic authority, but these remained instruments rather than defining principles. For Borowitz, the spiritual and moral challenge of postmodern and post-Holocaust Jewish life is to transform the instruments of liberal Judaism but not its ends, which are defined now, as before, by Israel's Covenant with God.

In sum, this dialectical postmodern evolution has brought much of world Jewry to a paradoxical spiritual situation. We are too realistic about humankind to return to the messianic modernism that once animated us. Instead, we sense we derive our deepest understanding of what a person ought to be and humankind ought to become from participating in the Covenant. . . . But not exclusively. The Emancipation was not altogether a lie. It taught us something about the dignity of each person and about the democracy and pluralism that makes it effective, and this must be carried over into our post-modern Judaism. . . . I understand it to be the task of Jewish theology today to give a faithful, thoughtful explication of this paradox.[23]

The Jewish postmodernism Borowitz favors is thus a non- rather than an anti-modernism: an effort to be bound neither by the terms of modernism *nor* by visions of whatever is opposite to these terms. His Jewish postmodernism is therefore not defined by the battles strictly *internal* to academe between modernist philosophy or science and anti-modernist criticism, nor by the supposed culture wars outside of academe between anti-modern religious orthodoxies and modern secularisms. Within academe, his postmodernism may have overlaps with various aspects of Jewish and of Christian pragmatism, process thought and post-liberalism. But his postmodernism may more properly be placed in that region between academe and the communities of what he calls "liberal, religious Jews," where Jewish "post-liberals" or "text reasoners" (with Christian and some Muslim parallels) now seek to reaffirm ancient covenants in non-orthodox ways.[24]

The task of this book is to discuss more precisely how Borowitz' Jewish postmodernism may fit within the modernisms, anti-modernisms, and postmodernisms of both academia and the religious communities. Before releasing the reader to that task, I offer one more set of preparatory exercises: three plausible ways that readers might situate Borowitz within the emergent history of postmodern or post-foundational Jewish theology.

BOROWITZ AMONG THE JEWISH POSTMODERNISTS: POSTMODERN JEWISH REASONING AS PERSONAL ODYSSEY: A BIOGRAPHICAL TYPOLOGY

Consciously challenging academic postmodernists' distaste for personalism, Borowitz makes his case for Jewish postmodernism by retelling his personal odyssey from a liberal and strictly Kantian Jew to a post-Kantian yet liberal advocate of rabbinic Judaism. However we interpret the starting and ending points of Borowitz' journey, I trust we may agree that there is a recognizable pattern to the *way* he moves from point to point: the pattern brings to mind the intellectual/religious odysseys of Hermann Cohen, Martin Buber, and Franz Rosenzweig. Since this book's collection of contemporary postmodern Jewish thinkers names these three among its primary teachers and resources, the general pattern of Borowitz' personal story may reveal something significant about his pedigree. On a previous occasion, I constructed the following typology to make sense of Max Kadushin's place among what I then labeled the "aftermodern" Jewish thinkers.[25] I now believe that the evolution of Borowitz' intellectual and religious journey fits into this typology as well, displaying what may be five prototypical stages of a postmodern Jewish reasoner's biography.

1. These reasoners were usually the products of a mixed Jewish socialization, trained in both traditional patterns of Jewish discourse and patterns developed in the Jewish Enlightenment, or *haskalah*. This stage applies to all three German Jews, to Kadushin, and to Borowitz, who notes that he was "a 1930s product of a Columbus, Ohio synagogue afternoon Hebrew school"—Jewishly identified, that is, but not traditionally trained.[26] He then pursued both Jewish studies (at the Hebrew Union College) and Western academic study (at Ohio State University and at Columbia University).[27]

2. Applying Enlightenment questions to traditional practices, these reasoners emerged from their Western-university training as critics of traditional forms of Jewish behavior and, often, of Jewish self-understanding. They believed that rabbinic Judaism failed to provide reliable norms of critical inquiry, in particular, norms for evaluating systems of ethics. They assumed these norms would be disclosed, instead, through some of the various practices of modern philosophy.[28] Cohen, of course, was the great scholar of Kantian critique; Buber and Rosenzweig acquired their critical eye from Georg Hegel and from leading existentialist and phenomenological thinkers, as well as from their teacher, Cohen; Kadushin entered graduate rabbinic studies as a process thinker and pragmatist, close compatriot of Mordecai Kaplan's and of his early Reconstructionism. Adopting Kantian, universal principles of critical rationality and personal autonomy, Borowitz began his theological work by extending the Jewish Enlightenment's critique of oppressive and dog-

matic dimensions of traditional Jewish law. In their place, he promoted such Enlightenment ideals as "the dignity of the individual, democracy, pluralism and our limited knowledge of God."[29] On the pursuit of universal principles, he argued, for example, that for liberal Jews, "the Torah texts seemed almost provincial in their concentration on the present and on the Jewish people. By contrast, the ultimate goals of human history, and thus the destiny of all humankind, constitute a major motif in prophetic literature. For those no longer restricted to the affairs of their own folks, these were liberating ideals."[30] Liberal Judaism "reverses traditional Judaism's attitude toward the Torah. . . . Because 'no one can see God's face,' our teachers gave absolute credence to the books and interpretations they believed came from God as revelation. Liberal theologians believe people are as much responsible for the Torah and tradition as is God. But now, because 'no one can see God's face,' we cannot accept any human description of God as absolute."[31]

3. From the start, however, these reasoners also remained suspicious of strictly philosophic attempts to construct ethical norms a priori, and they tended to favor philosophies with hermeneutical tendencies.[32] For example, Buber's existentialism also challenged Western rationalism and was linked, early on, to his study of Hasidic mysticism; Rosenzweig developed a phenomenological method at the same time that he criticized the metaphysical basis and use of phenomenology in Western philosophy; and Kadushin quickly separated himself from Kaplan's naturalism as well as from Whitehead's and classical Jewish philosophy's abstract and disembodied conception of religion.[33] We have already noted the dialectical tension in Borowitz' early Jewish modernism. Within his early proposals for modern Jewish theology, he also protested that "theologians in the past century have acted as if they knew a truth superior to Judaism. . . . I do not have a faith more basic to my existence than my Judaism."[34] And within his early, voluntaristic proposal for Jewish ethical choice, he also insisted that his choice is "a matter of religious belief," ultimately articulable only within his "internal Jewish religious discourse."[35]

4. Eventually, these reasoners became disillusioned, in various ways, with the Enlightenment or modernist sources from which they had previously derived norms for reforming traditional Judaism. This disillusionment accompanied another movement in their thinking:

5. They became conscious of remediable (as well as irremediable or perennial) conflicts within their Jewish yet modern theologies. They came to experience their own theological projects as unnecessarily conflicted, rather than as creatively dialectical. In different ways, they each then claimed to discover intra-Jewish rules (criteria or guidelines) for transforming the conflictual poles of their modern Judaism into the different yet complementary poles of a postmodern Judaism, coining various, new names for their new approaches to Jewish reasoning. This discovery was the subject of their later writings and, beyond their personal odyssey, the basis of proposals for reforming Judaism more broadly and, secondarily, for contributing to the reformation of Western philosophic or academic thought more broadly.

For example, Cohen offered a *Religion of Reason Out of the Sources of Judaism*. He drew on the biblical prophets as resources for rejoining Plato (philosophy) and Isaiah (prophecy) as partners in the reformation of modern ethics and thus modern philosophy. Buber offered a *dialogic philosophy* of I-Thou relations or mutuality. From out of the sources of Hebrew Bible, Jewish prayer, and Jewish mysticism, he articulated a Jewish yet conceptual (and in that sense philosophic) means of reforming modern ethics, social praxis, and philosophy. From out the sources of biblical and rabbinic religion and textuality, Rosenzweig offered his Jewish yet philosophic method of *speech-thinking (Sprachdenken)*: an alternative and corrective to the reductive logics of modern philosophy and ethics. Kadushin drew on readings of classical rabbinic midrash as resources for refashioning organicist and pragmatic social sciences into instruments of rabbinic hermeneutics—or of what I would label "rabbinic pragmatism." He offered his analyses of *rabbinic value-concepts* as a means of reforming both liberal and orthodox Jewish ethics, and the kinds of modern epistemology and value theory that academics tend to apply to religious ethics.

Analogously, Borowitz' claim to a *postmodern Jewish theology* marks his decision to articulate in a comprehensive and normative way a part of his theological project that previously remained in competition with other themes and tendencies. He labels this part his *postmodern theology*, identifies it with a contemporary renewal of Israel's Covenant with God, and adopts it also as a rule for transforming liberalism and rabbinic Judaism into complementary rather than competing modes of thought and practice.

POSTMODERN JEWISH REASONING AS JEWISH MOVEMENT:
AHISTORICAL AND TRANSHISTORICAL TYPOLOGIES

The individual biographies of these pioneers in postmodern Jewish theology belong to histories of late modern (or twentieth century) European and American Jewish life. As noted earlier, Borowitz has offered a history of this kind, and his history displays stages that correspond roughly to the stages of our biographical typology:

1. *Pre-modern Judaism:* If Jewish modernism is the Jewish response to emancipation and Enlightenment, then it presupposes a pre-modern stage of pre-emancipated Judaism. In Borowitz' history, this is, in an immediate sense, "ghetto" and "shtetl" Judaism; in an extended sense it is "traditional rabbinic Judaism." This telescoping of earlier history simply represents the perspective from out of modernity.

2. *Jewish Modernism:* the Jewish response to emancipation and Enlightenment, from notions of personal autonomy, rational choice, and universal human rights, to individualism and a suspicion of authoritative tradition.

3. *Jewish Anti-modernism:* from disillusionment with the Enlightenment project to projects of secular criticism or religious neo-traditionalism.

4. *Jewish Postmodernism:* the subject of this book, as illustrated in Borowitz' or in other, competing or complementary forms of Jewish non-modernism.

Viewed historically, these stages are set in the context of four periods in European Jewish history, appearing at somewhat different times in different societies, but roughly according to the same chronology: from medieval Europe to modern Western Europe (appearing later in the East) to late modern Europe (early twentieth century) and its cultural outposts, like the Americas. This is not to imply that all Jews after a certain time are postmodernists (!), but it does suggest that postmodernism does not appear before a certain time in the history of modern Europe. In this view, Borowitz offers his postmodern theology as a theology *for* Jews who are responding to the conditions of life in late modern European civilization and after.

These stages may also be viewed trans-historically, however, as four se-
quential stages in any cycle of Jewish religious evolution. From this perspective, each stage represents a reiterable *type* of Jewish religious life and
Jewish theology, where a given type appears before (sets the context for)
only one other type and appears after (is a response to) only one other
type. I believe a strong argument for adopting this kind of typology is that
historical typologies must themselves be constructed from out of some
interpretive perspective and that the specific typology I applied to
Borowitz' history appears to reflect a modernist perspective, broadly conceived. Jewish modernism, for example, introduces the dichotomy
between Jewish tradition (or "medievalism," or "the pre-modern") and
that which enlightens or emancipates it. When Jewish postmodernists
construct historical typologies, it may be out of a desire to legitimate their
criticisms of modern Judaism to other modernists: and Jewish postmodernists remain Jewish modernists in the sense that they have participated
in the modern, academic critique of religious tradition and now seek to reform or redeem that critique. In the hand of a postmodernist, the modernist distinction between modern (2.) and pre-modern (1.) is simply dou-
bled. Jewish postmodernists, for example, may expose Jewish modernism
as merely a revision of, rather than a substitute for, traditional Jewish life;
they would then argue that Jewish modernists become disillusioned (3.)
when they try to live their modernism as a substitute, and they would offer
their Jewish postmodernism (4.) as a remedy for that disillusionment—re-
valorizing *modernism*, more modestly, as making a helpful contribution to
the reform of traditional Judaism.

Such a postmodern account would be *trans*-historical because it could
conceivably apply to contexts other than that of modern European civilization. From Second Temple days through the Roman period and within
particular Jewish settlements throughout the Diaspora, "Jewish modernism" *could also* correspond to the following tendency of Jews at certain
points of their communal experience: to lose faith in inherited traditions
of belief and conduct and in the leaders previously authorized to administer these traditions; to believe that there may be wholly new ways of re-
founding and readministering the rules and principles of Jewish life; to
seek immediate knowledge of these rules and principles, and to claim a
new authority to administer them; to impose this new or renewed knowledge on self and others; or, failing any conclusive discovery of new rules

and principles, to construct methods and found communities dedicated
to this discovery and rededicated to it despite any resistance, and despite
repeated failures and the anxieties that accompany them. This tendency
may dominate a thinker's work, as illustrated in Spinoza, or it may appear
as only one among several tendencies or sub-themes in a Jewish work: illustrated, for example, in passages of the scriptural books of *Job* and of *Ec-
clesiastes;* in passages of the midrashic collection *Lamentations Rabbah;* as a
more significant motif in Philo's allegories or, perhaps, as an element of
every Jewish thinker's effort to question Jewish tradition or simply to
understand Jewish tradition from out of the context of some strange
"land"—from Maimonides' Moorish Spain to the Baal Shem Tov's Poland
to Eugene Borowitz' postwar America. In these terms, "Jewish postmodernism" would correspond to the tendency of modernist Jews, at any time
in history, to lose faith in their own efforts to reconstruct Judaism autonomously and to seek, instead, a renewed dialogue with antecedent (or abo-
riginal) Jewish tradition.

Such a postmodernism, however, would display many levels of belief,
doubt, and reaffirmation. In fact, what we have labeled four historical or
trans-historical stages of Jewish religious thought could also be viewed
ahistorically as four elements of Jewish postmodernism. We could say, in
other words, that a Jewish postmodernism would display the following
four tendencies simultaneously:

1. *An element of Jewish traditionalism:* In Borowitz' terms, this is a tendency to reaffirm Israel's Covenant with God, epitomized in the classical rabbinic community's hermeneutical, ethical, and legal re-reading.
2. *An element of Jewish modernism:* In Borowitz' terms, this is a tendency
   to affirm the autonomy of the Jewish person within Israel's Covenant,
   the dignity and rights of all persons universally, and rational standards
   for evaluating rabbinic rereadings of the Covenant.
3. *An element of disillusionment with modernism:* In Borowitz' terms, this
   is a tendency to recognize the finitude or context-specificity of human
   reason and of humanly constructed ethics and justice.
4. *An element of textual reasoning:* In Borowitz' practice, this is a capacity
   to transform the modern, anti-modern, and pre-modern elements of
   Jewish postmodernism into complementary, rather than competing
   tendencies: generating what we might call a covenantal movement of

rational *and* faithful Jewish persons, for whom the discipline of re-
reading the biblical and rabbinic sources of Judaism is a means of reforming the ethical and hermeneutical practices of the modern academy and modern secular society as well as of traditional Judaism.
"Textual reasoning" is a term coined by a community of Borowitz'
younger colleagues to identify this mediating capacity in Jewish postmodernism. Borowitz has welcomed the label enthusiastically, thereby
offering some evidence to support two final claims that fill out this
introduction's thesis: that *Renewing the Covenant* introduces a project
of textual reasoning, and that this project achieves its life and definition in the practices of the community that adopts it. In this book,
members of an emergent community of "textual reasoners" comment
on *Renewing the Covenant* as a movement from Jewish modernism to
Jewish postmodernism. Commenting on the comments, we mark a
first of what we hope will be many defining moments in the life of this
community.

THE COMMUNITY OF POSTMODERN "TEXT REASONERS" GATHERED HERE — THE SOCIETY FOR TEXTUAL REASONING

In the same year that Borowitz' book appeared—1991—ten of his junior
colleagues in the Academy of Jewish Philosophy invited him to join them
in a new project, *The Postmodern Jewish Philosophy Network*. In the early
issues of the Network, members simply described their current projects,
comparing their patterns of work and then gradually constructing models
of their shared or differing paradigms. At the same time, members began
to gather for annual face-to-face sessions, the first one hosted by Borowitz at the Hebrew Union College–Jewish Institute of Religion in New
York, followed by annual gatherings at the American Academy of Religion meetings, along with increasing numbers of smaller gatherings. By
the year this book was redacted (1996), the Network—now of three hun-
dred electronic subscribers—changed its name to *The Journal for Textual
Reasoning*;[36] reflecting its members' sense that the dominant paradigm of
postmodern Jewish philosophy is one of reading, dialogue, and reasoning. Both reflecting and extending the direction of Borowitz' postmodern Covenant theology, this is a communal practice of religious and crit-

ically rational rereading of the classical, medieval, and modern rabbinic literatures. Informed by academic but non-reductive disciplines of interpretation (literary, historical, and philosophic-hermeneutical), these re-*readings* become new forms of interpretive *reasonings* as they emerge from out of the texts into the community's efforts to address its most pressing issues; for example, how to relocate moral authority and redefine religious belief in the shadow of the Holocaust and in the face of disillusionments with modern rationalism and irrationalism. For "text reasoners," it is still possible, in an age of disillusionment, to *reason*, at once religiously and critically, without succumbing to the temptations of despair, of obscurantism, or of false universalism. This reasoning is, however, no longer a private affair, but a *renewal* of the classical rabbinic tradition of interpersonal inquiry rooted in commentary and conversation about Judaism's sacred texts. This is a *postmodern* renewal, because it mediates a dialogue between the pre-modern imperatives of scriptural and rabbinic texts and what Borowitz would call the "modern autonomy of the individual reasoner." As indicated in the essays to follow, many of Borowitz' junior colleagues would abandon the notion of autonomy altogether and speak, instead, of the critical rationality that the modern academy still contributes to this dialogue.

Society Members and Friends Gathered in This Book

Among the community of readers collected in this book, David Novak offered his comments at a session on Borowitz' book at the 1991 annual meeting of the Association of Jewish Studies in Boston (Novak reprinted a version in *Sh'ma*). The J. Richard and Dorothy Shiff Professor of Jewish Studies at the University of Toronto, David Novak writes on modern Jewish philosophy and on rabbinic ethics, most recently on Judaism and natural law and on various phenomenological approaches to Jewish philosophy.[37] Norbert M. Samuelson's reading appeared in *Zygon*. He is the Harold and Jean Grossman Professor of Jewish Studies at Arizona State University and writes on medieval and modern Jewish philosophy, most recently on doctrines of Creation, from the Bible to Rosenzweig to contemporary astrophysics.[38] Yudit Kornberg Greenberg, Edith Wyschogrod and Thomas N. Ogletree offered their comments in a symposium on Borowitz organized for the 1991 annual meeting of the American Academy of

Religion. Professor of Religion at Rollins College, Greenberg writes on modern Jewish philosophy, most recently on Rosenzweig's esthetics.[39] Wyschogrod holds the Rayzor Chair of Philosophy and Religious Thought at Rice University and is former President of the American Academy of Religion. She writes on postmodern philosophy and the philosophy of religion, most recently on the philosophy of community and on God and postmodernism. Professor of Theological Ethics at the Yale Divinity School, Ogletree writes on Christian ethics and postmodern Christian thought, most recently on the challenge of pluralism in the public witness of the ecumenical Protestant churches.

We may linger on the introduction of Ogletree, since his participation contributes in unique ways to identifying the meaning of a community of postmodern Jewish thinkers. Ogletree begins his reading with these words: "As a Christian theologian, I am the stranger who has been welcomed into this conversation." By self-definition, he is thus the group's *ger toshav*, or "resident alien": in academic terms perhaps a "participant observer," whose presence serves as a check on the group's collective perceptions, a point from which to identify both their collective difference from other groups and collective differences, one from the other. In other ways, however, Ogletree participates within the community as a postmodern community. He is only a more conspicuous reminder that community members belong here as well as elsewhere, that membership is established through participating in certain kinds of activities and thus relations (here, for example, the activity of thinking about the connections among various aspects of Jewish theology), and that any such community also belongs to wider networks among communities.

NOTES

1. See David Ellenson's biographical note about Borowitz in the preface to this book.
2. Edith Wyschogrod, "Trends in Postmodern Judaism Philosophy," *Soundings* 76, no. 1 (Spring, 1993), 129–38 (p. 129), citing Jean-François Lyotard, *The Postmodern Condition: Report on Knowledge*, trans. F. Bennington and B. Massumi (Minneapolis: University of Minnesota Press, 1984), 31–37. Wyschogrod's essay introduces a "Symposium on Jewish Postmodernism"

that might interest readers of the present volume. The Symposium includes essays on postmodern Jewish philosophy by Peter Ochs, José Faur, Robert Gibbs, and Jacob Meskin, with an afterword by Edith Wyschogrod.

3. Eugene Borowitz, *Renewing the Covenant: A Theology for the Postmodern Jew* (Philadelphia: Jewish Publication Society, 1991), pp. 3–4.

4. Eugene Borowitz, *Exploring Jewish Ethics, Papers on Covenant Responsibility* (Detroit: Wayne State University, 1990), pp. 26ff.

5. Ibid., pp. 27–28.

6. Ibid., p. 27.

7. Jürgen Habermas, "Modernity versus Postmodernity," *New German Critique* 22 (1981), 9. Cited in Edith Wyschogrod, "Trends in Postmodern Jewish Philosophy," *Soundings* 76, no. 1 (Spring, 1993), 129–37 (p. 131).

8. Ibid.

9. Ibid.

10. Borowitz, *Renewing the Covenant*, pp. 13–14.

11. See above, Note 1.

12. Borowitz, *A New Jewish Theology in the Making* (Philadelphia: The Westminster Press, 1968), pp. 187–88.

13. Ibid., p. 189.

14. Eugene Borowitz, *Choosing a Sex Ethic* (New York: Schocken Books, 1969), pp. 116–17.

15. Eugene Borowitz, *Choices in Modern Jewish Thought, A Partisan Guide*, 2nd ed. (West Orange, NJ: Behrman House, 1995), p. 283.

16. Borowitz, *Exploring Jewish Ethics*, pp. 30, 31, 32.

17. Ibid., pp. 33, 34, 35.

18. Borowitz, *Renewing the Covenant*, p. 41.

19. Ibid., p. 135.

20. Ibid., p. 40.

21. Ibid., p. 76.

22. Ibid., pp. 243, 245, 247, 248.

23. Ibid., p. 51.

24. To the degree that a strict, liberal/orthodox distinction may itself remain a symptom of modernism, some of us may prefer "non-Orthodox," or "not-strictly-Orthodox," to the term "liberal."

25. "Max Kadushin as Rabbinic Pragmatist," in *Understanding the Rabbinic Mind* edited by Peter Ochs (Atlanta: Scholars Press for the University of South Florida, 1990), p. 167ff.

26. Eugene Borowitz, "How a Discipline Became Established," *CCAR Journal* (Spring, 1997), 66.

27. See David Ellenson's biography, Note 1. For applications of this pattern to Kadushin and the German Jewish thinkers, see Ochs, "Max Kadushin as Rabbinic Pragmatist," 167ff.

28. Ochs, "Max Kadushin as Rabbinic Pragmatist," p. 168.

29. Peter Haas, "A Symposium on Borowitz' *Renewing the Covenant*," paper presented at the annual meeting of the Association of Jewish Studies, Boston, MA 1991. An abridged version of the paper appeared in *Sh'ma* 22/426 (January 24, 1992).

30. Eugene Borowitz, *Liberal Judaism* (New York: UAHC, 1984), p. 298.

31. Ibid., pp. 8–9.

32. Ochs, "Max Kadushin as Rabbinic Pragmatist," p. 168.

33. See Theodore Steinberg, "Max Kadushin, An Intellectual Biography," in *Understanding the Rabbinic Mind*, edited by Peter Ochs, pp. 4ff.

34. Borowitz, *A New Jewish Theology*, p. 189.

35. Borowitz, *Choosing a Sex Ethic*, pp. 116, 117.

36. The Journal's current editors are: Aryeh Cohen (University of Judaism), Charlotte Fonrobert (Syracuse University), Nancy Levine (Harvard), Jacob Meskin (Princeton University), Michael Zank (Boston University). Emeritus Editor and Founder is Peter Ochs. The Journal's electronic address is "owner-tr_list@bu.edu"; for editorial questions, "mzank@bu.edu".

37. Novak is also co-founder and chair of The Society for Textual Reasoning.

38. Samuelson is also founder of the Academy of Jewish Philosophy; he introduced the first electronic dialogue network of the *Postmodern Jewish Philosophy Network*.

39. Greenberg is also a founding member of *The Postmodern Jewish Philosophy Network* and contributing editor of *Textual Reasoning*.

2

Postmodern Judaism: One Theologian's View

EUGENE B. BOROWITZ

I am a believing Jew who seeks to understand, as best he can, the nature of Jewish faith and the religious life its beliefs entail. Jewish tradition classically and many believing Jews today do not share my great interest in this reflective aspect of Jewish spirituality. Some consider it a foreign importation into Judaism, and hence an activity no serious Jew should be associated with. Despite this, I carry on an activity I and some others loosely call "Jewish theology." I do so because I enjoy thinking and because I believe that trying to give words and intellectual structure to what I most significantly believe will make me a better Jew. I am encouraged in my uncommon Jewish religious activity by those people in our long history whom I perceive to be my predecessors: those authors whose writings indicate that they lived in cultures that honored Hellenic ways of thought and who therefore also pursued abstraction.

One of my major theological concerns is generated by an issue unknown to my theoretical forebears, traditionalists all of them. While my Judaism is as primary to my existence as their faith was to their lives, I do not live the life of Torah within the parameters of its classic interpretation, but in a modernized adaptation of them. Intellectually, it seems odd to me that my modernity has impacted on me sufficiently that I dissent from my tradition in significant measure. I say that because I know that no contemporary point of view is more basic to my life than is my Judaism. I would therefore like to understand this somewhat curious spiritual stance of mine—one, incidentally, that I believe the overwhelming bulk of modernized, believing Jews share.

I am not the first modern Jew to devote a good portion of his professional life to thinking about this matter, yet, to add to my puzzlement, I find serious fault with all the prior efforts to give an adequate intellectual description and cultural validation to this amalgamated Jewish faith which we thinkers have lived. I have sought, therefore, to create a new theoretical structure for my Judaism, and that of many other present day Jewish believers. The resulting work of giving an orderly, abstract articulation of my life's truth, I call "Jewish theology."

Having my most fundamental stance within Judaism drives me to understand myself theologically in relation to the classic Jewish tradition, a lifelong effort currently moving toward intellectual completion in a project currently under way. Nonetheless, since I also stand firmly within contemporary culture, I have been involved in the related work of seeking to understand my Judaism in terms esteemed by one of its significant intellectual currents. It is this cultural task, what theologians call "apologetics," that led me to my concern with the postmodern mind. The results of my mediating between Judaism and postmodernity, as I understand it, are now visible in my book *Renewing the Covenant*, a work whose theory and content provide the substance for this discussion.

I cannot directly continue the patterns of thought created by my teachers, the non-Orthodox Jewish thinkers of prior modern generations, because I do not share the unbounded confidence in culture that animated them. I have only a modest regard for the spiritual vitality of contemporary culture and the secular methods it commends as our most valuable ways of finding meaning. What troubles me about it is not so much its increasing fragmentation and contradictoriness, but its low moral standards. And the university, which once seemed to offer the hope of providing a guiding humane vision for our civilization, now seems, with many individual and some institutional exceptions, as much the cause and victim of our social malaise as its antidote.

To be more specific, my teachers and their teachers before them followed the accepted liberal Protestant method of doing theology. First they turned to the university and allowed it to prescribe a manner of speaking about religion that it considered acceptable. Then they sought to adapt their faith to it, glorying in those traditions which had long anticipated the new truths, yet occasionally calling for certain modifications of the accepted secular wisdom in the name of their old faith. Thus, in my lifetime, various Jewish thinkers have demanded that we speak of Judaism in the terms of philosophies as varied as neo-Kantianism, naturalism, logical analysis, existentialism, process thought and neo-pragmatism. Others, abandoning the philosophic standard, have found their formative truth in the social sciences, particularly sociology and its offshoot, anthropology, while some seek cultural legitimation from one of the humanities like literary theory or the study of religion. In part because it has itself been fractured by this experience of rapidly shifting plausibility structures, in part because of its own honest critique of its own assumptions, neither the university as a whole nor any one of its disciplines can today easily command the spiritual authority it took as its due perhaps as recently as a generation ago. The root difficulty is that our academies and the modern ethos they advocate project far more expertise as relativizers of values rather than as the leaders whose secular vision can provide us with a freshly commanding ground for them. It is this value-vacuum, I contend, that has spawned the utterly unanticipated spiritual search and religious revival going on in Western civilization—one seen most dramatically in the reborn vitality of classic fundamentalisms.

Sharing in religion's new self-respect, if not in the certainty of those who know they possess God's own verbal revelation, I cannot, as my teachers did, allow the university to define how modern Jews should understand and live their faith. Nonetheless, respecting greatly what the university might still teach us, I, like many others, seek the fresh understanding that might come from articulating my faith in a university-refined language. I find the dialect that seems most likely to allow me to speak least faithlessly of my Jewish truth among the babble that makes up the postmodern conversation.

I turn now to what seems to some of my academic critics my idiosyncratic use of the term "postmodern," and I shall then sketch in something of the results that flow from the application of my interpretation of it. To begin with, I find the accents of postmodernity particularly congenial because they impose few restraints and tolerate considerable ambiguity.

People far more learned than I am in the intricacies of French philosophic and literary thought wish, however, to draw a line at this point. They find it odd indeed that anyone would want to speak of himself as a postmodern and not follow the paths laid down by Derrida or perhaps pursue the fresh developments suggested by Lyotard or others. I find this suggestion strange. How can deconstruction be applied to everyone else's foundationalism, but not to its own when it finally seeks to move from criticism to positive statement? Is not a Derridean orthodoxy an oxymoron?

I prefer to read as the critical text of our time the actual history of people questing for reliable meaning. Seeking an ultimate and solid ground of values, a significant minority of people in our civilization have turned from the university to religion to help them understand what they intuitively know to be true, that not everything is relative and that humanhood is intimately bound up with acts we do not do, and others we are bound to try to do. As I see it, many of us find ourselves in the situation of experience seeking understanding. The great French deconstructionists have brilliantly cut the ground out from under the pretensions of others, but they have not yet explained convincingly how they can move on to ground values in a commanding way. Thus, in my religio-intellectual quest, they can only be of secondary, not primary, help to me.

Fortunately, the cultural horizon of postmodernism has been much broader than French critical theory. It embraces a rather broad-scale concern with how we might think if we did not take ourselves to be Cartesian selves. Its emphasis on the linguisticality of thought does not create impenetrable barriers for the assertion of religious truth, as positivism and many forms of rationalism did. To a Jew, its concern with creative linguistic misreadings awakens memories of rabbinic midrash—the classic language of Jewish theology—while its stress on usage rather than pure idea immediately involves us in community and historicity, two notions critical to Jewish faith yet problematic for prior modern Jewish thinkers. It is this amorphous linguistic, communitarian postmodernity that provides me with the least inadequate cultural language I know for speaking of the truth by which I and most other modern Jews live.

Three other features of my variety of postmodern discourse require comment. First, I endorse its polemic against our language's hidden metaphysics or prescriptive logic. I then move beyond its critical preoccupations to positive apologetic formulations by way of its vague appreciation of the truth of personal experience, of which I take relationship to be the critical instance; I shall say more about this later. Here I only want to make note of the controversy arising from my decision to assert my Jewish conviction that, in contemporary terms, we can have unmediated, compelling, quality-laden religious experience. I devote chapter 19 of my book to my reasons for affirming this position against the challenge of many philosophers. Although I necessarily do so in a non-philosophic manner, I believe what I do is not only understandable but a variety of thoughtful postmodern discourse. (For the record, let me indicate that I do not there discuss this issue in its prior Jewish incarnation, Hermann Cohen's radical neo-Kantian notion of the priority of reason to all experience.) This is but one example of the way my understanding of postmodernity allows me regularly to find a language for my disagreements with modern rationalisms that negate or vacate God, devalue community, and practically reduce the self to the mind. Positively, I can clarify much of the Jewish richness of the connections between God, community, and self by means of the metaphor of personal relationship.

Second, as is already evident, my thinking exhibits a certain circularity. My experience as a believer provides me with a measure of certainty and thus, too, with my most fundamental criterion of judgment. Thus, not surprisingly, as the fuller contours of my faith emerge from my reflection, they very much resemble the barely articulate ones with which I began. As a postmodern I see no scandal in this procedure. Once we acknowledge the situatedness of all our thought and deny Cartesian introspection a privileged transcendence of human particularity, we recognize that all serious thinking is significantly circular. That is, no methodology escapes the shaping of time and place, of language and person. The method we choose as appropriate to a given topic cannot claim more than guild or community objectivity—and perhaps only reflects class or person—yet it substantially determines the content that will result from its employment.

Third, the postmodern mood has considerable tolerance for the limitations of system. In fact, my apologetic thought has less coherence than the academic modern mind commonly desires. It is not nearly as tidy as I may have previously intimated. Although I claim to give Judaism priority in my thought, on occasion, most notably with regard to the notions of revelation and authority, I deviate from my community's classic teaching and allow influences from the culture to reshape my faith. Were I, like most other Jewish thinkers, to insist on the priority of tradition or that of culture, or, indeed, bow to the necessity of settling the issue, my thought would reflect the pre-modern tones of the one or the modern notes of the other. But in the languages for increased self-understanding the culture now puts at my disposal, I find I cannot be true to my Jewish relationship with God and myself by forcing myself into a linguistically determined systematic coherence.

I am grateful to postmodern discourse for authorizing those who admit they cannot give reasonably unambiguous voice to the *logos* to speak their truth, sloppy in structure as it may seem to some. This structural un-tidiness is abetted by my writing with conscious imprecision, a choice de-signed to warn my reader that my theology does not allow for geometric clarity. Against some postmoderns, however, I do not glory in unsystem-atic thought. God being one, I seek as much personal and intellectual inte-gration as I can find, so I try to present my ideas in as orderly and reason-able fashion as I can. I have no rule which explains or authorizes this procedure. If I did I would be a rationalist, at least as rationalisms cur-rently present themselves in our culture. Accepting my temporality, I re-main open to the possibility that a new construal of thoughtfulness and/ or the human condition will allow for more fully integrated Jewish theol-ogies. Until then I look forward to what our community's liturgical use of Zec. 9.14 teaches, that only in the Days of the Messiah will *Adonai's* name be one as *Adonai* is one.

Perhaps all this will be clearer if I speak in less than 320 pages of the substance of my book, *Renewing the Covenant: A Theology for the Postmod-ern Jew.* It consists of four unequal parts. The first of these provides the ex-periential foundation for the three analytic, more abstract sections that follow.

Thinking as a postmodern, the religious experience which I turn to is that of my community, the Household of Israel, as I individually have experienced and now interpret it. Moderns thought quite individualisti-cally and thus inevitably had the problem which so plagues us today of authorizing community, a polemical issue of great concern to me. While the university has supplied us with a number of ways of dealing with per-sonal religious experience, it offers no help in speaking directly of what a community has "personally" undergone. I have no presently legitimate hermeneutic by which to validate such a reading; no clear set of criteria by which I arrived at my judgments; and many thoughtful people see things quite differently, although I argue that they and much of our community have misunderstood our situation. I am, however, emboldened in my interpretation of our response to recent events by the uncommonly great breadth of data my view explains: to my mind one much more encompassing than that of alternative explanations. I can only submit my views to the judgment of the academic and believing communities and hope that a significant segment of each will agree with me.

In my view, the particular Jewish turn to postmodernity must be envisioned as an aspect of western civilization's disillusionment with the modern ethos: a consequence of our thorough Jewish modernization and secularization. Intellectually and spiritually, this change of ethos has grown out of our loss of a ground of values. The resulting disenchantment with modernity on this score has resulted in a renewal of Moslem, Christian, and Jewish fundamentalisms as well as a proliferation of new religions. Against those who believe that postmodernity means that God is dead—a peculiarly dogmatic assertion for a movement that prides itself on deconstruction—I associate myself with all those who know that our values are not mere word play but are rooted in the universe itself. But against all orthodoxies, I know that some of the spiritual truth of modernity remains valid, specifically, that human dignity involves a significant measure of self-determination and thus now must find a place in a postmodern religiosity which grounds the self in God and community. I am confirmed in this view by the fact that, for all their appeal, orthodoxies have not won the hearts of most thoughtful believers in the West, troubled by modernity as they are.

Our particular Jewish version of this development stemmed largely from our response to the Holocaust. Most observers concluded from it that God was dead. I see this, ironically enough, as the high point of the modernistic view of religion, one in which ethics and reason are foundational and God secondary if not dispensable. This judgment failed even as a descriptive observation; the significant post-Holocaust Jewish movements have not been atheist and secular but religious, even mystical, and that among non-Orthodox as well as Orthodox Jews. Intellectually too, the Jewish death of God movement collapsed as ethics themselves became problematic and the steady evidence of human perversity made a humano-centric faith wildly optimistic. For many Jews, an educated, cultured humankind that can produce or abet a Holocaust is no longer worthy of confidence.

But now a paradox confronted these once enthusiastic moderns. If the moral chasm between the death camp Nazis and their Jewish victims cannot be relativized but points to a standard of absolute value, if that standard can no longer be found in a secular assertion about universal human rationality, then they needed a new ground of value. They thus came to realize, almost despite themselves, that this conviction of theirs was a matter of faith, that they believed much more than they thought they had. Now a postmodern deconstructive reading of the assertion that God was dead is possible. Following Ludwig Feuerbach we can say that the opposite of its assertion was true, that the "god" who died in the Holocaust was not the God of Israel's tradition—in Whom few had believed in any case—but the functioning "god" of moderns: humankind, ourselves. And it is this loss of primal self-confidence that so shook the Jewish community and has given it its own version of our civilization's endemic aimlessness and depression.

A second result of our spiritual upheaval as a result of the Holocaust was our turn from enthusiastic universalism to a pronounced particularism, our version of the communitarianism so characteristic of the postmodern ethos. Many commentators have spoken about this as a result of world Jewry's experience of the Israeli Six Day War of 1967. I do not see how that phenomenon could have taken place had it not been for the discussion of the Holocaust which had been so prominent a feature of the preceding few years. In the threat to the survival of the Jewish community, a new issue was posed for the community: was it sufficient for modern Jews to be good people in general with a few Hebraic adornments, or was there something in corporate Jewish existence that had a touch of absoluteness about it? Our community is still divided on that question, but the rate of intermarriage and its consequences for Jewish continuity continue to force the issue to the center of Jewish consciousness. Clearly, Jewish particularism, in both non-Orthodox and Orthodox manifestation, has reasserted itself as a central aspect of postmodern Jewish faith.

Yet it is precisely in both these manifestations that a third insight makes its claims on the bulk of our community: most of us newly believing particularists know that it would be against our most fundamental sense of who we are called to be in our relationship with God as part of the people of Israel if we had to surrender, utterly, our right of self-determination. That is to say, in our new postmodern religiosity we cannot be Orthodox, nor can we non-Orthodox particularists be unreflective supporters of the State of Israel. Rather we know we need to retain a place for individual autonomy even if our freedom must be rethought in terms of its new context. It is from this continuing appreciation of selfhood (reshaped by its postmodern context) that the desirability of democracy and pluralism, and thus our refurbished sense of universalism, arises.

The three affirmations resulting from this experiential foundation set the topics of the theological reflection which follows and takes up the bulk of the book. It should be noted, however, that the idea of the responsible self, so fully adumbrated in modern Jewish thought, is not given independent treatment but is accepted as a common item of contemporary exchange. I analyze it only in terms of its new postmodern understanding. That is, I ask what it would mean to speak of the self when it is substantially structured, not by pure autonomy, but by its grounding in a relationship with God, a relationship it shares in community as part of the Jewish people's historic Covenant with God. The result of all this is a new theory of non-Orthodox Jewish duty, the acts of which constitute the primary expression and medium of Jewish holiness.

I then deal, in the first substantive section, with what it might mean that God rightly commands us yet is intimately involved with us. This requires a reworking of the notion of transcendence that is true not only to God's authority but also to human freedom and corporate relationship with God. Two other old religious themes require postmodern reconceptualization. First, what can we say about the nature of God, and thus about evil, now that rationalisms have only a limited hegemony in theology? Second, what dare we assert God actually does now that science has been demythologized into a construction of reality?

Given our postmodern situatedness, these issues, like all others, must be treated holistically. Thus, questions about God necessarily involve me in two other theological motifs, Jewish particularity and, in my non-Orthodoxy, with a self dignified by Covenantal autonomy.

The second substantive section deals with the people of Israel and is founded on briefs for the sociality of selves and the communitarian ground for universalism. All observers agree that Jewish particularism increased as a result of the Holocaust, but we differ over whether this imperative has an essentially secular, ethnic root or a theological one, and that a certain cosmic quality attaches to Jewish peoplehood before God. Practically, the Holocaust radicalized the question of the significance of Jewish survival and the threats to the State of Israel kept it current. Today it arises in more benign form as Jewish intermarriage increases Jewish assimilation. One hears the echoes of an extreme of modernization in the resigned notion that Jewishness is only another if a laudable cultural form, one which is secondary to being a fine, ethical human being. For a sizable minority among us, including me, good people are not simply Jews without Hebraism, but Jewish religious living teaches us that our ethnicity involves a singularly valuable relationship with God. Intellectually, how can we not be particularists? In a postmodern time how shall we justify beginning with the universal—a theory of religion or of human rationality or experience—and only then seek such particularity as our theory allows? In postmodern humility we must acknowledge that all thought begins particularistically, that giving up our group may mean giving up our universalism. Hence, I inquire how the self-legislating single self and this folk related to God fit together, how their particular relationship with God can be characterized and what this new particularity says about universalism and how it is affected by it.

These two postmodern religious motifs—the turn to God and the particular—are common to Orthodox and non-Orthodox Jewish postmodernity. Their divergent understandings arise, however, from the non-Orthodox insistence on the continuing spiritual validity of a central theme of modern Judaism: that personal dignity necessarily involves a substantial measure of self-determination. My religious holism substantially rejects Kant's secular autonomy by incorrigibly linking the autonomous self to God as one of the people, Jewish or human, while rejecting the classic Jewish notions of verbal revelation and God-authorized human law. The issue of feminism as good as settled that question for many of us, but there have long been other good reasons for thinking of religion as a more human project than our tradition acknowledged, as chapter 17 of my book indicates.

All this comes to a climax in a theory of Jewish duty, one elaborated by employing the Buberian notion of human relationship as its key metaphor, and I defend this teaching against its critics. I epitomize these ideas in the classic notion of Covenant now seen relationally rather than in its traditional sense as contract. This makes it possible to understand how a self can be commandingly involved with God and with a people, yet remain true to its individuality. It is my hope that this exercise in thinking carefully about our Jewish belief will make it possible for many in our community to live more faithfully as part of the Covenant.

Readings of Borowitz'
Renewing the Covenant

3

Gene Borowitz'
Renewing the Covenant:
A Theology for the Postmodern Jew

YUDIT KORNBERG GREENBERG

Borowitz' recent book addresses issues in the cognitive and practical forms of contemporary Western Jewish religiosity in light of what he discerns as the postmodern spiritual pulse. He names his theology "postmodern" and his audience "postmodern Jews." His theological project is driven by the need to reconceive the theoretical foundation of liberal Judaism in an effort to show the validity of maintaining a distinct Jewish life in a pluralistic world. His explicit aim is to develop a theory of Jewish duty as an alternative to a liberal Judaism that has failed to generate in its practitioners an unwavering commitment to a uniquely Jewish life. He believes that Jews have a moral duty to live according to their Covenantal obligations: their specific Jewish duties, among which is the duty to affirm a common humanity in the face of one God.

Borowitz assesses the extent to which patterns of Jewish behavior, beliefs, theologies, and philosophies promote or hinder the truths of postmodern Judaism. These are: (1) transcendent reality (2) individual autonomy (3) community and (4) pluralism. These represent the spiritual and philosophical convictions on which he refuses to compromise. In his effort to place himself in the history of modern Jewish theology, he develops three postmodern theological directions: (1) a cultural critique of liberal and Orthodox Judaism (2) a critique of linear modern philosophy, and (3) the construction of a theology of covenantal renewal through the return to genuine spirituality and the promotion of community.

BOROWITZ' CRITIQUE OF LIBERALISM AND ORTHODOXY

As part of his strategy to point out the vices and virtues of modernist religiosity, Borowitz evaluates the two ideological extremes: liberalism and Orthodoxy. Borowitz' criticism of both Orthodoxy and liberalism is motivated primarily by political and social concerns. He concludes that neither liberal Judaism nor mainstream Orthodoxy are viable options for the postmodern Jew. Liberal Judaism has failed to command from its practitioners specific Jewish duties, while Orthodoxy's hierarchical authority, sexism, and intolerance of pluralism are exclusivistic and offensive.

In his critique of Orthodoxy, he finds offensive not only *halakhic* authoritarianism, but also the Orthodox dogma of Jewish chosenness. The belief in chosenness has traditionally justified Jewish particularism, whose elitist and hierarchical connotations Borowitz dismisses as immoral. In objecting to the claims of Jewish particularism, Borowitz follows a long tradition of modern thinkers—initiated by Spinoza and later reiterated by Moses Mendelssohn, and others. Mordecai Kaplan, perhaps more than any other thinker, vehemently rejects chosenness, both because of its irreducibility and because of its historical propensity to perpetuate political and social segregation and hostility.

Borowitz desires to provide an antidote to traditionalist and modernist conceptions and their hierarchical and separatist entailments. He asserts that modern Jewish thinkers failed in their own way to interpret the idea of a Covenant. Hermann Cohen and later Leo Baeck upheld the notion of chosenness even as they affirmed Judaism as the religion that has provided the finest example of ethical monotheism. While they emphasized the notion of "mission" rather than of privileged election, Borowitz is suspicious that their stringent universalism could not be reconciled with a distinctive commanding particularity. He therefore proposes to replace the notion of chosenness with "Covenant," underscoring, in the spirit of Buber and Rosenzweig, the sense of a relationship rather than the legalism implied by the traditionalist notions.

He argues that the liberal Jew must come to terms with the positive and instructive aspects of traditional Judaism, and that Orthodox Jews must learn to absorb the liberal spirit and value of personal autonomy and universalistic morality. The liberal Jew, who is the one addressed by Borowitz, must consciously live in the dialectic of religious particularism and universal humanism and mediate between these two. He is optimistic that such mediation is possible without jeopardizing the uniqueness of the Jewish heritage and its historical ties to the land, culture, and people of Israel.

Liberal Judaism's past failures to underscore the uniquely Jewish world view and ethos stemmed from its willingness to compromise Judaism for the sake of the Enlightenment's ideals of universal reason and morality. Liberal Judaism thus produced a universalistic ethical monotheism that failed to support a distinctive cultural and religious Jewish life. By contrast, postmodern religious attitudes entail a commitment to preserve ethnic and cultural distinction, while embracing democratic pluralism.

Borowitz argues that, since Judaism already endorses autonomy by virtue of its notion of a Covenant, liberal Jewish thought only carried this premise of autonomy further. Liberal Judaism rejected the absolutist claims of *halakhic* Judaism, yet had not modified the traditional Jewish concept of God as the Ultimate who grants human autonomy. Therefore, rationalist modern Jewish thinkers such as Hermann Cohen and Mordecai Kaplan only "changed the classic Jewish balance between God and Humankind by transferring the power of legislation from God to the human mind." In other words, Borowitz defends the liberal notion of Covenant exercised in autonomy. His theology may be post-liberal, but it preserves the liberal understanding of substantial self-determination vis-à-vis Jewish law; he is post-*halakhic*, but is committed to a normative Jewish existence shaped by the love of traditional values and his fellow Jews.

BOROWITZ' POSTRATIONAL CRITIQUE OF MODERN JEWISH PHILOSOPHY

Borowitz launches a postrational critique of modern Jewish philosophies in an attempt to move towards intuitive, nonlinear models of cognitive and practical spirituality. This is the dominant feature of Borowitz' theology.

He examines the philosophical underpinnings of modern Jewish thinkers who exerted direct as well as more subtle influence on Jewish beliefs and practices. Toward the goal of balancing the norms of autonomy and divine authority, Borowitz measures the extent to which each philosopher succeeds in properly adjusting the power dynamics of the human and the divine. In the process, he boldly attacks the self-centered premises of modern rationalism and of the social and political behavior associated with it. Despite his objections to modern philosophy's overconfidence in the rational subject, he nevertheless advocates "substantial self-determination," as a necessary means to authentic religious beliefs and practice.

Borowitz' critique of modern Jewish philosophy is divided into rational and nonrational approaches to religion. As the Enlightenment's child, modern Jewish philosophy's objective has been to reconcile individual freedom with the validity of traditionalism. The reduction of Judaism to rationalist morality is epitomized in the philosophy of Hermann Cohen. Later reworking of rationalistic approaches to Judaism can be seen in the idealistic thought of Leo Baeck, who grounds the essence of Judaism in the universal idea of ethical monotheism yet extends Cohen's neo-Kantianism to include a personal spirituality. Kaplan's naturalistic interpretation of Judaism is another mode of rationalist philosophy, which displaces God with human self-realization, yet legitimates secularized Jewishness and develops a strong Jewish ethnicity.

Borowitz categorizes Buber, Rosenzweig, and Heschel as nonrationalist Jewish philosophers. Buber and Rosenzweig emphasize a personal relationship with God as the means for validating Jewish life and beliefs, a theological position to which Borowitz is sympathetic because, broadly speaking, it confirms transcendence without undermining the authority of the individual self. Despite Borowitz' resonance with Buber's personalism, he concludes that Buber fails to address the question of normative Jewish practice. As Borowitz puts it, "If Jewishness is merely a personal, existential stance . . . what will give structure to Jewish life in the Diaspora? In what sense do these Jewish individuals function as the people of the Covenant?" In fact, this is the central problematic with which Borowitz is engaged, since he, too, finds himself holding on to a type of religious personalism.

The challenge of maintaining a religious personalism is to reconcile existentialist inclinations with Jewish traditionalism. One extreme version of a personalist traditionalism is the recent return of a minority of contemporary Jews to religious fundamentalism. It is in the context of considering the intellectual underpinnings of such religious resurgence, or neo-Orthodoxy, that Borowitz underscores Heschel's postsecular philosophy. He identifies Heschel as a precursor of Jewish postmodernity insofar as his philosophy gives voice to the sublimity of God, who is the most basic premise of our existence. Heschel's passionate rendition of "actional" piety is credible to Borowitz, but the complete subordination of the self to God in his system is not. His paradigm of absolute transcendence, which leaves no room for self-determination, is inadequate for Borowitz' theology of postmodern spirituality. Borowitz notes that Heschel's theocentric theology and his view of Jewish law as grounding our values offer a moving validation of neo-traditional Judaism and, consequently, could supply the foundation for a postmodern Jewish theology. Nonetheless, he concludes that Heschel's ahistoricism and his lack of concern with ethnicity would pose difficulties for such a theology.

In place of Heschel's and Michael Wyschogrod's authoritarian theism, Cohen and Baeck's rationalist model, and Kaplan's socially based philosophy, Borowitz proposes a new, postmodern notion of the Jewish self that both continues and discontinues different aspects of Buber's approach. Of all modern Jewish thinkers, Buber's work best approximates Borowitz' postmodern Jewish theology. Buber's notion of the "I" and "Thou" entails an absolute commitment to a moral action out of a free response to the "Thou" whom we encounter. Yet the shortcoming of Buber's personalistic view of God is that neither its personalism nor its universalism can generate a life structured by normative Jewish values and behavior. Borowitz resonates with Buber's personalistic view of God and speculates that if its starting point were the historically constituted Jewish self, it could support a theory of Jewish obligation.

Even though Borowitz is philosophically close to Buber's and Rosenzweig's personalism, manifested in the concept of relationship with God who chooses and commands, he argues that Buber and Rosenzweig lack the theological discourse to link a private experience of revelation with particular Jewish obligations. Both the anthropocentrism of Buber's notion that Israel chose God and his antinomianism are problematic to Borowitz, for the former lacks a strong concept of God and the latter challenges the notion of Jewish obligation. Rosenzweig's concept of chosenness is problematic because it is meta-historical: ignoring the historicity of the Sinai event and other central events in the history of the Jews. Because Rosenzweig aimed to establish the eternity of Jewish existence, over and against the temporary existence of other religions, he erroneously ignored the historically embodied foundation of Jewish life. Furthermore, even though Rosenzweig favors a return to Jewish observance and, in distinction from Buber, validates the authority of Jewish law, he does so through a dogmatic assertion of the binding power of Jewish law. Borowitz criticizes Rosenzweig's failure to situate Jewish obligation within his central notion of revelation: revelation's command in *The Star of Redemption* may be love, and the individual may be transformed by this miraculous overflow, but the event is still devoid of specific Jewish law.

BOROWITZ' POSTMODERN JEWISH THEOLOGY

Having rejected, in part or completely, earlier paradigms for structuring Jewish belief, Borowitz introduces his constructive theology of renewing the Covenant. Providing an historical context for his theology, he reminds us that while modernity ended as pseudo- or anti-spirituality, postmodernity involves a return to genuine spirituality, born out of disenchantment with modernity and, at the same time, a refusal to despair over its failures. At the foundation of his thinking is an unwavering belief in God, or what he refers to as the "Absolute." Drawing upon biblical and rabbinic notions of a God who is known only in His relation to the world, he notes the ambivalence in traditional Judaism's treatment of God: even as tradition insists on the absoluteness of the self-disclosure of God's will, embodied in the Oral and written Torah, it envisions a limited notion of God as "self-conditioned by creation and Covenant." Unlike the Greek philosophical idea of an absolute as a self-contained, immovable reality, Borowitz asserts that Judaism's notion of a relational God knows of an Absolute only in the weak sense of the word.

Borowitz' theological method is a retrieval of biblical theology in the context of a liberally defined religious existence informed by history and modernist sensibilities. He follows in the footsteps of his predecessors, Buber and Rosenzweig, who had rendered the biblical views of God as Creator, Revealer, and Redeemer in existential and phenomenological terms. The Covenant life, Borowitz suggests, is a traditional Jewish life, devoted to family and community and affiliated with the Hebrew language, religious custom, and the land of Israel.

Borowitz' concept of Covenant implies a Jewish self constituted by its commitment to historical continuity, but it fails to justify the obligation to such particularist claims. For Borowitz, Covenant is not bound by the authority and embodiment of the Torah but is a lived experience. Renewing the Covenant is an existential move subject to one's personal and privileged moment of contact with God. It is only upon such a moment that one's relatedness to the historical body and fate of the Jewish people is absolutely dependent.

Borowitz shifts from an individual to a communal notion of the self, on the premise that the Jewish self is constituted by its relation to the history and life of the Jewish people, but is nevertheless not completely determined by these. Assuming a living encounter with God, Borowitz is optimistic about the capacities of a responsible Jewish selfhood that would, to paraphrase his words, sufficiently limit itself to leave room for community and God. Echoing postmodern notions of the fragmented self, he suggests that, since the constitution of such a self is an ongoing process of mediation between lived experience and memory, the result can only be a temporary and fragmented identification of personhood with Jewishness.

The postmodernist angle of Borowitz' thought is epitomized by his quest for the proper balance between autonomy and tradition. On the one hand, he is emphatic in his belief that reason and individualism (and not corporate loyalty) are our moral guide to responsibility. He rejects the normative principle that authentic Jewish continuity requires the *halakhic* process or our obligation to all Jewish law. Instead, he proposes a "newly flexible *Halakha*," which assumes the persons' right to self-legislation and choice of action. On the other hand, he claims that community must structure one's being in the world, even if ethics and human dignity may outrank the critical needs of the group. Citing examples of clashing values in the case of the Israeli government's insistence that Russian immigrants must come to Israel and not the United States, Borowitz sees it as a moral imperative to support the free choice of Russian prisoners of Zion over our support for the political needs of the State of Israel.

Another way of conveying the tension he sees between particularism and universalism is in terms of the boundaries of ethnic identity and transcendent religiosity. If Covenant is the central theme for his dialectical thinking, redemption is one of its important manifestations. Borowitz rejects liberal and rationalist efforts to identify redemption with political and social action. He believes that such notions are divorced from their transcendent grounds and therefore cannot sustain unique Jewish religiosity. Even Buber and Rosenzweig fail to link redemption with an explicit divine act, and therefore they, too, share in the humanistic concept of redemption characteristic of modern Jewish philosophy. While Borowitz speaks of humanity's role in redemption, echoing the Lurianic paradigm of Tikkun Olam, he also speaks of a transcendent redemption, as displayed in the traditional notion of the Messiah. It would have been interesting to see what he means by the notion of a Messiah. He seems to offer a personalist view, which would be in tension with his universalist aspirations; furthermore, his association of such events as the Civil Rights movement, the Six Day War, and the fall of Communism with redemption is questionable in light of his earlier critique of anthropocentric notions of redemption.

While Borowitz denies any secular interpretation of the idea of redemption, he is willing to associate its meaning with the outcome of certain historical events. At the same time, he is reluctant (in his assessment of contemporary Jewish root experiences), to identify either the State of Israel with redemption, or the Holocaust with revelation. He cautions against letting these govern our theological affirmation of the Covenant. He argues that while the Holocaust should be a dominant motive in our search for a postmodern spirituality, it nevertheless does not faithfully teach us the reality of Jewish existence.

In Borowitz' effort to affirm both Jewish ethnicity and Jewish spirituality, ethnic or historically based identification sometimes takes the back seat to spiritual absolutism. This theological position conflicts with Borowitz' advocacy of Jewish social action as a means of fulfilling Covenantal duties. He argues that both Emil Fackenheim's and Irving Greenberg's theological interpretations of post-Holocaust Jewish will fail to offer us an absolute ground, a transcendent. Rejecting the revelatory meaning which thinkers such as Wiesel, Fackenheim, and Greenberg attribute to the Holocaust, he seeks, along with Michael Wyschogrod, to exhibit the logical weakness in any theological stance that suggests that evil can lead to good. Dissenting from Greenberg's claims that, after the Holocaust, God no longer has a right to command Israel and that only the Jewish will can determine the continuation of Jewish existence, Borowitz insists that only a belief in the Absolute can explain and guarantee Jewish survival.

ISSUES IN BOROWITZ' POSTMODERN THEOLOGY

Borowitz' remarkable theological constructions also raise some pertinent questions:

The Notion of a Strong Absolute. Borowitz seeks "an absolute weak enough to allow for human self-determination yet absolute enough to set the standards for autonomy's rightful use." He suggests that our cognitive freedom in relation to God "weakens" God. However, his distinction between a strong and a weak absolute remains unclear. How strong can God be if we are to maintain an autonomous subject? In what ways does Borowitz' notion of a strong absolute manifest and imply specific Jewish duties that do not follow from "weaker" notions of God such as Rosenzweig's?

Covenantal Community vs. Individual Autonomy. In his construction of a postmodern Jewish theology, Borowitz asserts that God has made a Covenant with all humanity, but that at the same time, the Jewish Covenant is unique and historically binding. Unlike pre-modern and modern notions, however, Borowitz' concept of Covenant lacks any exclusive claims to God's special love for the Jews. He argues that the Jewish self is constituted by its ties to its historical roots, and the Covenant implies fundamental Jewish obligations. This notion of historical roots, however, is in tension with Borowitz' notion of a personalist type of religious experience. Like Rosenzweig, Borowitz believes it is a duty to sustain and live a specifically Jewish life, whether or not one feels personally commanded to do so. At the same time, their focus on what constitutes a religious obligation is different: Rosenzweig speaks about liturgy, scholarship, and law as primary features of Jewish life, while Borowitz speaks primarily about community, history, and ethnicity. Still, the same problematic Borowitz raises in response to Rosenzweig can be asked of Borowitz: How can one grant the individual self the dignity of making independent decisions, while at the same time require that it live in accordance with certain ethnic, historical, and social requirements?

Torah Is Not an Authoritative Source. While both Rosenzweig and Borowitz affirm the authority of person and God, both fail to designate the authority of the Torah as the text which dictates specific Jewish duties and to which Jews are eternally subject. Bypassing this traditional authoritative basis of Jewish obligation, their views of the validity of specific Jewish duties rest on their presupposition of the reality of the living God and his ongoing relationship with the Jewish people. This is a major shortcoming in both theologies. The difficulty with their claim about the human/divine relationship is that it is not an established or necessary condition derived from rational thinking or the acceptance of historical fact; rather, it is a spontaneous occurrence which must be discovered through personal experience rather than derived from the absolute truth of the Torah.

Insubstantial Theological Wrestling with History. One of the central questions for a postmodern Jewish theology is: Can it (comfortably) bypass the catastrophe of the Holocaust, the rupture of order and meaning of the God of the Covenant? Another way of posing this question: Can postmodern Jewish theology distinguish itself from post-Holocaust theology? Borowitz desires to establish the continuity of the biblically secured Covenant and messianic future at the price of ignoring the abyss of the Holocaust. On the one hand, he grants that transcendence can be experienced in time and history. If so, how can he efface the ontological implications of the Holocaust?

Related to the Holocaust issue is the State of Israel. Given his commitment to social and political reality, why does Borowitz not accept an event such as the creation of the State of Israel as a manifestation of the Absolute that dictates our Covenantal obligations? Responding to such a question, Borowitz suggests that apprehending the meaning of the State of Israel in theological terms may threaten the boundaries between nationalism and spirituality. As he puts it, "as a matter of Jewish principle, no political entity deserves being so exalted." Here the tension between history and metaphysics is at its highest. Borowitz is not consistent in his call for Jewish duty and ethnic loyalty. If there is a Jewish duty of political solidarity and support for Israel, then the Covenant must be renewed through this participation in history rather than through a reiteration of a metaphysical reality divorced from historical events. His response to the question of Israel weakens the ground of Covenantal piety, for the metaphysical claim of transcendence seems to replace the claim of ethnic loyalty and the bond of community.

Fackenheim clearly understands Jewish moral duty in light of his theological interpretation of the Holocaust and the State of Israel. Borowitz, on the other hand, maintains the tension between ethnic loyalty and what he claims is Absolute Transcendence. Would Borowitz agree that the balance he wishes to achieve between particularism and universalism may be threatened at the expense of justifying certain Jewish particularist claims?

Such difficulties only attest to the challenging project Borowitz has undertaken. Living in the dialectic between particularism and universalism is suggestive of new possibilities in Jewish experience and self-understanding. Borowitz engages us in a most timely intellectual self-examination. In a way the book ends where it might have begun, or better yet, where his next book would begin. Related to my earlier questions of the implications of a strong Absolute, I would also be interested in hearing what creative contributions to traditional Jewish life are envisioned by postmodern theology? Would a postmodern religiosity engage us in new liturgical and textual tasks, for these are the central building blocks for the Jewish community? If postmodern Jewish theology is post-*halakhic*, what specifically is a Jew's obligation to issues of social and political injustices such as racism and sexism? How should Jews respond to ecological issues?

Borowitz' thought provokes us to take seriously the challenge of discovering an appropriate response to the rupture in our individual and corporate psyche that characterizes our postmodern reality. Borowitz is a paradigmatic teacher of Jewish thought and values. He comes forward with a constructive effort to relate his personal religious experience and values to those who are philosophically informed and spiritually awake enough to listen to the critical issues that currently face us. His call prompts us to share in the task of renewing the Covenant.

4

Reading the Covenant:
Some Postmodern Reflections

EDITH WYSCHOGROD

In 1983, Gene Borowitz, one of the most perceptive Jewish theologians at work today, wrote that the key question for the emancipated Jew, even after the Holocaust remains: "How can one be modern and Jewish?"[1] For many Jews, he maintained at that time, modernity was inextricably bound up with the world view of science and with a universalist ethics. Modernity, as refracted in Jewish communal sensibility, was identified with three crucial assumptions: first, with the verificationist model of truth in science as providing the paradigm for understanding truth in most other domains of human experience; second with the claim that all of humankind is the reference point for moral action; and third with the insistence that the highest value is to be attributed to personal autonomy, together with its corollary that life derives its worth from self-affirmation and self-realization. Borowitz does not repudiate these taken for granted claims of modern Jews, but he brings out their inconsistencies: not only their discord with normative Judaism—this was the work of modernity itself—but also with one another. In fact, many postmodern analysts of modernity claim, mistakenly, that modernism's rationality is a fabric of suppositions that are all of a piece. Borowitz shows that the autonomy criterion leads in two directions, the Kantian one of universality as the standard for moral action and the other, the valuing of pure self-affirmation. At the same time, he insists in his earlier work and continues to insist now that modernity's claims must be reined in by the affirmations and exactions of Jewish particularity. The curbing of modernity's value scheme is one important present-day meaning of the Covenant with Israel.

The fine-tuning of the reciprocal adaptation of modernity and Jewish particularity is, on his reading, the task of contemporary Jewish theology. Thus, he explained:

> The contemporary agenda is set by the need to maintain the gains of universalism . . . while giving equal priority to the people of Israel and its distinctive way of life . . . I give Jewish tradition priority in my thought. Tradition makes authoritative but not irresistible claims upon me and I respond to them out of my Western culture situation in a personal . . . way.[2]

During this period, Borowitz examined the tension between liberal Reform and Reconstructionist thinkers and the claims of Jewish existential thought, especially that of Buber and Heschel, to whom Borowitz was and remains sympathetic. As early as 1968, Borowitz had written: "Buber fills the traditional concepts of religion with new power and thus makes possible a contemporary religious practice which is more pious than the older liberalism and more sophisticated than unrefurbished traditionalism."[3]

More than two decades have elapsed since Borowitz first began to formulate his position, a Reform theology tilting towards a religious existential personalism. The extraordinary historical, social, economic, and philosophico/theological transformations of the intervening period have not vitiated Borowitz' previous insights. His views, newly articulated and with significant additions, stand up remarkably well to the challenges of postmodernity as these are recounted in this significant and thoughtful new book. This is not, however, because the work itself is a postmodern theology. In what follows I shall state my understanding of Borowitz' position, point to some difficulties in his interpretation of postmodernity, offer some emendations, and conclude by going beyond his extremely suggestive readings of Covenant to propose some postmodern additions.

BETWEEN TWO COVENANTS

Borowitz' introduction lays out the work's ground plan and defines many of the terms of his analysis, a vocabulary whose semantic density grows richer and more complex in the course of the development of the Covenant idea. He defines theology as "orderly reflection on Jewish belief." He goes on to posit "substantial self-determination" as both a criterion and a necessary outcome of theological reflection. Thus, the theologian's freedom of thought and the actions which flow from such free reflection, an assumption of Reform theology, are not abandoned in Borowitz' work. What distinguishes his position from normative Reform Judaism is his stress upon the meaningfulness of Covenant, a term that, for him, has a twofold meaning. Covenant (capital C), denotes the special relation of Israel with God whereas covenant (lower case *c*) refers to God's compact with Noah and, through him, with all humankind, the compact with Noah functioning as a trope for modernity's universalist ethics. Freedom for the Jew who is both a member of Israel and of humankind is exercised within the constraints of these covenants.

Borowitz identifies six root Jewish experiences: Covenant, settlement, rabbinism, Diaspora, Emancipation, and post-Holocaust, terms for which the idea of covenant is the primary and controlling template key that governs the interpretation of the rest. In the book's first section, Borowitz chronicles the sociological and theological impact of the release from the ghetto and the Jewish entry into modernity, and the resulting split in Jewish communal existence between the private or Jewish and public spheres. The naturalism of Kaplan and the existentialism of Buber and Rosenzweig reflect, respectively, affirmative and negative responses to these developments. In Heschel's critique of the meaninglessness of a secularized reality and the affirmation of "an immutable ground of universal value," Borowitz finds a precursor to postmodernity.[4] Although I tend to agree with Borowitz about Heschel's importance, I cannot imagine any card-carrying postmodern endorsing an unchanging ground of value, a point to which I shall return. Like Heschel, Borowitz claims that "God and the individual self are the two axes around which [his] faith pivots."[5]

The break with Messianic modernity and the thrust into postmodern consciousness is configured by the advent of and subsequent debate about the Holocaust. Borowitz repudiates the sacralization of the Holocaust and the reading of a destructive dimension into divine being. Instead he stands by his earlier affirmation that trust in God "held fast through centuries of trial . . . and every new Exodus experience."[6] The Holocaust is not a Sinaitic event although it is an ineradicable part of Jewish identity formation. If any *conceptual* outcome of the Holocaust can be predicted, it is that a distinction must be drawn between victim and perpetrator, a distinction that makes sense only when some unqualified good can be affirmed.7 Like Fackenheim, Borowitz saw the Six Day War as a (somehow) counter-Holocaustal affirmation of God's saving power. I want to demur that if one sacralizes history, it is hard to posit the redemptive dimension without implicating the divine in its nadir moments. I shall return to this point when I consider Borowitz' treatment of theodicy.

Borowitz' faith is articulated in terms of the traditional Jewish themes of God, Israel, and Torah. God is to be understood relationally in the context of Torah and of communal continuity, a framework in which Covenant is central.8 The Covenant makes Israel God's people, a people obligated to Torah obedience. He sees these motifs as articulated in recent Jewish thought through four paradigms: the revelationism of Heschel and Rosenzweig, the Enlightenment rationalism of Hermann Cohen and Leo Baeck, the naturalism and pragmatism of Mordecai Kaplan, and the "mediating self" of Martin Buber. Borowitz' own model is that of "the Jewish self," one that he designates as a "holism" in which God, Israel/self (the slash expressing the indissolubility of self and community) and Torah are co-implicated in reciprocal relations.

THE WEAK ABSOLUTE

This Jewish self model, he argues, demands a God who enters into covenants, a relational God. Such a God is "a weak Absolute,"9 an Absolute that is transcendent but "a close-enough-Other to stand in intimate relation to us."10 The Absolute's immanent aspect sustains and unifies our lives but requires transcendent support if it is to command belief. Transcendence is encountered in human existence through religious awe, through the exalted character attributed to it, and through its power to orient the exercise of freedom.11 Borowitz also argues for the entry of transcendence, of the divine sparks in Buberian/kabalistic terms, into everyday experience through charity, blessing, and prayer.

The idea of a weak Absolute is a bold move. It is easy enough to demonstrate the impossibility of such an Absolute on logical grounds. What Borowitz intends, however, by this apparent oxymoron is something like a distinction between the Absolute in-itself and the Absolute for-us, transcendence and immanence, a distinction that resists Hegelian dialectical sublation. Divine transcendence, God who remains "the most high," opens up the sense of astonished reverence attested in Borowitz' moving descriptions of the Jewish understanding of God's numinosity.

One would welcome a more extended development of the implications of this idea. Although Borowitz may not want to pursue this course, a logical and phenomenological analysis of a weak Absolute suggests a fissuring within divinity, a play of differences within the divine nature itself. Such differentiation would result, not in an allotment of stable spheres or functional distinctions between transcendence and immanence, but rather in a postmodern reconfiguring of our grasp of the divine "nature" as one in which a dynamic interplay of difference is intrinsic. This reading would be consistent with biblical stories of a divine change of heart, of God differing with himself in response to human supplication. Borowitz states his rejection of nihilistic, rationalistic, and process approaches to God in favor of a God whom one cannot know, but who emerges in personal encounter, a God who grounds our values and allows for human freedom, a position that remains well within the ambit of modernist perspectives.

GOD'S JUSTICE AND ETHICS

The problem of theodicy is also worked out from the standpoint of traditional frameworks. First, he suggests the standard argument that evil must exist if human beings are to be free, that God's justice, limited by the need to grant human freedom, can only be rough and ready. That there is such justice, he claims, is clear from the fact that most people receive more bounty than is deserved. The use of this argument in relation to human suffering generally is puzzling, but is especially surprising in a post-Holocaust context and, I suspect, reflects the residual optimism of the liberal aspect of Borowitz' theology. In his earlier work, he adduces a more compelling Dostoevskian argument. "If God is dead," he reasons, "then Auschwitz was not despicable and Treblinka was permitted. If there is no transcendent standard of holiness by which all men are bound, then why should the strong not rule . . . ?"[12] What should be concluded is, of course, that since Auschwitz *is* despicable, God *cannot* be dead.

Borowitz' liberal side is at its best in his compelling account of religious hope, the belief that God is not only Creator and Revealer but Redeemer as well. His position is equally forceful in his critique of the narcissistic self-centeredness that is a fall-out of modernist self-determination.[13] Here he takes "a postmodern yet rabbinic position [that] individuality implies community" both with others and with God.[14] This stress on community is "genuinely" postmodern, a point to which I shall recur, as is the idea that we may not think of ourselves as "individual selves in general . . . [but] must end the distinction between . . . personhood and . . . Jewishness."[15]

Yet Jewish particularity demands that we not abnegate universalism either, which, for Borowitz is not based on homogeneity but takes account of the richly diverse peoples of the world.[16] Borowitz' point suggests an interesting *aporia* for a Jewish postmodernism to ponder: What is to be done with a universality that postmodernism abjures, when this universality is itself the product of Jewish difference or particularity, so that it is a universality that can only be thought in its endless differing from the particular? For Borowitz, the Jew must not tip so far towards the covenant of Noah, universalism, that she or he forgets the Covenant of Sinai.[17] "Postmodern religiosity," he says, "acknowledges God as the ground of. . . . personhood . . . and find[s] something sacred in exercising . . . personal autonomy in relation to God."[18]

POSTMODERNITY AND COVENANT

The elaboration of Borowitz' covenant doctrine in the final portion of the book should appeal to postmoderns who want to cope with the problem of justice. Borowitz stresses the inequities of the relations of the Covenant partners, and claims that the contradictions in rabbinic hermeneutics stem from this difference. Israel is "particular, historical, limited," whereas the other Covenant partner, God, is "universal, enduring, perfect, and unlimited."[19] He goes on to affirm that, as Covenant partner, Israel is entitled to the land that God promises, an aspect of Covenant that governs his understanding of the contemporary state of Israel, which is bound by the moral claims of the Covenant. In a concession to modernity, Borowitz grants that the individual who enters into Covenant relations must be autonomous and self-determining if she or he is to be a Covenant partner.

It is in this context that Borowitz testifies movingly to his own divine-human encounters, to the penetration by numinosity of the most banal events of his everyday life. Rejecting the identity of Covenant fidelity with strict *halakhic* (legal) observance, Borowitz posits "a non-Orthodox self that is autonomous yet so fundamentally shaped by the Covenant that whatever issues from its depths will have authentic Jewish character."[20] Such a self is linked covenantally to prior and future Jewish generations.[21]

It should be clear from the preceding analyses that Borowitz' earlier existential personalism, with its stress on the emergence of transcendence in dialogue, is augmented but not replaced by a stress on ethnicity and particularity, "a postmodern Judaism [that] manifests a resurgent particularism."[22] Postmodernism, he argues, is a disillusioned response to modernism's "belief that secular enlightenment would make people ethically self-correcting."[23] He also speaks of postmoderns as carrying with them modernity's "dedication to autonomy even as they seek to transcend it,"[24] as well as its pluralism and democratic spirit.[25]

Because Borowitz does not focus on the term postmodernism, I have adduced these meanings from his comments in various contexts. Postmodernity most often seems to function as a chronological grid, the period of the 1960s and after. But postmodernity must be construed as a conceptual matrix and not as a chronological parameter. Were postmodernity merely a function of clock time, any post-1960s theology, including the theology of ultra right-wing orthodoxies would qualify as postmodern insofar as they are alive and flourishing today.

While there can, of course, be no standard definition of postmodernism, a term that folds into itself a repudiation of normative discourse, it cannot mean what the history of the term, its uses in architecture, literary criticism, and French thought, shows it to have explicitly excluded: that there is a foundation for values, that we are selves and can become whole selves by virtue of our relation to a divine ground. While Borowitz offers a compelling critique of reason, it is largely an existential rather than a postmodern one. A careful elaboration of the difference between existentialism and postmodernism would take me beyond the scope of the present comments. I can only suggest that the idea of bypassing Enlightenment rationality, by appealing to personal encounter is an existential and not a postmodern strategy, that the postmodernism of a Foucault, a Derrida, or a Deleuze, is as antithetical to the ontological framework of encounter—encounter is, after all, rooted in an ontological ground—as it is to Enlightenment reason. Postmodern critiques of reason rely on such strategies as uncovering the differential infrastructure in reason itself (Derrida), or undermining the grand meta-narratives of theory (Lyotard), whereas existential attacks on reason, at least those of Kierkegaardian provenance, appeal to the Absurd.

A second criterion often invoked by postmodernism is double coding, in which two meanings, one generally identified as high modern and the other as popular, are built into a text, which results in a reciprocally interpenetrating critique. A case could be made for reading rabbinic texts as doubly coded, but this is not the focus of Borowitz' work. He is, however, in accord with what is generally recognized as postmodern in his appeal to particularity or otherness, the otherness of the people covenanted to God who are other than the others within a differentially-structured humankind and other than God.

It is just here, in relation to alterity or otherness, that Jean-François Lyotard's analysis of the differend may help to extend and elaborate Borowitz' own rich reading of Israel's Covenant. Lyotard, in the interest of developing a metaphor for the expression of powerlessness in contemporary societies, turns to a juridical model. He argues that, ideally, the plaintiff in a court process makes an accusation which the accused has a chance to rebut. But "imagine the case where the plaintiff is divested of the means to argue [accuse] and becomes for that reason a victim."[26] He calls this situation a "*différend*." The trial takes place as if there were no damages, because the conflict is regulated "in the idiom of one of the parties while the wrong suffered by the other is not signified in that idiom."[27] He goes on: "The differend is the unstable state and instant of language wherein something which must be able to be put into phrases cannot yet be. . . . This state includes silence. . . . A lot of searching must be done to find new rules for forming and linking new phrases"[28] to disclose the victim's feeling of inarticulateness. It is not irrelevant that Lyotard develops his account in the context of the voicelessness of the victims of Auschwitz.

Recall now that Borowitz emphasizes the inequities of the Covenant partners, and suggests that the contradictions of rabbinic hermeneutics issue from this inequity. Could one not claim that rabbinic language always already (in postmodern idiom) recognizes the doubleness of Israel's status as litigant in an endless trial? Is this not a situation described as a differend in which Israel is as "victim" always already voiceless, but as elect always already bold and in quest of a divine language so that it might question divine justice? Such, I suggest, would be the doubleness of Covenant yielded by a postmodern reading.

NOTES

1. Eugene B. Borowitz, *Choices in Modern Jewish Thought* (New York: Behrman House, 1983), p. 19.
2. Ibid., p. 279.
3. Eugene B. Borowitz, *A New Jewish Theology in the Making* (Philadelphia: The Westminster Press, 1968), p. 135.
4. Eugene B. Borowitz, *Renewing the Covenant: A Theology for the Postmodern Jew* (Philadelphia: The Jewish Publication Society, 1991), p. 29.
5. Ibid., p. 31.
6. Eugene B. Borowitz, *How Can a Jew Speak of Faith Today?* (Philadelphia: The Westminster Press, 1969), p. 43.
7. Borowitz, *Renewing the Covenant*, p. 42.
8. Ibid., p. 56.
9. Ibid., p. 73.
10. Ibid., p. 82.
11. Ibid., pp. 100–102.
12. Borowitz, *How Can a Jew*, pp. 33–34.
13. Borowitz, *Renewing the Covenant*, p. 172.
14. Ibid., p. 168.
15. Ibid., p. 181.
16. Ibid., p. 183.
17. Ibid., p. 204.
18. Ibid., p. 212.
19. Ibid., p. 218.
20. Ibid., p. 284.
21. Ibid., pp. 291–92.
22. Ibid., p. 5.
23. Ibid., p. 21.
24. Ibid., p. 20.
25. Ibid., p. 50.
26. Jean-François Lyotard, *The Différend: Phrases in Dispute*, trans. Georges Van Den Abeele (Minneapolis: University of Minneapolis Press, 1988), p. 9.
27. Borowitz, *Renewing the Covenant*, p. 9.
28. Ibid., p. 13.

5

Post-Modern or Chastened Modern?
Eugene B. Borowitz' Vision
for Jewish Fidelity

THOMAS W. OGLETREE

As a Christian theologian, I am the "stranger" who has been welcomed into a conversation about postmodern Jewish thought. Because I am a stranger, I will be learning more than teaching, listening more than speaking. My primary interest is to deepen my understanding of a companion heritage of faith; yet I am also struck by parallels in Jewish life and thought to my own struggles for Christian fidelity in the contemporary world. I recall the way Peter Ochs, my friend, describes the "face-to-face" experience: two people treading water, nothing but their bobbing heads showing above the surface.[1] Neither begins to know all that is involved in the life of the other, but each, to his surprise, recognizes something of himself mirrored in the other's face. So I also find something of myself mirrored in the work of Eugene B. Borowitz, even though the greater part of his life world remains unknown to me.

I consider *Renewing the Covenant* highly important, in part because it informs my own faith journey, but also because it advances an ongoing conversation within Judaism. I identify with Professor Borowitz' project. I read it as an attempt to recognize the importance of the European Enlightenment—its emancipatory power, its critique of traditional religious life and thought—while also holding in view its limitations. He underscores our need to recover, in a new manner, the formative power of the great traditions of faith that have sustained us over many generations. When he focuses upon God, Covenant, Torah, where Covenant refers to Jewish particularity and Torah to Jewish obligations, I am reminded of an equivalent triad in Christianity: the reality of God, ecclesial existence as the new people of the God, and the critical mediation of normative traditions of faith and practice as resources for responsible Christian life in church and society.

POST-MODERN OR QUALIFIED MODERN?

Having heard our responses to him, Professor Borowitz may by now regret having given the term "postmodern" such prominence in his vision for Jewish fidelity. Instead of conveying the central aims of the book, this term may actually have distracted his readers, disposing us to expect something other than what we found. By the same token, we respondents may suspect that we have devoted too much attention to explaining what postmodernism *really* is, as though our central task is to demonstrate energetically that Professor Borowitz' book does not quite fit the label. Rather than directly engaging the argument presented in the book, we may occupy ourselves with telling him what he should have written had he truly grasped the logic of his project. Had Professor Borowitz used other terms to characterize his perspective—for example, a modernist case for Jewish particularity, or perhaps simply, a theology for committed, non-Orthodox Jews—we would have had to rewrite our papers.

Even so, what Professor Borowitz offers is essentially modernist, albeit a chastened and qualified modernism. His stated aim is to reaffirm, authentically, Jewish understandings of God, Covenant, and Torah without falling prey to neo-traditionalist repudiations of the modern world. He correctly discerns the dangers in straight-forward reversals of modernism, whatever their specific religious bases. Apart from modernist constraints, neo-traditionalism can unleash cruel and vicious conflicts among human beings who have diverse moral and religious identifications. To protect his own position from such neo-traditionalist misunderstandings, Professor Borowitz builds his case for distinctive Jewish understandings and practices by relying upon modernist categories and strategies.

My primary interest is to examine the modifications in Enlightenment thought that figure in Professor Borowitz' account of Jewish fidelity. Two are pivotal: (1) his qualifications of the Enlightenment stress on universality in order to heighten our appreciation for Jewish particularity; and (2) his qualifications of the Enlightenment insistence upon moral autonomy in favor of a stronger emphasis on the formative significance of moral community. In regard to both of these themes, Professor Borowitz qualifies and yet retains modernist insights.

UNIVERSALITY AND JEWISH PARTICULARITY

Professor Borowitz qualifies, yet retains, the modernist emphasis on universality by offering a universalistic case for the continuing importance of Jewish particularity. That is to say, although he gives new weight to Jewish particularity, the controlling categories of his thought remain universal in both form and content, and hence, abstracted from the density of concrete historical existence. This claim arises directly from my surprise that he did not do quite what I expected him to do, especially as I consider my own efforts to reaffirm Christian particularity in a world that is morally and religiously pluralistic. My reaffirmation of concrete particularity reflects a judgment that experiential awareness, and even critical inquiry itself, are conditioned and constrained at every point by established social structures and concrete historical dynamics. These complex processes configure the operations of critical reason in concrete life settings.[2] Claims to universality that presume some radical transcendence of human sociality and historicity are pretentious and self-deceived. To do justice to Christian particularity, for example, I must focus my reflections on the critical retrieval and constructive mediation of normative Christian traditions that remain vital to concrete faith communities enduring over time. In this frame of reference, theology becomes a hermeneutical enterprise.[3] In contrast, Professor Borowitz devotes relatively little attention to the critical retrieval and mediation of the normative traditions that constitute Jewish particularity. If anything, he appears nervous about giving himself over too strongly to that undertaking, as though it might lead him back to some kind of *halakhic* imprisonment in a cultural ghetto.

What Professor Borowitz offers is a critical assessment of the work of a series of modern and anti-modern Jewish thinkers, as described in Edith Wyschogrod's contribution to this volume. These thinkers represent streams of thought that we associate with naturalism, rationalism, and revelationism, respectively. The first two are clearly modern; the third, less postmodern than antimodern. What we get in Professor Borowitz' study, then, is not an engagement with the concreteness, density, complexity, and ambiguity of Jewish particularity, but, rather, a critical portrayal of an ongoing debate among selected Jewish intellectuals, mostly Western European or American, about the meaning of being Jewish in the modern world. In relation to this debate, Professor Borowitz seeks to develop a credible case for the significance of Jewish particularity on terms that are in principle universally intelligible. By intent, his account of Jewish particularity is accessible not simply to the non-Orthodox Jew who has fully internalized modernist currents; it is also available to open-minded adherents of other religious traditions. Potentially, his claims might prove persuasive even to those who have no self-conscious religious identifications, provided they remained receptive to cogent arguments in support of religious sensibilities.

Professor Borowitz' concept of Jewish particularity builds chiefly upon the naturalism of Mordecai Kaplan. It amounts to a sociological theory of Jewish civilization. It also draws upon Martin Buber's existentialist, personal account of the experience of God. These thinkers provide the lynch pins of his constructive claims. Mr. Kaplan underscores the fact that moral and religious practices require a social and cultural base, a civilizational grounding. While this theory may function to justify attention to the maintenance, preservation, and development of particular civilizations, it is itself universal in form. It can inform theological inquiry, but it does not itself venture any explicit theological claims or hypotheses.

To grasp the significance of the Jewish particularity, Professor Borowitz recognizes, we must do more than simply show that moral and religious existence require civilization. They do not, after all, require *Jewish* civilization! To get at Jewish particularity, one has to link Jewish existence to God's covenanting initiatives in forming the Jewish people with a distinctive vocation in the life of the world. This move is prompted by questions that are internal to Judaism. At stake is the religious significance of the continuity of the Jewish people over time. When Professor Borowitz begins to elaborate his understandings of God's presence in the existence of the Jewish people, Martin Buber emerges as his principal guide. Initially, he commends Buber's portrayal of what it means to be in relationship to God, because he finds it congruent with his own personal experience. Yet, his interpretation of Buber's thought by no means highlights its distinctively Jewish features. Here, too, universal elements, those likely to prove intelligible at least to persons nurtured in one of the monotheistic religions, are in the forefront of attention. In this connection, it is well to keep in mind that Christians read Buber as avidly as they read any other twentieth-century religious thinker. Buber's language about "I and Thou" struck a deep chord. Christians draw upon his insights as readily as Hermann Cohen utilizes Immanuel Kant's moral philosophy.

Professor Borowitz states that critical reason by itself cannot establish a comprehensive, universally compelling view of the world. On this point, I am in complete agreement. At the same time, he also insists that reason can do two very important things. First, it can display the unacceptability of religious assertions that claim exemption from critical scrutiny. In this respect, it can rule out of further consideration irrational and anti-rational perspectives. Therefore, Professor Borowitz subjects all Jewish thought, both traditional and contemporary, to canons of rationality that reflect modern philosophical and scientific thinking. Resurgent Orthodoxy, various forms of fundamentalism, and neo-traditionalism are all rejected on this basis.

Second, reason can offer a description of religious awareness that is at least potentially intelligible, perhaps even plausible, within the context of the contemporary world. A rational account of religious awareness is intelligible and plausible because it is formulated in terms that are not incompatible with the rest of our critical knowledge of the world. Broadly speaking, this claim is precisely the modernist project. A bona fide postmodern view would have to acknowledge in a more thoroughgoing way the historicity of all thought and awareness. In my view, such historicity also entails the relativity and ambiguity of all human thought and awareness, including notions derived from allegedly absolute divine disclosures. There is no definitive way to transcend the limitations of finitude or of flawed human existence. Having recognized the historicity of all human thought and awareness, we then have to come to grips with an irreducible plurality in the forms of religious and moral existence. We also have to accept a comparable plurality in human accounts of what constitutes authentically rational thought. The challenge is to learn to live amid such plurality in a manner that resists the nihilistic repudiation of all normative standards. The fundamental problem with much so-called postmodern thought is that it is essentially nihilistic and skeptical. Once the pretensions of modernism have been exposed, then human reason itself tends for many to degenerate into mere rationalizations of arbitrary preferences, or what is more likely, into economically and politically motivated "spins" on contemporary public issues. Persons of faith rightly resist such nihilism.

When we accept the historicity of all human thought, the normative traditions that guide our own existence as participants in concrete faith communities by no means lose their authority. On the contrary, we are then set free to appropriate critically the truth and the practical wisdom they embody, not simply in our thought, but also in our daily practices. These practices include the active observance of rites that constitute us as a people of God. At the same time, we discover anew the moral urgency of honoring and protecting space for the plurality of perspectives that flourish among diverse cultures and subcultures throughout the world. When I contend that all thought is relative, I do not by any means wish to imply that the traditions that shape my own patterns of worldly existence are trivial. For me, and for those who share my faith pilgrimage, they are definitive, however much they are also limited by human frailties. Likewise, I would in no way concede that one person's viewpoint on life or conception of reality is as good as any other, as though basic life stances were merely matters of personal taste. Some life stances are manifestly better than others. One does not need a universalistic perspective, for example, to know that the Holocaust atrocities were evil! Many traditions can display for us the horror of such deeds! Besides, German intellectuals who accommodated themselves to the Nazi agenda were hardly ignorant of Enlightenment thought. Not even abstract, universal principles can shield us from deceit and cruelty when we have allowed ourselves to become entrapped in the power of evil.

My central point here is that Professor Borowitz does not himself move as radically into a full sense of historicity as his opening comments might suggest. He limits his embrace of historicity by a continuing search for standards that transcend the relativities of our historical existence. He wants to hold on to a bit of ahistorical universalism as an ingredient in genuinely rational thought. My own contention is that the European En-lightenment is itself a highly important piece of tradition within the total sweep of civilizations that structure and inform life in the world as we know it. I consider it quite urgent to retain Enlightenment traditions within the body of contemporary thought and practice, in no small meas-ure because of their contributions to the moral substance of American po-litical and economic institutions. Yet, we can embrace Enlightenment cri-tique of traditional religious and political thought without presuming that it is itself an ahistorical or history-transcending phenomenon capable of delivering the final rational truth on the nature of things. It has its own singular strengths and its own absurd pretensions. We learn best what it has to offer us when we appropriate it critically within the context of our more encompassing quest for ultimate truth and meaning.

MORAL AUTONOMY AND COMMUNAL SOLIDARITY

Professor Borowitz qualifies, yet retains, the modernist emphasis on moral autonomy, especially its highly individualistic forms, with a new apprecia-tion for communal solidarity and social accountability. He recognizes that it is not enough to speak in universal terms of the moral self. He calls upon his readers to affirm the Jewish self. In my own context, I would add as well, the Christian self. Stanley Hauerwas reminds us that we cannot say ethics without a "qualifier." We can speak of Jewish ethics, of Roman Catholic ethics, of Mennonite ethics, or perhaps of Enlightenment moral philosophy. We cannot speak simply of ethics as such. When attending to ethical matters, we are always dealing with a particular tradition.[4]

The Jewish self means a self formed and sustained within Jewish com-munal and social processes that endure over time. I am impressed by Pro-fessor Borowitz' willingness to take on some of the sensitive practical im-plications of this elemental fact. He reasons, for example, that it is quite proper to caution Jews about intermarriage with Gentiles. It is also quite proper to emphasize fidelity to Jewish practices and to insist upon active participation in Jewish communal life. These points, it seems to me, are entailed by his emphasis on community. Yet with all the stress on commu-nity, covenant, and peoplehood, Professor Borowitz' position still rests to a considerable degree on a notion of moral autonomy. Over against any form of heteronomous authority, whether sacral or social, he continues to insist upon the right of the free individual to follow his or her own conscience. The case for Jewish obligation, then, finally rests upon the consent of the individual, doubtless the individual who has experienced the presence of God in his or her life. The emphasis on community has not yet been fully incorporated into his account of moral selfhood.

My own project is to try to show more clearly how even my capacity for independent moral judgment and action is derived from and sustained by the communal bonds that nurture me. This capacity is also conditioned and shaped by the social and institutional processes that provide order for my life. Here we must move beyond a simple dichotomy between I-Thou and I-It. I-Thou is not a meeting that occurs in a vacuum. It occurs in concrete social and historical locations, which bear shared human understandings of a specific sort. These shared understandings facilitate, shape, and perhaps also inhibit the I-Thou meeting of which Martin Buber speaks. The central point is that I cannot simply opt out of the formative bonds that figure in my moral identity and still hold onto my moral autonomy. I can exercise my free conscience in opposition to the teachings of my formative community only by means of resources also supplied by that community. My struggle with my community probably reflects tensions already present within my communal heritage. When I become alienated from the community that formed me, my moral autonomy is itself at risk, both my capacity for discerning moral judgment and my powers of implementing my judgments in concrete life practices. My moral autonomy remains unsettled until I can reconstitute it anew in a new relational matrix. In fact, my alienation from my primary community of reference is, more than likely, a reflection of the fact that other attachments, other associations, have already gained preeminent importance in my life. Freedom of conscience and communal solidarity are not independent phenomena, but interrelated poles in the complexity of self experience.

Professor Borowitz is probably correct when he contends that the explicit consent of individuals to norms established through participatory democratic processes cannot, by itself, bring about a strong concept of obligation. Much depends, of course, upon what we mean by consent. Immanuel Kant might argue, for example, that consent is about making and keeping promises. To make a promise without intending to keep it is a moral contradiction. To honor a promise once made, even when it becomes inconvenient or dangerous, is a mark of moral integrity. The crucial question is whether a formal analysis of the moral logic of consent is sufficient in itself to disclose the true nature of moral obligation. I would argue that consent gains its full moral significance from my awareness of deep, enduring, and life-sustaining bonds with fellow human beings, bonds that persistently figure in my own deliberations and actions. Consent expresses my recognition that the common social good finally depends upon the readiness of all people to observe civil laws and public policies arising from constitutionally established principles of representative decision-making. For ethical inquiry, the challenge is to describe in a more complete way the complex communal and interpersonal dynamics that constitute our moral and religious understandings, indeed, that establish their authority in our lives. Within Judaism, and derivatively, within Christianity, the legacy of God's gracious, life-giving Covenant with Israel furnishes a far more profound doctrine of the moral meaning of consent than can be found in purely formalistic analyses.

Moral and religious authority is itself constituted and maintained in and through communal processes. Such authority certainly cannot rest simply upon the claims of individual leaders who presume the right, perhaps by virtue of their office, to define the nature of Jewish obligation. Professor Borowitz rightly resists authoritarian assertions by traditionalist rabbis, which accounts for his opposition to the possible reinstitution of *halakhic* processes within the Jewish community. Authority derives from rich, communal sharing in relation to the normative traditions of Jewish existence, or in my case, of Christian existence. In the pre-modern period, the authoritative interpretation of normative faith traditions did, in considerable measure, reside with rabbis or priests or bishops or a consistory of clergy. In a postmodern world, however, the activity of interpreting is necessarily more dispersed, more interactive, more responsive to diverse perspectives and experiences. It involves the continual re-examination, re-interpretation, and perhaps transformation of formative faith traditions. Nonetheless, it is through and through a communal process.

I cannot develop my own private convictions as a morally autonomous being, wholly isolated from my faith community, without cutting myself off from essential dimensions of my own moral identity. I begin by attempting to understand the vital traditions that disclose the identity of my faith community. So far as possible, I attempt to express clearly and faithfully the shared convictions of that community. I can then position myself to offer suggestions to the community about how it might live and work creatively within the life-giving resources of its normative traditions, preserving their substance yet formulating anew their central understandings in ways that disclose more forcefully their contemporary import for faithful existence.

In attempting to speak to and for my faith community, I may voice views that do not fully accord with my own private understandings. To be sure, I can certainly continue to press my own interpretations. Yet, I cannot simply go my own way, wherever and however I might please, without cutting myself off from essential and indispensable sources of my own fidelity in the life of the world. What we now require is a more nuanced account of communally mediated moral and religious authority, one that embraces the distinctive insights and concerns of individual members, yet retains an appreciation for our deeper communal bonds. The point is not to reestablish traditionalist models of authoritarian control that require us to submit to authority without regard for our own deep moral and religious sensibilities. It is to display more clearly how our own perceptions of obligation are themselves integral to communal belonging.

A RELATIONAL GOD

The personalism lifted up by Professor Borowitz is precious to me. Respecting that personalism, I do not believe that human beings have direct access to absolutes. I have difficulty thinking of God as absolute precisely because God relates to us. A relational God is improperly described by the term "Absolute." The term is too abstract, too detached from the concrete matrix of creation. Absolute moral norms are, likewise, too abstract to expose concrete instances of social evil, basically because we interpret abstract concepts in terms of our own concrete social and cultural locations. The alleged equality of all human beings, celebrated in the Declaration of Independence, was presumed by our "Founding Fathers" to be fully compatible with chattel slavery and with the restriction of the ballot to males who owned property. They took it for granted that some were more equal than others.

It is a mistake to believe that nothing short of an absolute grasp of a universalistic moral imperative will equip us to be outraged by evil. If we will not listen to Moses and the prophets, why do we think that we will be more attentive to Enlightenment moral philosophy? Convictions that are relative to one's own social, cultural, and communal existence are still normative. They have binding authority. Universality is not something we possess, but something we propose, something we seek in discourse with the plurality of human communities. It is, however, more an ideal and a hope—shall we say, a messianic hope?—than a concrete historical reality.

In emphasizing historicity and relativity, my intent is not to dissolve or even to weaken normative authority. It is to recognize that all human thinking is both finite and flawed. To be finite is to be limited in what we are able to see and to understand, even when we attempt to bestow universal form on our central moral convictions. In this respect, I would suggest that the covenant with Noah is a particularistic Jewish way of reaching toward universality. Its virtue is that it does not fall prey to the Kantian claim of direct access to universality through the application of pure practical reason.

Similarly, I would say that the Enlightenment project is a West European way of reaching toward universality. Yet, even this way is not fully adequate to the richness and complexity of diverse human experiences in the cultures of the world. Thus, to seek an apologetic that begins with a recognition of the irreducible plurality of moral and religious perspectives is by no means to trivialize moral standards. It is rather to examine those standards in the concrete historical and communal settings that render them authoritative for human life.

CONCLUSION

In conclusion, I want to take special note of Professor Borowitz' comments in this volume about the importance of history and community. He states quite succinctly the themes that are pivotal to his goal of formulating a "theology for the postmodern Jew." This book by no means marks the end-point of his quest, but rather a crucial step within an on-going inquiry. I shall follow with interest subsequent stages in his attempt to elaborate the meaning of Jewish obligation in terms of history and community. He will almost certainly aid my own efforts to advance a parallel project within Christian thought and practice.

NOTES

1. Referring to Peter Ochs, "A Rabbinic Pragmatism," in *Theology and Dialogue,* ed. B. Marshall (Notre Dame, Ind.: University of Notre Dame Press, 1990), pp. 213 ff.

2. I have elaborated these points in *Hospitality to the Stranger: Dimensions of Moral Understanding* (Philadelphia: Fortress Press, 1985). See also my "The Public Witness of the Christian Churches: Reflections Based Upon Ernst Troeltsch's *Social Teaching of the Christian Churches,"* in *The Annual of the Society of Christian Ethics* (Washington DC: Georgetown University Press, 1992), pp. 43–74. Themes in the latter essay will be elaborated in a monograph scheduled for publication by Westminster/John Knox in the fall of 2000, entitled *Times of Trial: Rethinking the Public Vocation of the Churches.*

3. I have outlined my understanding of hermeneutics in the first chapter of *The Use of the Bible in Christian Ethics* (Philadelphia: Fortress Press, 1983).

4. Stanley Hauerwas, *A Community of Character: Toward a Constructive Christian Social Ethic* (Notre Dame, Ind.: Notre Dame University Press, 1981).

6

Is the Covenant a Bilateral Relationship? A Response to Eugene Borowitz' *Renewing the Covenant*

DAVID NOVAK

Of the many seminal passages in Eugene Borowitz' magisterial theological statement, *Renewing the Covenant*, the core of its argument, it seems to me, is expressed on (p. 273). "The model of relationships . . . [is] that rightful authority arises *between* the parties involved," and this is what "exercise[s] normative power upon them." Borowitz' position is clearly one that builds upon Martin Buber's phenomenology of interpersonal relationality, but which is very much tempered by Franz Rosenzweig's greater emphasis on community and its norms in Jewish religious life.[1] Thus, Borowitz must be seen as an original Jewish thinker, critically continuing the noble tradition of Jewish religious existentialism.[2]

Borowitz has located the essence of Judaism in the Covenant, which is primarily the relationship between God and Israel, and thereafter the relationship between Jews themselves. The designation of an "essence of Judaism" (although Borowitz himself does not, to my recall, actually use that term) is the prerogative of any systematic Jewish theologian, and not just a liberal one like Leo Baeck, who actually named his major theological statement *Das Wesen des Judentums*.[3] Systematic theologians are those religious thinkers who have been influenced by the methods of philosophy. Even for an existentialist like Borowitz, the act of systematically speaking *about* the Covenant requires the hierarchical use of essentiality for its ordered presentation, however much he refuses to equate the existence of which he speaks with the enunciation of meaning. Like all existentialists, in their common opposition to Georg Hegel and his followers, the rational is less than the real, not identical with it. But the rational is still rational nonetheless, although forever incomplete due to its inherent lack of totality. Existence precedes essence because of its transcendence, but it does not obliterate essence into absurdity.[4]

I agree with Borowitz in his location of the essence of Judaism in the Covenant (which is not the case with many other Jewish thinkers), and I agree with Borowitz that the presentation of this essence can only be done systematically.[5] Like him, but unlike a number of other Jewish religious thinkers, I favor the designation "theology" for Jewish religious thought, and assume that being influenced by philosophy is unavoidable for any Jew secularly well-educated. Hence, the theology of any such Jew can only be systematic, recognizing, of course, that there is no one model of "system." My disagreement with him, however, is over his designation of the Covenant as itself essentially a *bilateral* relationship between God and Israel.[6] Does the authority of the Covenant really emerge *from between* the parties of that relationship: God and Israel? Is its source what is *among* them? Is that the source of a normativity that corresponds to the overall tendency of Jewish tradition, and is that a normativity that is sufficiently coherent to govern Jewish belief and practice here and now? Basically, my question to my old friend is whether the more recent covenantal emphasis in his theology sufficiently overcomes his ongoing liberal emphasis of *autonomy*, which I consider to be the very antithesis of Covenant proposed by modernity.[7]

Borowitz, being very much in the tradition of Jewish religious existentialism, has the same problem as Franz Rosenzweig, who seems to have posited a non-propositional revelation, but one that leads to the formulation of laws, which are, of course, normative propositions. By doing that, Rosenzweig very much parted company with Martin Buber, who posited a non-propositional revelation that is antithetical to the formulation of any propositions, whether normative or descriptive. Thus, in his famous dispute with Buber in the early 1920s over the issue of the relation of commandment (that is, personal directive: *mitzvah, Gebot*) and law (that is, communal directive: *halakhah, Gesetz*), Rosenzweig insisted that revelation is not only consistent with law, but can actually lead to it.[8] Therefore, my essential question to Rosenzweig and to Borowitz is: How can this nonpropositional revelation create communal norms, which cannot be stated except as ethical propositions or rules, that is, as laws?

In this book, Borowitz emphasizes that he does not take normative authority in Judaism to be strictly autonomous, that is, reason self-legislating to itself, as Immanuel Kant and his Jewish followers (most notably, Hermann Cohen) assumed all morality worthy of human beings must be.[9] Nor does he take this authority in Judaism to be heteronomous, that is, the community legislating to its own individual members.[10] Neither of these alternatives, which are still seen by many Enlightenment-bound contemporary thinkers as the only moral alternatives, is adequate to Borowitz' relational view of Judaism. But what sort of relation are we talking about? It seems that there are three basic alternatives: contract, or personal relationship, or Covenant.

The notion of the relationship between God and Israel being contractual was first argued by Baruch Spinoza. He saw the biblical *berit* as a *pactio* or *contractum*.[11] Such a contract consists of four elements: (1) two equally present parties approach each other; (2) the partners come with their own preconceived ends that produce contractual agreement if enough commonality can be negotiated; (3) the contract is verbal, both in terms of the respective preconceived ends and in terms of the subsequent negotiated commonality;[12] (4) the contract has a real *terminus a quo* (it begins at a definite point in history) and a possible *terminus ad quem* (it can end by a breach of contract by either side, or mutual agreement to terminate it). And, for Spinoza and all those who followed him, that *terminus ad quem* of the contract / covenant between God and Israel is already a fait accompli. For him, the history of Judaism is over; the Jews no longer have a cogent identity worth preserving in the world. Therefore, those Jews who thought like Spinoza about Judaism in contractual terms, but did not act like him by exiting Judaism and the Jewish people, had to reconstitute the relationship between God and Israel by arguing that its termination had not happened, indeed could not happen.[13]

The notion of the relationship between God and Israel being personal is the one favored by Borowitz, who is admittedly under the strong influence of Buber.[14] In a personal relationship, there are also four elements: (1) two equally present partners approach each other, although Buber insists that the divine partner can sustain the directness of the relationship, whereas for the human partner it is episodic;[15] (2) the partners do not come to the relationship with their own preconceived ends but, rather, the relationship itself becomes its own end, often with unforeseen results—it founds its own history; (3) speech is not prior but only subsequent—it emerges out of the relationship and serves to sustain it in the present and extend it into the future; (4) the relationship has a real *terminus a quo* by beginning as an actual event in time. At least *ab initio*, though, it has no *terminus ad quem*. It intends its own perpetuity. If love is the epitome of this personal relationship, then authentic lovers always say to each other: "I will love you forever."[16]

The question to Borowitz—being the most distinguished contemporary advocate of this relational model for Judaism—is this: Does this "I-Thou" model adequately explain the Jewish covenantal reality and enable it to function with its full normativity? I respectfully submit that it does not, although it is certainly closer to it than the contractual model outlined above.

In the Covenant there are also four elements:

1. Two unequally present partners approach each other. The inequality is seen in the fact that the approach is initiated by the Creator and not the creature, in this case, Israel. At best, the creature can only respond, and that response is most often ambivalent, if not frequently absent altogether.[17]

2. The Creator comes with his own preconceived end. In principle at least, the Torah is already intact before revelation takes place. The first response of the creature so approached must be obedience. "All that the Lord has spoken we will do and we will heed." (Ex. 24:7).[18] Only thereafter may humans incompletely surmise what ends the Covenant intends by the law given within it *(ta'amei ha-mitzvoth)*.[19]

3. The Covenantal reality is verbal, but not dialogical. The Creator speaks and that speech is ipso facto normative, whether proposing human acts or eliciting human attitudes.[20] Only prophets engage in anything like a conversation with God, and only Moses as *the* unique prophet did so in what could be termed a "back and forth" manner on any regular basis.[21] The covenanted creature responds by praising God's power and wisdom in both Creation and the Covenant itself,

verbally accepting God's authority in the Covenant, devising means for its extension and protection, and petitioning God in prayer for the wherewithal to be more fully effective as the human participant in the Covenant.[22]

4. There is a *terminus a quo* of the Covenant: it begins at a definite point in time. It founds its own history.[23] But there is no *terminus ad quem*. Neither God nor Israel can terminate the Covenantal reality: Israel, because she has been unconditionally chosen by God, not God chosen by her (as is the case in Spinoza's notion of a contract between God and Israel initiated by Israel conditionally); God, because there is no higher authority that can dispense him from the Covenantal oath he took in his own name.[24] Unlike a personal relationship, where the absence of a *terminus ad quem* is only ideal (the parties do not intend it for the future in the present), in the Covenant the absence of a *terminus ad quem* is real because the Covenant and the cosmic reality of creation are linked. The Covenant is the very *telos* of Creation; creation cannot persist without the Covenant. "If my covenant does not endure day and night, then I have not established the laws of heaven and earth" (Jer. 33:25).[25] The Covenant is ontological, not just phenomenological, or what Buber liked to call "philosophical anthropology."[26]

The difference between a phenomenology of personal relationship and an ontology of creation as the best explanation of the reality of the Jewish Covenant with God is the philosophical core of the theological differences between Professor Borowitz and myself. (In an age when intellectual discourse in general and Jewish intellectual discourse in particular is so often debased, I do not take for granted the privilege of having a thinker like Eugene Borowitz with whom to have such an exalted disagreement—hopefully, one for the sake of God.)[27]

Our fundamental difference is whether the Covenant requires a God who actually speaks. Without a God who speaks I do not see how we can have a durable bridge from revelation to communal norms qua *mitzvoth* (namely, the commandments *of* God), and not just universal ethical imperatives as in Hermann Cohen's theology, or ethnic folkways or religiously significant sancta as in Mordecai Kaplan's theology. For Cohen's ethical imperatives are grounded in the autonomy of the self (following Kant as he does), and Kaplan's folkways and sancta are grounded in the heteronomy of the group (following Durkheim as he does). Indeed, in both contractual and interpersonal relationships as models of the Covenant, the theological problem is the equality of the partners, and that follows from the fact that the relationship itself requires that both parties speak to each other. But does the liberal theology that assumes that God's word is *bespoken* by humans not actually place humans at a decided advantage over God?[28] Is it not even more theologically problematic than the former two models, autonomy and heteronomy, for just that reason?

If only the human partner is able to speak the reality of the Covenant in the name of God, then how is that to be distinguished from autonomous or heteronomous *projection* of essentially human will onto an idealized God? Is this not the great critique of religions of revelation conducted by Feuerbach, Marx, Freud, and their respective followers? Of course, these enemies of revelation would attribute revelation and its norms to projection irrespective of how theologians constitute it.[29] Nevertheless, when theologians constitute revelation in a way more consistent with biblical and rabbinic teaching, both of which continually affirm the God who speaks his commandments, they have not seen in it a meaning that cannot answer the charge of projection. Therefore, the debate with the enemies of revelation is not only about its truth (which cannot be settled until the "end of days") but about its meaning as well.[30] Meaning is always more accessible than truth; being immediately public it can be authenticated here and now.[31] To lose the battle over meaning leaves nothing left to be won by the final revelation of truth. Since truth and normativity are so intimately linked in Judaism, this leads to what can only be termed the crisis of authority in the liberal, religious, Jewish community, of which Borowitz is in the mind of many the leading theorist.

It is not that the liberal, religious, Jewish community is devoid of *halakhah*, for *halakhah* simply means "law," and no human community can exist without law of some kind or other.[32] But this community seems to have law only in the area of interhuman relationships—what the tradition calls the "realm *bein adam le-havero*."[33] The best example of this is the virtually unanimous consensus in this community on the issue of gender equality as a moral norm. But in the area of the relationship between God and humans—what the tradition calls the "realm *bein adam le-maqom*" —

there seems to be virtual antinomianism, if not anarchy, whether the issue be the observance of the Sabbath, the content of the liturgy, the status of mixed marriages, or even the identity of members of the Covenant.

Why is this the case? I think it is the case because a nonverbal revelation at the core of the religious reality, not having a God who speaks, must revert to either the voice of an individual human being (namely, *auto*-nomy) or the voice of a community (namely, *hetero*-nomy). Considering the general preference for autonomy by contemporary liberals, especially evidenced by the prominence of highly individualistic "rights-talk" in our current political and social discourse, it is little wonder that contemporary Jewish liberals, even religious ones, look to liberalism, not classical Judaism, for their normative model. In the liberal community, made up as it is by autonomous selves, religion as the relationship between a human person and *his* or *her* God is essentially a matter of individual preference. Only what is strictly interhuman is a matter of social concern here. Law can never be anything so individual, operating as it does by generalizing categories.[34]

What is needed to get us out of this theological impasse is a constitution of the classical Jewish doctrines of election and verbal revelation. This need not back us into a position of fundamentalist literalism, which has enjoyed such a resurgence of late in certain traditionalist circles, Jewish and otherwise, as part of a concerted attempt to repeal modernity in the name of a pre-modern utopia. Clearly, classical texts which record revelation have a history of communal transmission and cannot be understood apart from it.[35] At this point in time, it cannot be understood without a judicious incorporation of the methods and findings of modern critical-historical scholarship. Nevertheless, this requires the far more profound theological task of a philosophically cogent constitution of the classical Jewish doctrine of verbal revelation. Only a theological project of that magnitude can insure us that the incorporation of these modern methods and findings be truly incorporated *into* Judaism and not vice versa. Without such a constitution, I cannot see how there can be any real covenantal community between God and Israel, which is true to the reality of God and the nature of human creatures. And without it, I cannot see how any truly binding norms can emerge from this understanding of the Covenant.

I eargerly await Eugene Borowitz' response.

NOTES

1. See Borowitz, *Renewing the Covenant* (Philadelphia: Jewish Publication Society, 1991), p. 16f.; p. 104ff.

2. Note Eugene Borowitz' first book, *A Layman's Guide to Religious Existentialism* (Philadelphia: The Westminster Press, 1965).

3. Leo Baeck, *Das Wesen des Judentums,* trans. into English by V. Grubenwieser and L. Pearl as *The Essence of Judaism* (New York: Schocken Books, 1948).

4. See Franz Rosenzweig, *The Star of Redemption*, trans. W. W. Hallo (New York: Holt, Rinehart, and Winston, 1970), p. 381ff.

5. Any Jewish thinker who asserts the immutability of God (e.g., Halevi, Maimonides) cannot make the Covenant, which entails both action and reaction both on the part of God and humans, central to his or her theology. That is why the concept of *berit* plays almost no role in medieval rationalist Jewish theology. Cf. Abraham Joshua Heschel, *The Prophets* (Philadelphia: Harper and Row, 1962), p. 226ff.

6. I use the term "bilateral" as put forth by José Faur in his important article, "Understanding the Covenant," *Tradition 9* (1968), p. 42. Cf. D. Novak, *Jewish Social Ethics* (New York: Oxford University Press, 1992), p. 33ff. for a critique of Faur that could apply to Borowitz as well.

7. See Borowitz', *Exploring Jewish Ethics: Papers on Covenant Responsibility* (Detroit: Wayne State University Press, 1990), p. 163ff. Cf. D. Novak, *Jewish-Christian Dialogue: A Jewish Justification* (New York: Oxford University Press, 1989), p. 148ff. for a critique of the notion of autonomy, which should not, however, be confused with the notion of freedom, which is absolutely essential to any Jewish theology (see Maimonides, *Mishneh Torah*: Teshuvah, chap. 5).

8. See Franz Rosenzweig, *On Jewish Learning*, trans. W. Wolf (New York: Schocken Books, 1955), p. 85f. Cf. Martin Buber, *I and Thou*, trans. W. Kaufmann (New York: Scribner, 1970), p. 157ff.

9. See Borowitz, *Renewing the Covenant*, p. 64f.

10. Ibid., p. 66f.

11. See Baruch Spinoza, *Tractatus Theologico-Politicus*, chap. 16.

12. Although Spinoza's God does not literally speak as does the God of the Bible, humans can still relate to him as if he had agreed to be their sovereign. See ibid., chap. 17. This same type of "as if" retrojection is common to all social contract theories from Thomas Hobbes to John Rawls. See Plato, *Crito*, p. 50Aff., who anticipated it all.

13. See D. Novak, *The Election of Israel: The Idea of the Chosen People* (Cambridge: Cambridge University Press, 1995), p. 22ff.; p. 50ff.

14. However, Borowitz is not slavish in following Buber, being willing to differ with him on occasion. See Borowitz, *Renewing the Covenant*, p. 68f.

15. See Buber, *I and Thou*, p. 128.

16. See Novak, *Jewish Social Ethics*, p. 96ff.

17. That is why the rabbinic doctrine "Israel is still Israel even when she sins" (*Sanhedrin* 44a) eventually came to mean that Israel, whether collectively or individually, is never released/abandoned by God from the Covenant. See *Teshuvot Rashi*, ed. Elfenbein (New York: 1943), no. 171.

18. See *Shabbat* 88a and Rashbam, *Commentary on the Torah*: Ex. 24:7.

19. See *Sanhedrin* 21a-b.

20. See Maimonides, *Sefer Ha-Mitsvot*, pos. nos. 1–4 for the prescriptive character of elicited attitudes.

21. See Maimonides, *Mishneh Torah*: Yesodei Ha-Torah, 7.6 re Ex. 34:34; Num. 12:8; Deut. 34:10.

22. All of these points are best and most accessibly expressed in the heart of the liturgy, in *the* prayer *(ha-tefillah)*, the *shemoneh esre* or *amidah*, to be found in any traditional *siddur*.

23. Hence, the constant reference to the exodus from Egypt in the Bible and the liturgy. See *Tosefta*: Berakhot 1.13.

24. See *Berakhot* 32a re Ex. 32:13.

25. See *Pesahim* 68b.

26. Martin Buber, *Between Man and Man*, trans. R. G. Smith (New York: Macmillan Pub., 1955), p. 119.

27. See *M. Avot* 5.17.

28. Hermann Cohen had the same theological problem in constituting God's love *of* humans as distinct from humans' love of God or fellow humans. See Hermann Cohen, *Religion of Reason Out of the Sources of Judaism*, trans. S. Kaplan (New York: F. Ungar Publishing Co., 1972), p. 146f.

29. Thus, Freud, most famously, argues that any attempt to conceptualize religious attitudes and actions theologically with some sort of philosophical rigor and clarity, nonetheless is "an insubstantial shadow and no longer the mighty personality of religious doctrines" (*The Future of an Illusion*, trans. W. D. Robson-Scott, rev. ed. J. Strachey [Garden City, NY: Anchor Books, 1964], p. 52). These original religious attitudes, for Freud, come from "our wretched, ignorant and downtrodden ancestors" (Ibid., p. 53). Of course, could not one say the same for Freud's own attempts to conceptualize unconscious forces? One can see the efforts of a modern pagan like D. H. Lawrence or even Carl Jung (Freud's erstwhile disciple) to counter Freud's rationalism on just this point, namely, to remythologize these unconscious forces.

30. For the notion that the validation of truth is eschatologically transcendent, see *Berakhot* 34b re Isaia. 64:3; *Bekhorot* 24a re Hos. 10:12.

31. See Ludwig Wittgenstein, *Philosophical Investigations*, 2nd ed., trans. G. E. M. Anscombe (New York: Macmillan, 1958), nos. 242ff.; Jürgen Habermas, *The Theory of Communicative Action* 1, trans. T. McCarthy (Boston: Beacon Press, 1984), p. 307ff.

32. For the correct etymology of *halakhah* as "law," see Saul Lieberman, *Hellenism in Jewish Palestine*, 2nd imp. ed. (New York: Jewish Theological Seminary of America, 1962), p. 83, n. 3.

33. For the phenomenological distinction between these two types of *mitzvoth*: divine-human or interhuman, see M. Yoma 8.9; also, Maimonides, *Mishneh Torah: Berakhot*, 11.2, and R. Joseph Karo, *Kesef Mishneh,* thereon. For the ontological unity of all the *mitzvoth*, however, see *Berakhot* 5a re Ex. 24:12; *Hagigah* 3b re Eccl. 12:11 and Ex. 20:1.

34. See Maimonides, *Guide of the Perplexed*, 3.34.

35. See George A. Lindbeck, *The Nature of Doctrine: Religion and Theology in a Postliberal Age* (Philadelphia: Westminster Press, 1984), p. 114f.

7

A Critique of Borowitz'
Postmodern Jewish Theology

NORBERT M. SAMUELSON

I met someone recently at a concert who asked me what I do. I said that I teach at Temple University. She became interested because she was a student there. Then she asked me what I teach and I said Jewish studies. She became slightly more interested, because she was also Jewish. However, when she asked me more specifically what kinds of courses I offer, she became perplexed. I said that I teach courses in Jewish philosophy, and she said (as she moved away), "Really, I didn't know that Jews have philosophy!" Her sentiments would be shared by a large number of other Jews whom I know, particularly colleagues in Jewish studies and Jewish-by-birth professors in philosophy, all of whom would agree that there is no such thing as Jewish philosophy (because there is only philosophy), and if there was (in the case of ancient anachronisms like Maimonides), it certainly doesn't exist any more. There certainly is some basis for this judgment, given the fact that the publications of some of the most prominent names in general philosophy show (at least overtly) neither concern with nor influence from Judaism.[1] This judgment could also be echoed by some of my colleagues in general (which really means Christian or, more specifically, Protestant) philosophers of religion who find little of their obsession with epistemology reflected in the concerns of Jewish philosophers (past and present).[2] However, they are wrong. The truth is that Jewish philosophy has never been more active than it is now, and much of the activity is going on in the United States.

The contemporary tradition of Jewish philosophy that is best known in philosophy circles can be found in France, thanks largely to the writings and influence of Emmanuel Levinas. However, to repeat, it can also be found in the United States. Through professional associations such as the American Academy of Religion, the Association of Jewish Studies, and (last but not least) the Academy for Jewish Philosophy, people committed to thinking Jewishly as philosophers and philosophically as Jews have been meeting and sharing ideas and papers for more than a decade. Now some of their activity is beginning to emerge as books in constructive Jewish thought. Among the more important American recent products are David Novak's *Halakhah in a Theological Dimension*,3 Menachem Kellner's collection of the Jewish writings of Steven Schwarzschild,4 and Kenneth Seeskin's *Jewish Philosophy in a Secular Age*.5 It is into this company that I would locate Eugene B. Borowitz' *Renewing the Covenant: A Theology for the Postmodern Jew*.6

Another way to catalogue contemporary Jewish thinkers is as popular or technical, as religious or secular, and as liberal or conservative. In terms of the first pair, Borowitz' writings bridge the ever increasing chasm between works directed at an educated laity (such as Neil Gillman's)7 and those directed at professional scholars in universities (such as Steven Schwarzschild's).8 Borowitz is an integral part of the community of scholars who do constructive religious thinking. In this role he is an active participant in groups like the American Theological Society and the Academy for Jewish Philosophy. Although his colleagues are not at the forefront of his arguments in this book, he knows their work and their concerns are easily detectable behind the surface of his words. At the same time, in terms of a popular audience, Borowitz is a professor at a seminary that trains American Reform rabbis, most of whom enter a career of service to Reform synagogues, and his writing reflects his involvement with these students. As such this book should be required reading for anyone interested in the best of Reform Jewish thinking at the close of the twentieth century.

Renewing the Covenant brings together, into a more cohesive whole, the main theses that Borowitz has advocated in his earlier books. He argues vigorously as a religious liberal against all forms of Jewish secular-ism and religious Orthodoxy. More positively, he sides with the central tradition of contemporary Jewish liberals in personal and political ethics, and with modern religious thinkers who could call themselves biblical and / or Covenantal theologians.[9]

Borowitz' conclusions emerge from a dialogue with many of the most important religious thinkers of the nineteenth and twentieth century—Immanuel Kant, Georg Hegel, Alfred North Whitehead, Hermann Cohen, Leo Baeck, Mordecai Kaplan, and Nachman Krochmal (all of whom Borowitz labels as rationalists), and Franz Rosenzweig, Martin Buber, and Abraham Joshua Heschel (all of whom are called nonrational-ists)—and many of his Jewish contemporaries, including Henry Slonim-sky and Alvin Reines in the Reform movement; David Hartman, Michael Wyschogrod, and Yeshayahu Leibowitz in the Orthodox movement; Neil Gillman and Elliot Dorff in the Conservative movement; William E. Kaufman and Harold M. Schulweis in the Reconstructionist movement; Arthur E. Green and Lawrence Kushner as voices of contemporary Jewish spiritualism; and Emil L. Fackenheim, Irving Greenberg, and Richard L. Rubenstein as voices of Holocaust theology. However, the most important partner in Borowitz' dialogue is Steven Schwarzschild, whose presence is constantly felt throughout the book. The only explicit reference to Schwarzschild's thought is on p. 65, where he is identified as a disciple of Hermann Cohen. However, on p. xii Borowitz acknowledges the Schwarz-schild influence. In my judgment, Borowitz' argument with rationalism, a major theme of this book, appears to be an argument with Hermann Cohen and others, but is really an argument with Schwarzschild.

Franz Rosenzweig argued in *The Star of Redemption* that thinking ought to be negative rather than positive. In part what he meant was that affirmation arises out of negating negations. In this sense Schwarzschild is the single most important philosophical source for Borowitz' theology, since Borowitz' non-rationalism, which is at the foundation of his con-structive thought, emerges from his (loving) arguments against Schwarz-schild's vigorous affirmation of Cohen's rationalism. Also present through-out the work, but not directly discussed, is feminist Jewish theology. In this case, the most important implicit voices are those of Judith Plaskow[10] and Ellen Umansky.[11]

BOROWITZ' THEOLOGY

Borowitz describes his book as a project in covenantal theology that seeks to clarify non-Orthodox Jewish faith. He further characterizes it as being written in a postmodern mood in a postmodern period. The problem that he addresses is how to make sense out of being more religious than secular, and more Jewish than universal-human, while affirming the seemingly conflicting right to individual moral self-determination. The mood of his work is associated with what he had learned from the late work of Ludwig Wittgenstein on the logic of language and how that understanding affected his philosophical understanding of *aggadah* and *halakhah*. In general, what he learned from both Wittgenstein and his Jewish (that is, classic) texts, was that in Jewish thought *praxis* has primacy over *doxis*. The context of his conclusions is consciously located at the end of a process that begins in the pre-modern (Biblical, Hellenistic, and Sassanid)[12] Jewish thought of the Jewish people, and continues through the disillusionment of modern Jewish thought with Western European secular culture and ethics in post-World War II United States.

As Borowitz understands Jewish intellectual history, the central issue for Jewish thought revolved around the apparent incoherence of affirming the modern world's commitment to freedom and secularism with traditional Judaism's authoritarianism and spirituality. More specifically, the general cultural faith in moral autonomy and universalism appears to contradict the historical Jewish acceptance of the authority of Jewish law *(halakhah)*. Borowitz notes three main strategies for maintaining both sets of values.[13] Hermann Cohen (1) and Mordecai Kaplan (2) offered rigorous defenses of Judaism based on a total commitment to rationalism. In the former case, the rationalism was rooted in the philosophy of Immanuel Kant; in the latter case, it was rooted in early twentieth-century social science, notably sociology. Finally, Martin Buber and Franz Rosenzweig (3) changed the theological paradigm from ideas (like Cohen's God and Kaplan's peoplehood) to a view of the whole person. This personalist paradigm is the cornerstone of Borowitz' own postmodern Jewish theology. It enables him to move beyond grounding modernism's moral values in secular humanism; he moves to a specific form of spiritualism (Covenant theology) in which the source of the ethical becomes the word of God.

In a single phrase, what Borowitz calls postmodern is disillusionment with the values of modernism. More specifically, modernism is associated with placing ultimate moral value on the ability of the philosophy and science of the secular university to provide criteria for truth, and on the power of the political democracy of the secular state to bring about good. Postmodernism arises because the individual quality of life has and is corroding in political democracies, while modern philosophies and science lead to moral relativism. In sum, the authority of revelation and rabbinic tradition in the pre-modern Jewish world gave way to the authority of universal human reason in the modern world. Now, in the postmodern world, we are left without authority. None of the contemporary candidates for faith are satisfactory: neither science, nor mysticism, nor ethnic nationalism, nor any contemporary form of Orthodoxy (be it Jewish,[14] Christian, Muslim, or Asian).

The constructive side of Borowitz' theology consists in a reconstruction of Martin Buber's theology from a postmodernist perspective. While Borowitz finds much of value in much of modern Jewish thought, no one else occupies as favorable a position in Borowitz' judgment as does Buber.[15] In a sense, Borowitz' constructive theology is Martin Buber's theology reconstructed to include a more adequate sense of Jewish community.[16]

With respect to postmodernism, Borowitz affirms the primacy of experience over reason[17] and proposes to ground ethics in relations rather than in individual autonomy. In addition, Borowitz' postmodernism affirms what he calls "moral realism" over "human optimism," by which he means that human beings cannot on their own bring about the redemption of the world because, while they do good, they tend more to do evil. Borowitz' Buberian theology is modified as both biblical and covenantal. It is biblical theology because it affirms a God who is personal rather than impersonal, and transcendent as well as immanent. The theology is Covenantal because the revelation and Torah of this personal transcendent deity are to be understood on a Covenantal model of divine and human interaction. In other words, Torah (whose content is the road map to redemption) is neither the gift of God nor the invention of humanity; rather it is the product of their interaction.[18]

A CRITIQUE OF BOROWITZ' THEOLOGY

I want to focus the analytic part of this essay on two of Borowitz' central concepts: first, on his understanding of what reason is, since that understanding is fundamental to his embrace of postmodernism; and second, on his concept of the self, since that is central to his continued affirmation of a concept of individual rights, which in turn is fundamental to his embrace of liberalism.

Concerning Postmodernism: A Jewish Understanding of Reason

What Borowitz means by postmodernism is disillusionment with modernism, and the most important characteristic of his modernism is what he calls "rationalism." His understanding of rationalism comes from reading, but (more importantly in my judgment) from years of conversation with his friend, Steven Schwarzschild. Schwarzschild's understanding of reason is based on his own reading of Jewish and philosophical texts under the influence of his intellectual master, Hermann Cohen.

Borowitz' ultimate dependence on the Jewish philosophy of Cohen for the critical concept that he is rejecting—rationalism—is part of the problem with his particular commitment to postmodernism. Cohen's understanding of Judaism as a religion of reason has much to recommend itself. First, it is foundational for what has been the dominant tradition of Jewish philosophy and theology in the twentieth century. The Jewish thinkers that Borowitz deals with in his book are the most important ones of this century, and all of their thought (with one exception, namely, Mordecai Kaplan) goes back to the influence of the writings and teaching of Cohen. Second, it is a rich tradition that has not as yet been given a fair hearing in either Jewish or Christian circles. Most of modern philosophy, both on the Continent and in Great Britain, has been a dialogue with modern science. Scientific theory, in turn, has rested to a very large extent on modern developments in mathematics, yet few modern philosophers have fully appreciated the radical way mathematics has changed scientific thinking.

The most obvious example of an attempt to root philosophical method in mathematics was Bertrand Russell's *Principia Mathematica*. However, the model for this work of Russell's was simple, static algebra as it applies to arithmetic, whereas the mathematics of modern science, from Sir Isaac Newton on, is based on the significantly more complex, dynamic nature of calculus. No other philosopher was Cohen's equal in taking seriously the consequences of the dependence of scientific laws on calculus.[19] Cohen's work had a profound effect on those Jewish thinkers who followed him, notably Franz Rosenzweig, but to this day it has had little influence on anyone else.[20]

Another virtue of Cohen's philosophy points to its problem for Borowitz' critique of rationalism. Cohen's rationalism is not the only kind of reason, in fact, it is not even characteristic of most of contemporary Western philosophy. Hence, at best, Borowitz' argument against rationalism is only an argument against one possibility. It is not an argument against rationalism as such.

Let me raise but one example of this last point, one that, in my judgment, is central to Borowitz' argument. He asserts that neither philosophy nor science is able to provide us with an absolute standard by which to decide either what is true or what is good. Hence, reason fails to save us from absolute relativism. Now, I suppose there are some people, both in the past and in the present (some of whom might even be or have been sophisticated, for example, Spinoza), who thought that they could or did have such an absolute standard. But most do not. Furthermore, it does not really matter. The general belief of most so-called rationalists is that what is logically demonstrated is more likely to be true than what is not, and, even though there is no way to be certain about truth, that situation is good enough. For example, I assume that the more I know about stocks and the stock market, the more likely it is that I will choose a good stock. I also know that in any particular case my most reasonable reflections may lead to a bad choice, and someone else, in total ignorance of the market, may make a better choice. There is no certainty, because in reality nothing that matters is certain. In other words, the non-absolute character of my decision-making reflects reality: to the extent that there is chance in the universe, there is no absolute knowledge, and there is always an element of chance in every actual, specific state of affairs. Hence, the uncertainty of any concrete application of rational thinking is in itself no argument against reliance upon reason. Rational thinking can tell us about probabilities; rarely can it tell us about absolutes, and this judgment itself is a dictate of reason. Now, if there were some other way of thinking that could give us absolutes, or at least give us conclusions that are more likely to be true in the concrete (for example, if Alice's Wonderland were reality), then we would reasonably choose not to be reasonable. But there is sufficient uniformity in the natural and the human world that no such choice is called for. In other words, the critical claim of rationalism is not that it can provide us with absolutes. Rather, it is that neither can anything else, and, given our available options, nothing is more likely to lead us to correct judgments (in science or ethics) than reasoning.

Nor is it in fact correct to claim that either Cohen or Schwarzschild claimed that reason can give us absolutes in the sense that Borowitz says that rationalism claims that it can. What Borowitz seems to miss (as do many other so-called Jewish postmodernists) is the force of understanding reason on the model of the asymptote. An asymptote is the limit towards which the succeeding values of a function endlessly approach, but never realize.[21] On this model, the functions express the sensual reality of our everyday lives as events or states-of-affairs, the variables and terms in those functions are the objects in our sensual world that are constructed out of (and dependent upon) those functions, and the asymptotes represent the moral ideals that make intelligible (that is, rational) the events themselves. In other words, reality is to be interpreted as a series of endless movements towards ends. It is the ends, not the movements themselves, that are the objects of reason, and the kind of reason to be employed here is ethical (namely, expressions of what ought to be rather than what is). This is what Cohen meant when he said that reality is a moral construct, and it is what Schwarzschild meant when he argued that practical judgments are to be ruled by moral ideals that are to be understood always in terms of hopeless hope: that is, in terms of our acting on a hope to succeed in full knowledge that we will not.

In more practical terms, the Cohen/Schwarzschild understanding of the life of reason as a life lived in hopeless hope clarifies much that we do as humans that matters to us. A trivial example is playing (or following) competitive sports. No matter how many teams are involved, and no matter how many games they win, in the end there is only one winner. Hence, the dominant experience in sports is losing. In a sense, one of the values of sports is that it teaches us, in a fairly trivial (and therefore safe) setting, how to live with failure. Whether we are players or spectators, we live (that is, we become involved) to win (that is we hope to win.) But if we lose, which we most often do, then and only then can we say, "it doesn't really matter." There is always the hope for tomorrow, even though we know that on most tomorrows we will lose again. A vastly more important example of the rational usefulness of hopeless hope is medicine. Ultimately the goal of all physicians, who are worthy of calling themselves physicians, is to save the lives of their patients, even though they know (if they are rational) that they will fail, for everyone, sooner or later, dies. The same analysis applies to most important pursuits in life—financial planning, learning, friendship—that is, everything that most of us would think constitutes the pursuit of happiness.22 To win is not to win, it is to delay losing.

Now none of this kind of thinking is the result of existentialism, or postmodernism, or any other kind of what Borowitz calls "nonrationalism." Rather it is a vision that was originally set forth by Jewish philosophy's greatest rationalist: Hermann Cohen.

Concerning Liberalism: A Scientific Understanding of the Self

What Borowitz means by liberalism is non-Orthodoxy, where the most important characteristic of Orthodoxy is that it affirms the authority of the leadership of a religious community over the conscience of its individual members. In classic terms, what Reform and Orthodox Judaism share in common, in opposition to Conservative and Reconstructionist interpretations of Judaism, is a conviction that Torah (in Borowitz' sense of Covenant, as what defines the relationship between God and the people Israel) is to be expressed in terms of moral obligations, and those obligations define Judaism.23 The issue between them has to do with what those obligations are. In the case of Orthodoxy, the obligations are determined · by the legitimate authorities of the community as a polity, that is, the rabbinate. In the case of Reform, the obligations are determined by each individual member of the community. From a Reform (or a Jewish liberal) perspective, the tradition's preservation of God's interface with the people Israel confronts every Jew with a demand both to believe and to act, but ultimately it is the inescapable obligation of the individual himself/herself to decide in good faith what is really true and what is really good.

In general, everyone ought to believe truth and do good. What these are is the word of God. That word confronts every Jew through rabbinic tradition. So far, there is no theological argument between Reform and Orthodoxy. The issue arises only at the point that we ask who makes this decision.24 For Orthodoxy, the answer is the community through its legitimate authorities. For Reform, the answer is each and every individual.25 At the core of this dispute are radically different philosophical judgments about the ontological relationship between individuals and communities.

In general, it is always possible to distinguish between collections, entities, and parts. Entities are the constituents of the universe. Collections are ways of grouping entities, and precisely because they are merely ways of thinking, they have no ontological status. Consequently, it makes no sense to speak of collections having rights. Conversely, parts are real, but they also have no rights. While an entity as such can be said to be entitled to exist (that is, it need not do or be anything to justify its existence), the real existence of parts depends on their value or usefulness to their wholes.

How the experienced world is to be parsed out in terms of these three categories is not self-evident. For example, particles form communities called "atoms," which form communities called "molecules," which form communities called "physical objects," which (in the case of human beings) form communities called "societies," which (together with other collections of physical objects) form communities called "worlds," which together form communities called "galaxies," which together form a community called the "universe." Which of these objects should be called entities is an arbitrary judgment. If particles are entities, then all else are collections. The consequence of this kind of view (implicit in Newtonian science), is that there is no logical reason why human beings should have rights, since, in reality, they do not exist.[26] Conversely, if the universe is the only entity, then everything else is a part, whose right to exist depends solely on its value for the whole. At both extremes any notion of an autonomous individual human being is unjustifiable.[27]

The modern notion of the moral and political autonomy of the individual is rooted in a mode of thinking that may be labeled atomism. It is the model for picturing the universe that was presupposed in the above summary of the interrelationship between parts, entities, and collections. On this view, ultimately what exists are things (atoms) which join together with other things to form relations, and what is fundamental in reality is the existence of the things, not their relations. Consider, for example, the statement, "John threw the ball." The atomist model presupposes that what exists are John and the ball (the objects), and the activity of throwing, which relates John and the ball, are secondary. Ultimately, the verb only expresses something about what the nouns name; it is the nouns that say something about existence. Atomism with respect to physics involves particles; with respect to politics and ethics, it involves individual human beings.

Note that before the modern period Jewish thinking never was atomistic. Rather, it was what may be labeled relationalist. This insight, which Borowitz acknowledges that he learned from Buber, is the ontological foundation of his Covenant theology. Using the above example, this way of picturing the universe presupposes that what exists are relations that may be analyzed into things (namely, terms) in relationship. In other words, things are to be understood as *relata:* not as independent entities, but as terms of relations. Hence, in the case of the sentence, "John threw the ball," what exists is a given dynamic state of affairs where the objects John and the ball are defined relative to each other by the action verb. In this sense, Jewish thought has always been relational and never atomistic.[28] Consequently, in terms of political ethics, Jewish thought has always (until the modern period) functioned with a notion of a community founded on some sense of Covenant, without any notion of individual rights of the sort that (for example) Thomas Jefferson expressed in his Declaration of Independence. In my judgment, it is Borowitz' move from atomism to relationism with reference to the self that properly entitles him to call his thought postmodern.[29]

It should be pointed out that Borowitz is not the only contemporary Jewish thinker to propose a covenantal approach to rethinking liberal Judaism. Of particular note in this respect is the work of Daniel J. Elazar and his associates.[30] What Borowitz approaches in terms of Jewish theology, Elazar approaches in terms of Jewish political theory. Conscious of the very same kinds of problems with modernism of which Borowitz speaks, Elazar has devoted much of his creativity to exploring how a covenantal model of political theory can be used to replace modern theories based on the notions of human rights to preserve the values but exclude the vices of contemporary Western secular society. In the cases of both Borowitz and Elazar, the primary sources for their covenantal enterprise are the texts of the Hebrew Scriptures and the inspiration of Martin Buber's theology.

The values of Borowitz' Buberian enterprise are self-evident in everything that is spiritually and politically wrong with our modern world from a Jewish perspective. First, Covenant theology provides us with a way to reread the traditional texts of Judaism that is more faithful to the texts themselves, be they biblical or rabbinic. Second, it enables us to make sense out of our faith experience that the Jewish people is no mere mental construct, and that its survival is something of inherent moral value.

Although it is less obvious, it also is important to note that Borowitz' enterprise provides us with a more rational way to understand the universe than does the old liberal atomism. By "rational," I mean a world and life view that is more coherent with contemporary logic and science. Let me allude to the kind of consideration I have in mind. First, in terms of formal logic, Aristotle's model[31] for logical thinking has given way to the model of Russell's *Principia Mathematica*. Briefly, Aristotle's formalism interpreted narrative sentences of the form "Allen is a boy" into propositions about particulars (Allen) and universals (boy), where the universal was thought to be some kind of thing that somehow inheres in the particular thing. Conversely, in Russell's formalism, "boy" expresses an external relationship to a particular relatum ("Allen"). Second, in terms of physics, while the laws of Newtonian-based dynamics were expected to apply to individual entities that have specific, determinate locations at specific, determinate times, Quantum Mechanics ultimately makes sense only when it is applied to collections of particles. When it is applied to individuals (for example, a photon), the scientific formalisms generate paradoxes.[32] While Newtonian science professed the ideal that it could make determinate causal statements about every individual thing in the universe, Quantum Mechanics professes as its ideal probabilistic statements about sets of things. Within this new, formal mathematical and scientific model for rationalism, collections have status more than particulars, and truth is about probability more than necessity. Consequently, Borowitz' moral and political covenantalism is no less rational than is his epistemology.

Let me conclude by saying another word about postmodernism. The term is used in many ways. With respect to epistemology, it is often used in the way Borowitz used it in *Renewing the Covenant*, namely, to express some sort of nonrationalism. However, the term is also used in a temporal sense to express thinking that moves beyond the modes of thought introduced in the Enlightenment of the seventeenth and eighteenth centuries. In these two senses we can say that Borowitz' theology is both modern and postmodern. In terms of epistemology, he believes that he is postmodern, but he really is modern. In other words, his rejection of modernist reason is really most reasonable. In terms of time, his theology truly is postmodern, that is, it is one of the few statements of Jewish theology in our decade that is coherent with the major breakthroughs that have occurred in our century in both mathematical logic and scientific theory.

NOTES

1. Paradigmatic examples would be Saul A. Kripke, *Naming and Necessity* (Cambridge: Harvard University Press, 1972), and Hilary Putnam, *Meaning and the Moral Sciences* (London: Routledge and Kegan Paul, 1978).

2. A recent example of a first rate study in Protestant thought that intends to be a study of religious thought is *A World Theology: The Central Spiritual Reality of Humankind* by N. Ross Reat and Edmund F. Perry. (Cambridge, New York et al.: Cambridge University Press, 1991). In spite of its sensitivity to the reality of other religions (especially Hinduism and Buddhism, but also Judaism and Islam), a sensitivity that far exceeds most works of this genre, its categories for understanding "theology" remain predominantly Christian, and nowhere in this (otherwise most interesting) book could I find even a trace of the kinds of discussions that have been central to Jewish philosophy in the past decade.

3. David Novak, *Halakhah in a Theological Dimension* (Chico, CA: Scholars Press, 1985). Also of interest is his *Jewish-Christian Dialogue: A Jewish Justification* (New York: Oxford University Press, 1989).

4. Mena Chem Kellner, *The Pursuit of the Ideal* (Albany: State University of New York Press, 1990).

5. Kenneth Seeskin, *Jewish Philosophy in a Secular Age* (Albany: State University of New York Press, 1990). There are many other works also worth mentioning. For example, Neil Gillman's *Sacred Fragments: Recovering Theology for the Modern Jew* (Philadelphia: The Jewish Publication Society, 1990) is a valuable statement of philosophic speculation in relation to the Conservative movement. I have not listed it because it did not grow out of the discussions in contemporary circles of academic studies in Jewish philosophy. However, Michael Wyschogrod's *The Body of Faith* (New York: Seabury Press, 1983) did; it is a valuable example of contemporary philosophical speculation on Jewish religious topics. I excluded it out of deference to his own desire not to be considered a Jewish philosopher. In fact one of the features of some (fortunately not all) contemporary Jewish philosophy is that it denies that there is contemporary Jewish philosophy. Much the same can be said about the important work of Emil L. Fackenheim, particularly his penetrating discussions of both Spinoza and Rosenzweig in his antiphilosophical *To Mend the World* (New York: Schocken Books, 1982).

6. Eugene B. Borowitz, *Renewing the Covenant* (Philadelphia: Jewish Publication Society, 1991).

7. Neil Gillman, *Sacred Fragments*. The best known example in this category would be the publications of Lawrence Kushner, notably *Honey from the*

Rock (San Francisco: Harper and Row, 1977), and *The River of Light* (Chappaqua: Rossel Books, 1981).

8. Borowitz' function as a bridge in this sense is an important feature of his literary work. When Jewish scholars were rabbis, most works of Jewish thought had this characteristic. Today, as more rabbis serve congregations and more scholars are trained in and work for secular universities, few works are like this. The danger of popular works directed at a laity (even an educated one) is superficiality; the danger of professional academic works is triviality. Bridge builders are in danger of being both superficial and trivial. Borowitz' work is neither. Furthermore, the fact that Borowitz has achieved both popularity (in academic and communal circles) and presents creative ideas with rigorous arguments falsifies the often verified thesis that quality and success are inversely proportionate.

9. Primarily Martin Buber. However, this category also includes Franz Rosenzweig, Abraham Joshua Heschel, Milton Steinberg (in his later work; cf. *Renewing*, p.103), and Michael Wyschogrod (cf. *Renewing*, pp. 132–34, and 245–46).

10. Judith Plaskow, *Standing Again at Sinai* (San Francisco: Harper and Row, 1990).

11. Ellen Umansky, "Females, Feminists, and Feminism: A Review of the Recent Literature on Jewish Feminism and the Creation of a Feminist Judaism." *Feminist Studies 14*, no. 2 (Summer 1988).

12. These terms are mine, not Borowitz'. Borowitz himself divides the premodern period into Covenantal, settlement, rabbinic, and Diaspora stages.

13. For Borowitz, other, less important strategies include those of the Holocaust theologians (notably Richard Rubenstein, Emil Fackenheim, and Irving Greenberg). It is against Rubenstein's affirmation of the death of God that Borowitz develops his argument that our modern disillusionment with traditional Jewish values (namely, with God's existence and providence and moral absolutism) is a consequence of general secularist humanism rather than the specific tragic events of the Holocaust. Fackenheim's theological argument for the Holocaust's radical uniqueness also is rejected for parallel reasons. Borowitz is unwilling to give anything as morally negative as the Holocaust a central role in redefining postmodern Judaism. Furthermore, against Irving Greenberg's attempt to ground ethics in Jewish ethnicity, Borowitz argues that ethnicity is again declining (hence, this would not be an effective strategy even if it were theoretically viable) and, even if it were not, it is not in itself sufficiently rich theoretically to do the job Greenberg wants it to do. Finally, the current moral conflicts that arise in connection with Israeli policy on the emancipation of the Palestinians, and Orthodox policy on women's rights, exemplify for Borowitz the inadequacy of modernism; democracy and individual autonomy must remain Jewish values.

14. Borowitz identifies one form of postmodern Jewish Orthodoxy that also maintains modernism's affirmation of universal ethics, namely, that of Abraham Joshua Heschel. What is attractive about Heschel's thought to Borowitz is that he moves beyond secularism to a renewed religious view of the world. His objections to Heschel's Orthodoxy are vocalized in terms of feminist Jewish objections to Orthodox gender discrimination. However, these objections are only examples intended to illustrate his major objection to Heschel, namely that Heschel's Orthodoxy is incoherent with continuing to affirm, as Borowitz does, the value of autonomy.

15. For example, "Buber's understanding of God otherwise substantially communicates what I take to be the core postmodern Jewish religious experience: The God whom we encounter is real, and great enough to ground our values, and yet respects us enough to give us personal freedom in our relationship with God" (p. 131).

16. The critical move in this respect is Borowitz' concept of what he calls "the Jewish self." Cf. p. 181.

17. This seems to be what Borowitz means by claiming to favor nonrationalism. It is not a rejection of the value of reason as such. Rather, it is an assertion that the sources of rational thought are not in reason in itself, but in experience. In these terms, it would have been more appropriate for Borowitz to claim that he is a radical empiricist (in the tradition [at least in this respect] of thinkers like William James), rather than a nonrationalist, for what he calls rationalism is largely limited to the thought of those philosophers (often misnamed "Idealists") who followed in the footsteps of Hegel.

18. It is this interpretation of revelation on a covenantal model that most clearly identifies Borowitz' thought as Reform. It reconstructs what Reform Jewish thinkers used to call "divine inspiration." The place where Borowitz most clearly emerges as a Reform Jew is in his discussion of saying the *motzi* over a fish sandwich at McDonald's (pp. 111–12). (It is a classic example of what Richard Israel once called "a kosher pig.") The context in which it arises is a discussion (chapter 8) of phenomenal examples of the experience of the transcendent in the mundane with specific reference to Peter Berger's "rumor of angels." While other Jews can relate to his other examples (namely federation Israel missions, Jewish community "tsedakah" campaigns, and saying the traditional blessing for urinating and defecating), only someone positively raised or involved in a Reform Jewish community could understand (as I do) how someone could say (let alone be spiritually moved by saying) a traditional blessing over a non-kosher meal. (Out of consideration of general Jewish sensitivities [I don't know what Borowitz' personal food regimen is] he says that he was eating a fish sandwich. The point would have been the

same [as it often is] even if he were eating a cheeseburger.) It is interesting that this most Reform example is (possibly) Borowitz' most personal (namely experiential or nonrational in Borowitz' terms) and least philosophical (namely rational in Borowitz' terms) in the book.

19. The sole possible exception to this judgment is Alfred North Whitehead.

20. Modern Jewish philosophy is a tradition of philosophy rooted in Cohen's argument that philosophical thinking should be based on scientific thinking, which in turn is an instantiation of the kind of dynamic reason that the formalism of calculus makes possible (in contrast to a tradition such as the one that followed from Russell's mathematical philosophy, where the model for philosophic thinking remains as static as it was at the time that Spinoza wrote his *Ethics*). Modern Jewish philosophy projects an understanding of the universe where to know consists not in grasping things, but in discerning purposeful processes towards infinitely remote limits. These limits are, in some significant sense, ethical ideals. Hence, another way that "Jewish thinking" has differed from modern Christian thought is that Jewish thought rejects the radical separation between the theoretical and the practical (or, science and ethics) that so typifies contemporary non-Jewish philosophical reason.

21. A fairly simple example would be the function $(x/(x+10))$. No matter what actual number we substitute for the variable x, the value of the function will always be less than 1. (e.g., if $x=10$, then the value of the function is ½; if x is 20, then the value is ⅔, etc.) However, the higher the value of x becomes, the closer the value of the function comes to being 1. In this case, the asymptote, that is, the limit of the function, is 1. As Cohen applied this kind of example to rational thinking about reality, limits were interpreted to be ideals, and ideals were seen to be the object of ethical thinking. Now, in what sense such an "ideal" can be called "ethical" is an important question. In fact, it ought to be the main question for those Jewish philosophers (whether or not they are Jewish) who follow the Cohen tradition in thinking that ethics is primary (at least critical) to scientific thinking.

22. The clearest example outside of lived life that I can give is the old video game of "Space Invaders." The goal is to stay alive by shooting down the space ships. As you succeed, the invaders travel faster and their bombs have a shorter distance to fall. In mathematical terms, the asymptote that expresses their speed is infinity, and the asymptote that expresses their distance is zero. Hence, death (i.e., losing the game) is unavoidable. To win is to delay losing.

23. This is the sense in which I would agree with Borowitz' judgment that in Judaism *praxis* is prior to *doxis*. It does not mean that for Judaism good action is more important than true belief.

24. The answer is not God. That only pushes the question back one step. For

both Reform and Orthodoxy what is true and good is the word of God. In these terms, the question is, who decides what that word is.

25. Consequently, in Orthodoxy rabbis use their knowledge of Jewish tradition to legislate, while Reform rabbis use their knowledge to recommend.

26. Because they are nothing more than a certain configuration of particles.

27. Hence, while this decision is arbitrary, it is anything but trivial. For example, if human beings are mere configurations of particles, then what right do "useless" individuals (such as the unemployed, the sick, the homeless, etc.) have, even to exist?! The same question could be asked if human beings are only parts of a larger whole. Whether or not to save a human being (from a political perspective) would be decided in precisely the same way that we would decide whether or not to perform surgery on a diseased body part!

28. For example, in biblical theology "entities" are nations, who are defined by the covenant relationship between peoples and their deity, while in medieval Jewish philosophy the sole entity is the universe, defined by the covenantal relationship between the Creator and His creatures.

29. In this sense he is more "postmodern" than many others in contemporary religious studies who call themselves "postmodern." Here, "postmodern" means moving to a new model for thinking beyond the one that has dominated European thought since the rise of the secular nation state. In nineteenth-century terms, it means thinking in patterns consciously in opposition to the patterns of Newtonian science.

30. Elazar has published more than thirty-one books in areas related to Jewish political theory through the work of his Jerusalem Center for Public Affairs and Center for Jewish Community Studies. Of particular importance in this context are, with Stuart Cohen, *The Jewish Polity: Jewish Political Organization from Biblical Times to the Present* (Bloomington: Indiana University Press, 1985), *Federalism as Grand Design: Political Philosophers and the Federal Principle* (Lanham: University Press of America, 1987), and *Authority, Power and Leadership in the Jewish Polity* (Lanham: University Press of America, 1991).

31. It is this model that Rosenzweig had in mind when he formulated logical, scientific thought in terms of the equations, "A is A," "A is B," and "B is B" in the first part of *The Star of Redemption*. The truth behind his argument for their limitations is the inadequacy of Aristotelian logic, and not (as he mistakenly thought) the inadequacy of reason.

32. For example, Schrödinger's cat.

Readings of the Readings

8

Borowitz and the
Postmodern Renewal of Theology

PETER OCHS

BOROWITZ IN THE FAMILY OF POSTMODERN JEWISH THINKERS

Postmodern theories of "readerly collusion" leave skeptics wondering what kind of coherent meaning a book could have if its meanings were as many as its readers. One assumption of this study has been that there are many kinds of postmodernism; the postmodernism the book seems to espouse responds to the question of coherence in the following terms: If you want the kind of coherence that may be thought, but not necessarily lived, then look for a coherent reader. If you want the kind of coherence that may be lived, then look for a finite community of readers, whose commonalities-amidst-differences may generate coherence of a "truer" or at least more enduring sort. This study has examined the work of readers who may, in fact, constitute a community of readers, loosely defined: with one exception (a Christian "guest"), they all allow themselves, with varying disclaimers, to be called "postmodern Jewish philosophers," and they are all in active dialogue with one another, at conferences and by way of an electronic journal now called *Textual Reasoning: A Journal in Postmodern Jewish Philosophy*.[1] One goal of this study has been to elicit a coherent reading of Borowitz' theology from out of this community; not because "coherence" is "truth," but because, if it is of the lived sort, it helps initiate communal dialogue.

An earlier, briefer version of this essay appeared in *Cross Currents* 43, no. 2 (Summer, 1993), 164–83.

These comments would sound like truisms if we were considering simply another academic community, like the "communities" of New Critics or of social anthropologists. A community of "postmodern Jewish thinkers" appears to be a more complex creature, however. By way of illustration, consider this characterization of the "postmodern Jewish philosophies" of the original members of *Textual Reasoning*, then called *The Postmodern Jewish Philosophy Network* (this was my contribution to the Network's attempt at self-identification):

> The variety of for-now-called-postmodern Jewish philosophy displayed by our members is a non-ontologizing, non-foundational philosophy, stimulated by concern for problems in our social or religious praxis and by a shared concern that the dichotomizing, reductive models of modernity (or also the trajectory of medieval-modern philosophy) do not foster adequate responses to those problems. This for-now-called-postmodern Jewish philosophy participates in the open-ended inquiry into human experience fostered by modern western philosophy, but seeks to refer all interpretations of such experience to context-specific paradigms of interpretation. Among the paradigmatic contexts preferred by for-now-called-postmodern Jewish philosophers are: Revealed Text (Bible); Prototypical Communities/Traditions of Jewish Text Interpretation (Rabbinics); The Social-Intellectual Practices of Jewish Communities.

Although a family of "thinkers" would include more than "philosophers," and although the philosophers in question are not about to wear a description like this on their team uniforms, the description serves to illustrate ways in which postmodern thinkers work in what were the boundaries between community-specific and "universal," academic discourses. This "in-between" location works both ways. If it means that postmodern Jewish discourse is irreducible, on the one hand, to the purportedly universal terms of what Borowitz calls Enlightenment science, it means that it is also irreducible to the strictly intratextual or indigenous vocabularies of this or that tradition of Jewish religious practice. We are not dealing here with an overthrow of the universal, but, rather, with an alternative to the standard dichotomization of universal and particular. In terms of this alternative, the postmodern Christian "stranger" may in fact belong to the postmodern Jewish discourse in as yet unforeseen ways. But more on such matters later.

BOROWITZ' COVENANTAL THEOLOGY
IN HISTORICAL CONTEXT

Borowitz offers his book as a situated statement, and the readers receive it that way. According to the readers as a whole, Borowitz offers a theology for the non-Orthodox, or liberal yet religious Jew. Borowitz calls this the "postmodern Jew," a modern Jew who remains loyal to the Enlightenment values of personal moral autonomy and of some form of non-exclusivism, but who is disillusioned with modernity's failed rationalism and moral optimism. As Peter Haas has summarized it, while many Enlightenment ideas remain essential to contemporary Jewish life, "for example, the dignity of the individual, democracy, pluralism and our limited knowledge of God," nonetheless, the violence and evil of this century have discredited Enlightenment optimism about human goodness.[2] According to Norbert M. Samuelson's words in chapter 7 of this volume, "The individual quality of life . . . is corroding in political democracy while modern philosophies and science lead to moral relativism." The postmodern Jew no longer trusts in the capacity of the secular university and secular science to respond to these ills, and none of the contemporary faith systems have proved capable of responding either: neither mysticism, nor ethnic nationalism, nor religious orthodoxy. The result, says Ogletree, is Borowitz' attempt

> to realize the importance of the Enlightenment critique of religious life and thought, to recognize its emancipatory power, but at the same time to recognize the inadequacies of that new development in Western culture and our own need to recover in a new form the formative power of the great traditions of faith that have sustained us over many generations . . .

Borowitz does not attempt to construct a new theology out of his religious imagination, but rather to clarify in an intelligible way the theology that is already embedded in the practices of the postmodern Jew. For Borowitz, these practices already commit this Jew to a binding relation to "the people Israel" (the traditional rabbinic term for "the Jewish people") and to God, but in a way that respects personal autonomy as well as theonomy. If this commitment to both personalism and religious duty appears self-contradictory, this is, says Borowitz, only because we are judging appearances according to the inappropriately dichotomizing standards of modern liberalism on the one side or anti-modern Orthodoxy on the other. The non-dichotomizing alternative is a "covenantal theology for the postmodern Jew." Borowitz brings this theology into words by examining the Jewish theologies that have served modern Jews until now and then revising the strongest theologies in a way that would enable them to speak directly to the postmodern condition. Among the strongest theologies, Borowitz numbers those of Abraham Heschel, Mordecai Kaplan, Martin Buber, and Franz Rosenzweig, but his single most important resource is Buber. In Samuelson's words, Borowitz' covenantal theology could be described as "Buber's theology [of dialogical personalism] reconstructed to include a more adequate sense of Jewish community" and, we might add, of the commanding voice of normative Jewish practice.

Samuelson notes that, in mode of presentation, Borowitz bridges the gap between popular and technical writing: he is an integral part of the community of scholars, but he speaks at the same time to the immediate experiences and needs of his community of reform rabbinical students. He is, one might say, a pastoral philosopher, bringing intelligibility to the everyday work of his rabbinical students at the same time that he brings concerns about everyday practice to the intellectual work of his philosophic colleagues. He links intelligence and practice through the medium of what Yudit K. Greenberg calls "autobiographical theology." To discover what relationship a given theology would have to actual experience, Borowitz asks himself (in a manner reminiscent of William James) what actual difference in his everyday life a given theological option would make and what difference a given experience would make in his theological understanding. Borowitz' survey of modern religious thinkers is, as he describes it, a way of taking stock of the ways in which his teachers and colleagues have and have not influenced his life.

Christians have a pre-modern prototype for this approach in the Augustinian tradition of confessional theology, but Jews have traditionally been wary, tending to consider autobiographical reasoning a mark of modernity and of "modern subjectivism." If Borowitz' personalism speaks to post-liberal Jews, it is because it is tempered, as he says, by his engagement in the life of his community and by fittingly postmodern disclaimers about the situatedness and fallibility of his theology. Beyond these methodological disclaimers, I suspect that Borowitz' personal accounts speak so broadly because of the particular person who offers them. He happens to have listened empathetically to the experiences of many of his contemporaries and to have thought-and-lived-out many experiences that have proved to be prototypical of the move into modernist religiosity and out of it.

Edith Wyschogrod reads *Renewing the Covenant* in terms of its author's own autobiographical approach. She notes that, ten years earlier, Borowitz articulated a religious, existentialist personalism consistent with the one he advances now: seeking, at that time, a way for the individual to be both Jewish *and* modern, by respecting both personal autonomy and Jewish particularity.[3] Borowitz' version of postmodern Judaism appears, in fact, consistent with his lifelong respect for traditional norms *and* personal choice: a lifetime, in his terms, of "reform faith seeking understanding."

THE COVENANTAL RELATIONSHIP BETWEEN
GOD AND THE POSTMODERN JEW

For Borowitz' readers, the central focus of his theology is the binding yet non-heteronomous relation between God and the "postmodern" Jew. In the last section of *Renewing the Covenant*, Borowitz offers what I take to be a fitting characterization of this theological stance as a whole. He refers to the implicit personalism of contemporary *posekim* (legal or *halakhic* decisors) who "claim the right to issue directives to the community simply on the basis of *daas Torah* (knowledge of Torah): . . . assert[ing] their authority in terms [only] of their general 'knowledge/sense' of Torah." He then says he interprets "this as pointing to the legislative authority of their personal intuition of our Jewish duty, one growing out of their learning and piety but finally valid as the insight of a Torah personality." He adds, climactically I believe, "I have in mind something similar, a non-Orthodox self that is autonomous yet so fundamentally shaped by the Covenant that whatever issues from its depths will have authentic Jewish character. The secular conception of autonomy must be transformed in terms of its Covenantal context." Here, the covenant appears to achieve its commanding presence *without* explicit law *(halakhah)*. But how? What grants the non-Orthodox self the capacity to fulfill its Jewish duty autonomously?

David Novak argues that, in Borowitz' account, the non-*halakhic* self cannot, in fact, fulfill its Jewish duty, because it is not engaged in the binding relationship with God that would establish that duty. Novak argues that, as displayed in the following passage, Borowitz has, following Buber, offered a theology of relationship, but not of Covenant.

> Authentic relationship obligates and does so in a curious dialectic of particular importance for postmoderns seeking to illumine their experience of being commanded by God. Its oddity begins with its shared authority. Were one of the partners dominant as in Orthodoxy, we would have something like a master-slave relationship, a figure we shy away from in recent centuries, translating *eved Adonai* as "God's servant" rather than the more literal "God's slave." Of course, our hesitancy has good biblical foundation, God being depicted there as attending to human will and not overriding human freedom. *We moderns have amplified that view of human dignity to include the critical power to share in the decisions that effect one. The model of relationship reflects this enfranchisement of the person by indicating that rightful authority arises* between *the parties involved. What they mean to one another, just who they discover themselves and this other to be in this relationship, the special depth and quality of what has and now continues to transpire between them, all exercise normative power on them*(273).[4]

Novak's reply is that, while *relationship* so defined does share some essential characters with the biblical/rabbinic notion of *Covenant*—such as a beginning in time and some degree of reciprocality—it is also lacking other essential characters. Most conspicuously absent is the ultimate inequality between God and creature: the Covenantal God *initiates* the Covenant by way of a revelation whose a priori and verbal character has no counterpart in the Buberian notion of relationship. It is this character that lends the *halakhah* its binding authority and its power to bind community together. We must therefore "posit a God who speaks, primarily, a people that responds, secondarily and subsequently and, without that . . . revelation cannot ever create *halakhah* and without *halakhah* there is simply no community."[5]

Greenberg shares Novak's concern to find a place for verbal revelation in the Jewish Covenant. She argues that, along with both Rosenzweig and Buber, Borowitz fails to identify the authority of the Torah text as the source of Jewish duties. She says that, without this authority

> their views of the validity of specific Jewish duties rest on their presupposition of the reality of the living God and His ongoing relationship with the

Jewish people. This relationship with God, however, must be derived from personal experience rather than from the absolute truth of the Torah. . . . Renewing the covenant is [thus] an existential move subject to one's personal and privileged moments of contact with God. . . . Borowitz is entirely too confident in the Jewish self . . .

Ogletree appreciates Borowitz' unapologetic description of the Jewish self as a "self formed and sustained within Jewish communal and social processes enduring over time." At the same time, he is concerned that Borowitz has not sufficiently articulated the historist implications of this description, particularly as it applies to the notion of individual "autonomy." He believes Borowitz' position rests too much "on a notion of moral autonomy over any form of heteronomous authority," as if the consent of the individual were not itself "derived from and sustained by the communal bonds that nurture [the individual] and also by the social and institutional processes that provide order for [the individual's] life." Ogletree explains that "when I refuse the normative guidance of my community, I place my moral autonomy at risk, that is, my *capacity* for discerning moral judgments." Because the community is itself implicated in any of my choices

> the task is not just for me to state my personal convictions over against dominant traditions within the community, but to try to put in words the shared convictions of the community of faith to which I belong, to give suggestions to the community about how it might live and work creatively with its normative traditions.

Samuelson appraises Borowitz' covenantal theology in terms that may be used to identify a common ground among Borowitz and his critics. On the topic of individuals and community, Samuelson regards the "modern" view as "atomistic": the claim that "ultimately what exists are things (atoms) which join together with other things to form relations [such as collections and communities], and what is fundamental in reality is the existence of the things, not their relations." He says that the traditional Jewish view, however, was "relationalist: . . . a way of picturing the universe that presupposes that what exists are relations which may be analyzed into things (namely, terms) in relationship. In other words, things are to be understood as *relata*—not as independent entities, but as terms of relations." He adds that "in this sense, Jewish thought has always been relational," rather than atomistic. Buber continued this theme, as has Borowitz, offering a liberal version of Jewish relationalism. What, then, does "autonomy" mean on these terms? Samuelson apparently believes that, whatever the terminology, Borowitz' position could accommodate Ogletree's. Borowitz understands the self, phenomenologically, to be constituted *in* relation, to represent in fact a *term* of relation. People enact their autonomy in *relation* to others and to God. In order to distinguish a liberal notion of religious *authority* from an Orthodox one, Borowitz retains the term "autonomy" (perhaps he could use a better term) as part of a political and juridical, rather than a phenomenological or ontological analysis. He believes that, in Samuelson's terms, in matters dealing with one's relationship with God, the leadership of the religious community does not have authority over the conscience of its individual members.

This still leaves us with the concerns of Greenberg and Novak to locate the self in a Covenantal relationship whose terms are introduced verbally and a priori. Here, I think it is possible to extend Samuelson's terms, to show how the relational self may be both autonomous, in Borowitz' sense, and bound by the authority of the Covenant's divine partner. We may say that the "self" refers to a relational location, in fact the matrix of an indefinite number of relations; for example, the love and dependency and mutuality and dominance or need that interrelate family members or friends or coworkers. To the extent that these relations are themselves brought into dialogue by way of the self, the self may also be described as a kind of community. As a matrix of relations, this "community" differs from societal or interpersonal communities only in its materiality, or in the qualitative idiom with respect to which its parts or members are interrelated. The self may be termed, for example, a psycho-somatic matrix of relationship, as opposed to cultural or linguistic matrices. In this regard, Julia Kristeva draws a useful distinction between what she calls the "semiotic" order (the somatic matrix of proto-symbolic relations) and the "symbolic" order (the public or cultural order of symbolic relations per se).[6] There are tensions between the orders, but each anticipates the other in a way excluded from modernist definitions of individual and community.

In Kristeva's approach, the semiotic order of the self remains prelinguistic and in this sense a source of the self's independence from societal intrusions. Within the province of rabbinic philosophy, Max Kadushin offered an analysis of self and society that places greater emphasis on the integrative role of public discourse.7 He described the religion of the Talmudic sages as an integrated system of "value concepts," named by such biblically-derived terms as "lovingkindess," "God's justice" and "God's mercy." These mutually interdependent virtues are defined only *in actu* but are illustrated for heuristic purposes in biblically-based, Talmudic stories about paradigmatic acts of virtue. He claimed that the virtue of these virtues (Kristeva would call them "symbols") is that they inform a communal process of socialization that enhances the individuality of community members (what Borowitz would call "individual human dignity") at the same time that it strengthens the relational bonds of the community.

Kadushin's and Kristeva's analyses represent contrary poles of a semiotic alternative to modernist discussions of self in society. Kadushin's analysis tends to hypostatize societal hopes and ideals, while Kristeva's addresses the lives of individuals in societies that are disillusioned with such ideals. Nonetheless, both describe the self as a participant in and contributor to symbolic relations, as dependent on its interpersonal life in symbolic orders as it is insistent on its own particular needs and life forms. Restated in these terms, Borowitz' Covenant might be written in the idiom of Kadushin's "value concepts," thereby presented *to* the individual in the idiom of communally interpreted biblical discourse. According to Kadushin, these value concepts lack a priori definition, and, according to Kadushin as well as to Kristeva, they must nurture individuality as well as community. *For these reasons*, we may suppose that the value concepts have retained their value over the centuries *because they possess a capacity at once to shape individual behavior and to be reshaped—continually redefined—by it*. For now, we might label this the value concepts' capacity for "relational authority"; that is, for exerting an authority that is defined only *in relation to* the community and the individuals it serves (the Talmudic sages referred to this as the attribute of divine *mercy—middat harachamim*). The value concepts command behavior (in this sense like legal imperatives), but they command in an indefinite way (in this sense like ethical values). They are brought to definition only by way of the *experiences* of individuals. Experience is therefore an essential, but not a foundational element of Covenantal life.

Borowitz' Covenantal theology would appear to meet the concerns of Greenberg and Novak if the Jewish Covenant it envisioned were written with words—value conceptual words—that exerted relational authority over the Covenant's human partners. These words would provide the verbal, a priori authority that Greenberg and Novak attribute to the revealed Torah. Their *relationality* would ensure the respect for individual human dignity (or "autonomy" in modernist terms) that Borowitz attributes to the postmodern Covenant. This is not to suggest that this play of definitions will get Novak and Borowitz to agree on the specific character of Jewish law—consistent with rabbinic as well as a postmodern conceptions, they participate in different religious subcommunities loyal to different juridical bodies—but it may show that they differ *in terms of* some shared conception of law. David Weiss Halivni has introduced useful terms for framing this conception:

> There exist three rabbinic positions on the nature of the revelation of the Oral Law. . . . [These] may be classified as maximalistic, intermediary and minimalistic. The *maximalistic* position claims that God revealed to Moses on Mount Sinai the entire Oral Torah consisting of all the legitimate arguments of, and all the legitimate solutions to, every issue that may arise . . . [Humanity] merely needs to uncover them. The *intermediary* position claims that God revealed to Moses on Mount Sinai all the legitimate arguments of every issue that may arise but not their solutions. The solutions were left for [human beings] to offer, and whatever [they] offer becomes a part of "the words of the living God.". . . The *minimalistic* position claims that God revealed to Moses on Mount Sinai directions for [humanity] to follow and principles to implement, but not detailed stipulations. . . . In contrast to the intermediary conception of revelation, in which only ultimate *halakhic* rulings were left for [humanity] to determine, the minimalistic position presents humanity with the opportunity, and authority, for the fleshing out of *halakhic* arguments and details from directional principles.[8]

Borowitz and Novak may agree to differ in these terms. Novak would adopt an intermediary position, for which the Covenant commands by way of specific, Talmudic argumentation. Borowitz would adopt a minimalistic position, for which the Covenant commands by way of the more general *value concepts* alone. As non-maximalists, both of them would acknowledge the role of human beings in defining the commands; that is, of human communities attentive to individual needs (Novak), or of human individuals attentive to communal needs (Borowitz).[9]

COVENANTAL THEOLOGY AS POSTMODERN THEOLOGY

Borowitz' use of the term "postmodern" has stimulated controversy. Ogletree suggests that, after hearing these responses, Borowitz may regret having called his theology "postmodern": "a theology for the caring non-Orthodox Jew [would have been preferable]. . . . What Borowitz offers is still essentially modernist. It is a kind of qualified modernism, a kind of chastened liberalism. His aim is to protect authentically Jewish understanding of God, Covenant, and Torah without falling prey to the neo-traditionalist repudiation of the modern world." Yet, Ogletree continues, "the controlling categories of Borowitz' book are universalistic in content and method," since they are presented through an analysis of concepts offered independently of a specifically Jewish hermeneutic."

Greenberg suggests that Borowitz has laid out a postmodern project, but has undertaken it in terms still beholden, in part, to modernist conceptions. Borowitz' postmodern concerns are displayed, for example, in his concerns for "egalitarianism, pluralism, and community," and in

> the return to a genuine spirituality born out of the disenchantment with modernity and at the same time the refusal to despair over modernity's failures. . . . The postrational critique of modern Jewish philosophy unlocks possibilities for intuitive, non-linear models of cognitive and practical spirituality. . . . [And,] the shift from an individual to a communal notion of the self [is based on the postmodern premise] that the Jewish self is constituted by its relations to the history and life of the Jewish people but is nevertheless not completely determined by these.

At the same time, she adds, Borowitz' robust portrayal of the Jewish self in Covenant with God does not also take sufficient note of the postmodern conditions of displacement and of decentered faith.

Taking note of these insufficiencies, Wyschogrod offers the most elaborate description of a postmodernism that is somewhat other than what Borowitz has undertaken. For her, "postmodernism" refers more strictly to the "conceptual matrix" that accompanied the postmodern movement in earlier twentieth-century art and architecture and that was enunciated since in Continental, mostly French and mostly deconstructive philosophy. This matrix has no place for Borowitz' notion of the *whole self founded* in God as *absolute norm.* Instead, the postmodernists repudiate the notions of normative discourse as a foundation for values and of God as divine ground of "whole selves." She argues that a Derridean deconstruction deconstructs personalist existentialism as well as modern rationalisms, laying bare all such modern theories as "grand meta-narratives." In Jean-François Lyotard's reading, the texts that deliver such theories are "doubly coded," revealing both a "high modern" meaning *and* a popular meaning that is in tension with it. The postmodern critic's task is, in attending to this double-codedness, to deliver meanings that would otherwise remain suppressed.[10]

As postmodern reader of Borowitz' work, Wyschogrod suggests that a theory of double coding is *almost* already present in his book. Nudging the theory out, she delivers her version of Borowitz' theology as a postmodern theology. Her move, as I see it, is to attend in particular to the *relation* between Borowitz' work and its rabbinic antecedents, thereby placing it in apposition to the work of both modernist critics of rabbinic tradition and neo-traditional disciples. How does Borowitz' approach differ from these two? Noting that, for Borowitz, inequity is built into the rabbinic Covenant, Wyschogrod suggests that, in these terms, discipleship and criticism need not be so far apart. As disciple, after all, Abraham *urges* God to act justly (rather than assuming God necessarily will): it makes sense in terms of his relationship with God for him to be critic as disciple and disciple as critic. Noting that, for Lyotard, inequity is built into language itself, Wyschogrod suggests that Lyotard's analysis of linguistic inequity may help extend Borowitz' analysis of covenantal inequity. She notes that Lyotard uses the term *différend* to refer to "the unstable state and instance of language wherein something that must be able to be put into phrases cannot yet be." The prototypical instance is when a language does not provide the means for a plaintiff even to put her arguments against an accused into words: *le différend* thus refers to "a condition of inarticulateness." Wyschogrod then asks:

> Could one not claim that [consistent with Borowitz' reading,] rabbinic language "always already" recognizes the doubleness of Israel's status as litigant in an endless trial . . . as 'victim,' always voiceless, but as elect always already . . . in quest of a divine language, so that it might question divine justice? Such, I suggest, would be the doubleness of Covenant yielded by a postmodern reading.

Restated as Wyschogrod suggests, Borowitz' Covenant would have written into it the capacity to speak to conditions of displacement and of decentered faith: one's very relationship with God and with Israel, that is, could be as complainant, but *in* relationship as complainant rather than out of relationship. Since Borowitz does not present his covenant in these terms explicitly, it remains to be seen what moves he would make if he chose to accommodate these terms. I will suggest that two moves would suffice. The first move, in line with Novak and Greenberg, would be to make more explicit the *textuality* of the Covenant. I say "more" explicit, since Borowitz has already made *Torah* a foundation of his theology. Thus, he writes, "whereas contemporary philosophy can at best only commend universal human dignity, Hebrew Scriptures command it. . . . With the one incomparable God of Hebrew Scripture as its source, universal human dignity cannot be compromised or qualified by any merely human authority" (pp. 185–86). The issue is more fully to articulate the role of *textual reading* per se in understanding what human dignity is all about, thus avoiding the experiential foundationalism Greenberg and Novak detect in both Buber and Rosenzweig. This appears, in fact, to be the goal of Borowitz' work since *Renewing the Covenant*: to describe his direct encounters with God as worldly experiences that are both brought to expression by way of, *and* give expression to, Jewish readings of the Bible.[11] In either way, this is to teach that Biblical discourse provides the predicates in terms of which otherwise extra-linguistic encounters enter into public discussion.[12]

Borowitz' second move would be to explain how *Covenantal textuality* would allow for displacement or decentered faith or for the other theological in-betweennesses he identifies, such as a commanding voice that allows for complaint, a *halakhah* that allows for personal objection ("choice" would represent a stronger option), or a textual hermeneutic that allows for personal experience. This is to locate the "postmodernity" of Borowitz' theology, in particular, in the relationship in his work between Covenantal textuality and displacement. The primary way to disclose Borowitz' account of theological displacement, however, is not merely to read his words and predict the direction of his theology. It is, rather, to articulate the *performance* of his theological work within the covenantal sub-community gathered near, with, and around him. This is because the "displacement" postmodernists discuss is only secondarily a trope in their writing but primarily an *event* of which their writing is a record or sign. Such events are measured by their actual force or effects on the writer, rather than in imitative representations or descriptions of them. Otherwise put, the events are disclosed only by way of a *différance*: both in the way their disclosure is deferred, or put off, to later signs and in the way these later signs represent the events: by marking befores-and-afters or differences in the words and actions of those affected by them. In the case of Borowitz' postmodern Jewish theology, the event we are talking about is the displacement of a modern practice of Jewish theology, which was primarily a practice of mono-logical and monographic writing. The primary sign of the displacement of Borowitz' *modern* theology is not his *writing about* postmodern Judaism, but his historically situated, non-modern practice: the way he engages with others in a dialogical and communal performance of writing, speaking, and doing, from teaching his postmodernism in rabbinical school, to helping gather meetings of the Society for Textual Reasoning, to *encountering* a sub-community of postmodern theologians *who will not let him respond alone* to the issues of this volume. This dialogical performance remains, moreover, a "place of displacement": a context in which, for example, a text tradition is both received and challenged, an individual thinker is both summoned by others and released to him or herself, or a community that both gathers away from other communities and is interrupted by them or for them.

GENE, YOU CAN NO LONGER RESPOND TO YOUR WORK ALONE

As modern Jewish theologian, Gene, you may have written your own monographs, but having now announced your postmodernism, you may find your autonomy challenged, if modestly, by the community that gathers around your announcement.[13] Your old friends, with whom you engaged in spirited and mutually respectful theological argument, may now join you again, along with many new ones, but the mode of engagement will be a little different. Just as your words now find part of their meaning in the way they help shape community as well as belief and opinion, so too, the community becomes a context in which your words are released somewhat from their authorship and its propriety. What is your postmodern Jewish theology? You will (in the next chapter) offer your own response to your readers, but throughout the rest of this volume your readers begin to answer the question by presuming to speak, to some extent, for you. You are displaced *to* us, you might say. This is how I understand the biblical prophets to have substituted themselves for the people Israel, and vice versa in Israel's memory of them, and how I understand the rabbinic sages to have become, collectively, voices of the Jewish people's dialogues with God and with each other. In our day, it may be time for Jewish scholars to accept, with whatever modesty, a substitutionary role of their own *within the particular communities of inquiry* that bring them not only some place in the western academy, but—certainly more significantly, in the context of this volume—also a specific place in Israel's Covenant with God. For the conclusion of this reading of your readers, I therefore want to turn, on your behalf, from you to them, as the community now with you. In my introduction, I sought to classify your postmodern work among other kinds of inquiry; now, to conclude this review, I want to imagine what place this community that includes you would have among other communities.

A POSTMODERN JEWISH COMMUNITY AMONG OTHERS

A Catalogue of Traits

The community of postmodern Jewish theologians (CPJ) to which I have referred in this chapter does not necessarily claim such an identity self-consciously; in fact, its identity as well as its existence is yet aborning, one might say. Nevertheless, enough sub-groups have emerged that *could* be associated with such a community (such as the Textual Reasoning Journal and Society), and enough individuals have linked their writing to the topic (starting with Gene Borowitz), that I feel it is appropriate to end this chapter with a catalogue of the community's identifying traits. The catalogue is partly descriptive of what I have seen taking place in the circle of thinkers that includes Borowitz and his readers; and it is partly predictive. The list of traits is partly unsystematic (where I am simply listing what I see somewhere) and partly systematic (where I have tried to discern certain communal rules; and, of course, the more I have tried, the less empirically reliable the results may be!).

Postmodern Jewish Theology. A good trait to start with is the irreducibility of the community's theological/philosophic tendencies—call them postmodern Jewish theology (PJT)—to any other categories of modern or postmodern thought. PJT represents a distinctive relation among the Jewish Covenant, a philosophic theology, and postmodernism. It cannot be categorized as some instance of a general type of either modern or postmodern philosophy or theology, but may be described as a philosophically articulated expression of another moment in the historical life of the Jewish Covenant.

Students of the various forms of contemporary postmodern inquiry, from deconstruction to pragmatism, will be among the significant dialogue partners of the CPJ; but PJT remains irreducible to any other form of postmodernism. Readers should not expect PJT to mirror the "postmodernity" of any other postmodern method of thought, or the "Jewishness" of any other Jewish philosophy, or the "philosophic" character of any other philosophy. Neither the "postmodern," the "Jewish" nor the "philosophic" attributes of PJT will be definable independently of the other two attributes. It would represent a species of modernist thinking to suppose, to the contrary, that any attribute could be defined independently, or that the defining features of a given "postmodern" philosophy could be determined, a priori, through the use of any one of the postmodern approaches mentioned earlier.

The "postmodernity" of PJT may be characterized, eclectically, with respect to selective traits shared with those of other postmodern orientations. In terms of the survey of postmodernism offered in the introduction, we might, for example, observe the following similarities and differences.

Derrideans and Other Continental Postmodernists. With Derrideans[14] and other Continental or, more generally extra-religious academic postmodernists, the CPJ shares in the deconstruction of onto-theology, or of the attempt to found theologies and philosophies on premises that are altogether removed from the embarrassments of historical particularity and historical change. They are all suspicious of the actual generality of conceptual universals, presuming that universal claims are abstracted from finite domains of reference and then over-generalized. They are, more generally, suspicious of the Western academic practices of epistemological foundationalism—the rationalist "quest for certainty"—and of the intellectual individualism, atomism, and egoism that accompanies it.

They are critical of various claims to self-presence, that is, that some knowledge or object of knowledge has "disclosed itself" (or its true being, and so on) to someone. This means they are suspicious of any claims to unmediated knowledge—that one just "sees" the truth—including literalist readings of the Bible, fundamentalist claims about religious truth, dogmatic claims about religious experience, and the claims of various ideologues to having certain knowledge based on some non-public experience, alone. They are all, finally, critical of the abuses that follow from the adoption of universalist, foundationalist or self-validating claims as the basis of social policy and political action. Among such abuses are totalitarian government, colonialism, imperialism, policies of terrorism.

The Biblical and Rabbinic Context of CPJ. Along with most groups of postmodernists, the CPJ acknowledges the communal, textual and performative contexts of postmodern thinking, theological or otherwise. For postmodern *Jewish* thinking, more precisely, they note that these contexts are biblical, rabbinic, and post-rabbinic—although different members of the CPJ offer different assessments of the relative importance and normativity of these contexts. This means that the CPJ is critical of Continental postmodernist tendencies to assimilate some central claims of Western biblical religion to the category of secular foundationalism or universalism: such as claims about the sacrality and behavioral authority of Scripture. Along with Hans Frei, George Lindbeck and other Christian postliberals,[15] the CPJ would argue that such claims about Scripture not only do not merit deconstructive criticism, but most likely introduce the transcendental conditions and historical foundation for Derridean methods of deconstruction. Acknowledging the community-specific normativity of Jewish notions of self, God and so on, they would argue that, where there is no pretension to universalism or a priorism—that is, to context-independent notions of the cosmos or of "cosmic" obligations—there should not be any deconstructive criticism.

Process Thinkers and Postliberals. With the process thinkers[16] and postliberals, therefore, the Jewish postmodernists do not abjure rational or normative discourse altogether. With the process thinkers, they believe that there is still a lot of reasoning to do and that this reasoning may have normative import. With the post-liberals, they describe this normativity in a way that is relational, but not relativistic. This means that they argue *with* other

members of given communities of discourse about what norms of discourse (including rules of thinking as well as rules of everyday comport-
ment) might best (or ought best to) serve those communities. These communities, moreover, may have expansive domains that render them
functionally bigger than "mere particularities," even if smaller than that
maximal domain moderns have called the "community" of human beings.
For postmodern Jewish thinkers, in other words, the modern dichotomization of universal and particular is useful only to describe opposing vec-
tors or idealized limits. The everyday business of reformatory, postmodern
Jewish thinking must make use of a modal logic that provides some third
term to refer to what lies in-between these limits. Such a logic would be
complemented by a postmodern hermeneutic that provides a third term to
refer to what lies in-between textuality and experience and in-between
general law and individual life.

Pragmatists. With the pragmatists, the CPJ understands postmodern
thinking as responsive, rather than as originative, generative or foundational thinking.[17] It is thinking that *responds*, moreover, to some experienced or suffered condition that they call the "postmodern condition."
Among the most conspicuous features of this condition is a perception,
to cite Samuelson's words, that "the individual quality of life has been and
is corroding in our political democracy, while modern philosophies and
sciences lead to [an apparently unresponsive] moral relativism." As reflected in the pattern of Borowitz' presentation, the first stage of postmodern thinking is to examine the presently available responses to this
condition and to find them wanting. The result is "disillusionment with
modernity," that is, with modern *thinking* as well as with modern living.
Judging by its positive energies, however, postmodern thinking does not
rest with this disillusionment, but offers new-old responses in its stead. It
should go without saying that the responses—Borowitz' included—will
retain elements of modern thinking and will therefore appear to be in
tension with themselves to varying degrees. This appears to be the character of all workable, reformatory movements: they are movements *from*
somewhere to somewhere else and, therefore, display traces of their past
as well as anticipations of their future. Postmodern reformers ought to be
wary, therefore, if their plans for reform appear too coherent or too good
to be true. "To be true to the mark," in this case—*emet* in Hebrew—

would mean to be true to those whose conditions of suffering the reforms are supposed to remedy. This is to be "true" in the sense of being faithful to them, as in the biblical phrase, "The Lord, The Lord, a God merciful and gracious, slow to anger and abundant in mercy and truth" (Ex. 34:6). The medieval commentator Rashi explains that "in truth" means "faithfully rewarding those who perform His will" (ad. loc. Ex. 34:6); Abraham ibn Ezra adds "'in truth,' fulfilling His word" (ad. loc. Ex. 34:6). The most powerful symptom of truth in this sense is the relief it brings, rather than its fulfilling any a priori conditions of coherence.

Articulated more specifically within the terms of PJT, responsive thinking is redemptive thinking, whose prototype is God's response to the Israelites' call: "God heard their moaning. . . . God took notice of them" (Ex. 3). In the biblical model, divine responses are offered in terms of the conditions of suffering, rather than creating new conditions *ex nihilo*. In the case of human responses, we would therefore have all the more reason to expect redemptive thinking to be meliorative rather than apocalyptic. Its method is, within the limits of what can be known at the time of action, to read occasions of suffering as indices (doubly coded) of what is both wrong *and* right within the context (community, relationship, tradition, etc.) of the sufferers. This is why the purpose of PJT is not to reject modernism, but to come to its aid: to read its foundationalist project *both* as a symptom of suffering (indicating that something is wrong in the antecedent or pre-modern traditions), and as an errant attempt to replace those traditions rather than repair them. The problem with modernist thinking is therefore not its criticisms, but its proffered solutions. The task of PJT is to re-respond to these criticisms, but in the terms made available in the pre-modern contexts in terms of which modern criticisms have meaning.

Religious Pragmatists and Postliberals. With religious pragmatists and post-liberals, the CPJ acknowledges a human capacity for direct knowledge of the Absolute. This is not a claim to unmediated, foundational knowledge, but to the possibility of entering into a direct relation to God. This is not a claim about self-presence, since the human cannot offer any self-validating propositions about or on behalf of God, except the claim that God has been encountered—which claim remains maximally vague, however, or subject to clarification only through a communal process of interpreting

the texts of any claims about God and testing their empirical consequences and implications. For the CPJ, the community's authoritative
record of such direct knowledge is Scripture and its rabbinic and post-
rabbinic tradition of interpretation. Direct encounter does not itself cease
with the cessation of prophecy, however; but individual encounter offers
only enlightened and creative insight into the hermeneutics of this tradition. With religious pragmatists and postliberals, therefore, the CPJ acknowledges the *non-exclusivity and fallibilism* of any discursive knowledge
that follows our encounters with the Absolute.

Textualists & Communalists. With post-liberals and some Derrideans, the
CPJ argues that the modern academy needs a hermeneutical recovery of
the textual and communal contexts of modern criticism. Textuality reen-
ters postmodern Jewish thought because text traditions *lie behind* the
modern project of academe as an essential part of the context of modern
criticism. Otherwise veiled by modernist constructions, this part needs to
be recovered, rather than reconstituted through arguments about the a
priori features of textuality. Part of the modern academy's error is to have
supposed that biblical and talmudic communal and text traditions were
the source rather than the context of modern suffering. PJP recovers the
context. To repair modernism in this way, however, is at the same time to
repair pre-modern traditions of text and community. Modernity com-
plained for good reason.

A Pragmatic and Postmodern Logic. With some pragmatists of a classic sort,
there are members of the CPJ who argue that contemporary postmodern
theology cannot win its arguments with the modern academy unless it
resuscitates a discipline of philosophic logic, but of a postmodern sort. A
"postmodern logic" would not offer any representations of the universe,
but only techniques for rendering the claims we make of and to each
other more precise and less misleading—including appropriately vague
claims about irreducibly vague beliefs, relations, and expectations. In the
post-Kantian era, Jewish thinkers have shown decreasing interest in the
use of mathematical symbols or in logical precision, but there is no reason to perpetuate this tendency *if* the use of symbols and the practice of
precision remain instruments of non-foundationalist, text-based Jewish
inquiry. Borowitz himself divides modern Jewish thinkers into groups of
"rationalists" and "nonrationalists." This is consistent with the tendency of

many postmodern thinkers, who then opt for a "nonrationalist" alternative to Enlightenment "rationalism." Samuelson adopts a mediating approach, suggesting that the dichotomization is itself a symptom of modernism and that the postmodern critique of modern foundationalism calls for new paradigms of reason, rather than for non-reason. He argues, in fact that

> this seems to be what Borowitz means by claiming to favor non-rationalism. It is not a rejection of the value of reason as such. Rather, it is an assertion that the sources of rational thought are not in reason itself but in experience.18

This, says Samuelson, makes Borowitz a radical empiricist in the tradition of William James and, for that matter, Franz Rosenzweig, who identified himself, in similar terms, as an "absolute empiricist."19

Such an empiricist is equivalent to the religious pragmatist who recognizes both our capacity to experience God directly and the fallibility of our discursive claims about God. To test and refine such claims, the pragmatist or absolute empiricist needs a logic that provides rules for clarifying our claims and reformulating them as empirically and hermeneutically testable hypotheses. The following three items illustrate a few traits of such a logic. (These items contain some technical sections that may not interest all readers. These sections will be marked with brackets [ ] so that less specialized readers may read through the items more readily, attending only to the main text.)

Critique of Substantialism. One basis for a postmodern logic is a critique of substantialism in modern and medieval epistemology and logic. Modern critics have justifiably raised concerns about such burdens of premodernity as authoritarianism, paternalism, and patriarchy. At the same time, modern reforms have failed when they have replayed rather than repaired other burdens, of which "substantialism" is of particular interest to postmodern philosophers. For our purposes, substantialism refers to the presupposition that the grammatical subjects of our languages refer to enduring entities, that the grammatical predicates identify attributes of such entities, and that there are hierarchies of enduring entities, at the top of which is the ultimate entity or substance *(ousia)*, to be identified with being itself *(to on)*. The presupposition implies, for one, that being ultimately discloses itself—or, in the Heideggerian terms that disturb Derrida, that it has "self-presence."

PJT renounces substantialism, because it provides the metaphysical and epistemological conditions for atomism, individualism, and foundationalism. PJT renounces propositionalism, because it provides the logical conditions for substantialism. For our purposes, "propositionalism" refers to an attempt to reduce all rules of reasoning to the terms of a propositional logic. [This is a logic that diagrams judgments as acts of predicating discrete qualities of quantifiable subjects: for example, "S is Q" or "Some S is Q" or "All S is Q."] Among the most well-known laws of propositonal logic are the law of excluded middle, which asserts that, as they appear in predicates, discrete qualities are mutually exclusive (a or $-a$); and the law of non-contradiction ($-(a$ and $-a)$).

Some postmodern thinkers attempt to replace propositional logic with no explicit logic, as if there were no alternative to classical/modern epistemology and logic, and as if, therefore, the critique of substantialism left us with contrary alternatives: either substantialist and thus propositionalist rules of rationality or else no rules of rationality. It is more likely, however, that postmodernisms that operate in terms of such a binary opposition are in fact—whatever their protestations—guided by the law of excluded middle that belongs to propositional logic. PJT would assume, instead, that modernist and postmodernist assertions represent logical contradictories, rather than contraries. This means that we know about postmodern reasoning only that it is irreducible to the terms of propositional logic, but not that it is positively not-logical in this sense; it remains to be seen what attributes postmodern reasoning may display.

Relational Logic. Another basis for postmodern logic is the use of a relational logic (or logic of relatives) in place of the propositional logics of classical/modern philosophy. This is a rule of logic that is neither classical nor modern, neither epistemologically substantialist nor logically propositionalist, but a rule nonetheless. The rule is articulated most clearly in the works of the American pragmatist, Charles S. Peirce, is developed by recent students of semiotics and pragmatics, and belongs to a family of logical claims that includes those of Ludwig Wittgenstein's *Investigations* and Alfred North Whitehead's *Process and Reality.*[20] Within the province of Jewish philosophy per se, such a logic is implicit in the work of

Max Kadushin and is anticipated in that of Franz Rosenzweig, particularly as articulated most recently by Samuelson.[21]

[A logic of relatives reverses the classical / modern prioritization of subject and substance over predicate and attributes. It diagrams propositions as relative predicates instanced on given occasions in indexical subjects. Thus, to diagram the sentence "This ball is red," we could write bR, where R = the character of being a red ball; b = "here!"(an indexical sign of some observable instance of the character, or relative predicate). To diagram the more complex sentence "Jack takes the ball," we could refer to the two subjects (a = Jack; b = ball) that on this occasion instance the two-part or dyadic relative, R = someone's taking something: aRb or a,bR. In this approach, relations are maximally triadic or three-part: all other relations may be reduced to these. To diagram the sentence "Jack gives the ball to Mary," we could write $aRbc$, or $abcR$, where R = someone's giving something to someone; and a = Jack, b = ball, c = Mary. In this approach, we would say that, epistemologically, simple qualities are represented by monadic relative predicates (such as "—red-ballness"; "—hot"), simple actions, brute events or reactions by dyadic relative predicates (such as "—hits—"; "—sees—"), and representations, words, activities and symbols by triadic relative predicates (such as "—means (says, appears as, gives)—to (for, on behalf of)—").

In terms of a logic of relatives like this, it is possible to describe the "relational self," for example, as a given mode of triadic relations *(aSbc)*, instanced in given contexts (social-historical-somatic). In this case, *"S"* itself would not be strictly defined (otherwise, we would end up with another kind of substantialism), but would be characterized as that relation or set of relations to which we could refer an indefinite series of triadically-linked relata: of which the prototypes are "—appears as—to—" and "—does—to—." At least one member of this series would describe the relations displayed in our attributing some *"S"* to the series itself.[22] Each member of the series S would belong to at least one other such series (the series are interrelated). And the series itself may appear as member of another series (communities may be defined, that is, as series of series).]

Logic of Vagueness. Another basis for postmodern logic is a logic of vagueness. A logic of relatives makes it possible to make intelligible claims about inherently vague things and, therefore, about a modality of things that lies

in-between what modern thinkers call "universality" and "particularity."
This modality is of central interest to postmodern Jewish philosophers,
because it is the most conspicuous feature of the various "in-
betweennesses" that they believe exceed the grasp of modern and classic
rationality. Edith Wyschogrod illustrates the postmodern concern. Reflecting on Borowitz' claim that his Jewish *particularity* is itself the source
of his universalism, she notes that, for Borowitz, "universalism is not based
on homogeneity, but takes account of the richly diverse peoples of the
world. [This] is an interesting *aporia* for postmoderns to ponder. . . .
What is to be done with the universality that postmodernity adjures, when
this universality is itself the product of Jewish difference or particularity?"
The absolute empiricist's response is to make use of a logic of vagueness to
identify a modality that is irreducible to the modernist alternatives.

Peirce introduced his logic of vagueness in terms of a doctrine of
signs, or *semiotics*, that differs in a significant way from the "semiology"
developed by Ferdinand de Saussure and adopted by most Continental
postmoderns. By way of illustration, consider some thinker's interpretation of a biblical text. Following de Saussure, we may describe the biblical
text as a sign *(signe)* that has some meaning *(signifié)*. We are now left to
debate whether the text possesses one true or universal meaning (which
the thinker's interpretation may approximate or not), or an infinite number of individual meanings (in which case the thinker's interpretation will
be true only to its own criteria of truth). In terms, however, of Peirce's
semiotics, we would describe the text as a *sign* that had its *meaning* (or referred to its *object) for some interpretant* (or some interpreting mind or
context of interpretation). Each interpretation of the biblical text would
thus represent a particular, triadic relation among sign, meaning, and
interpretation. Criteria for truth would be particular to each *relation*, in
each case engaging biblical text and interpreter in what Borowitz would
call a "Covenantal relationship." [In the terms of a logic of relatives, this
relationship (C), rather than the text, represents the *rule* that informs any
act of interpretation ($= Cxyz$, where $C =$ the Covenantal rule; $x =$ biblical
text; $y =$ interpreting context; $z =$ particular interpretation or meaning).]

According to the logic of vagueness, the modality of the relational
(in this case, Covenantal) rule is that of *vagueness*, rather than of either
universality or *particularity*. Peirce explains in the following way. He wrote
that, in relation to its object, a sign may have either of two characters. A

sign is *determinate* if its meaning would leave "no latitude of interpretation" or "in respect to any character which inheres in it or is (universally and affirmatively) predicated of it, as well as in respect to the negative of such characters," or if it "indicates an otherwise known individual."[23] Otherwise, the sign is *indeterminate*—describing in some way, but not completely, "how an individual intended is to be selected."[24] Of indeterminate signs, there are two kinds: the *vague*, or indefinite, and the *general*, which means indeterminate *but* definite. For Peirce, the *general* indicates the character of a merely possible individual and "turns over to the interpreter the right to complete the determination as he pleases."[25] The *vague*, on the other hand, denotes some of the characters of an *existent* individual and "reserves for some other possible sign or experience the function of completing the determination."[26] In our case, as described by de Saussure, the meaning of a biblical text would be *general* (either universal or merely possible); as described by Peirce, it would be *vague*: it would belong to an *existent* relation, of which the text itself is only a part. At a given time, we would be given only some of the characters of this relation, for example, the biblical text and general acquaintance with past interpretations and with the present context of interpretation. It would remain for the act of interpretation to supply the missing characters: on one level, *this* act of interpretation; on another level, an indefinite series of future acts.

A Rule for Action. Postmodern logic offers a rule for personal and communal transformation and action, not for making overly sharp pictures of a world outside. Members of the CPJ do not divorce their academic work from the reparative process of a covenantal theology, which means that their communal work as well as their academic work draw on the same rules of postmodern rationality and the same obligations of personal commitment and the same risks of personal and communal reform and transformation. PJT is irreducible to either pole of the modern academic disjunction of "confessional" theology (extra-rational) and objectivist academic inquiry (extra-relational).

A Postmodern Theo-logic

A logic of relatives provides a vocabulary for postmodern theologians to respond to difficult theological questions in a way that is clear and precise, albeit a touch technical. Here, then, is a sampling of responses of this sort to questions raised in this volume about the character of a postmodern Covenantal theology.

Textuality and Experience: Law and Dialogue. For PJT, the biblical text need no longer be portrayed as *either* a heteronomous authority (in the logic of relatives, this means a *determinate* sign, whose meaning is imposed on the interpreter) *or* a field of possible interpretations subject to the reader's autonomy (a merely *general* sign). Instead, the text may be portrayed as *one*, essential and immutable member of a triadic relation: the text is immutable (or functionally so), but its meaning is processual, bound up in the life of its relation to the other two members. The interpretive context represents another member and each finite meaning the third member: product of the interpreter(s)' concrete acts of interpretation. These acts integrate experience with text and with, finally, the recollected history of previous acts of interpretation. The "Jewish Covenant" refers to this triadic relationship itself, as described by members of the people Israel and in so far as this people sees itself as an interpreting member of the relation.

In this approach, the Covenant is "written" on two levels. As relation, the Covenant represents what the rabbis of the Mishnah and Talmud called the "Oral Torah": written in what Martin Buber called "fundamental words," such as I-Thou and I-It, or in what Kadushin called "value concepts." These words guide behavior in an authoritative sense, but they are prototypically vague: defined only by way of concrete relations among the text of the "written Torah," or the Bible per se, its contexts of interpretation (its interpreters' mind-set, language system, etc.) and the occasions which elicit its interpretation (communal or personal crises, etc.). On a second level, then, the Covenant is written explicitly in the words of the Bible. These words are determinate, but, as such, they do not govern behavior authoritatively. The authority emerges only out of the words' relations with the other elements of the Covenant. This approach leaves room for both Novak's conception of asymmetry (the Biblical words are determinate and the value-concepts govern authoritatively) and Borowitz' conception of dialogue (this authority is "responsive").

Individual and Community. In this portrayal, neither God nor Israel appears as a name for any one of the three elements of the Jewish Covenant. The logic of relatives suggests, instead, that these two are named only by

way of—and are thus irreducible to the specific terms of—an indefinite series of concrete triadic relations. To this list, the Covenant itself (as the
oral Torah) may be added as a third "person" to be known only by its
works, that is, its relations. This all means that there are concrete textual
traditions for characterizing God, Torah, and Israel; that these character-
izations may govern the beliefs and actions of various communities or individuals; but that they need not apply for other communities or individuals. Each "person" represents a fundamental relation *(R)* that enters into
relation with other such relations (that is, shares concrete *relata* with them,
the way *Rabc* shares "a" with *Sxya*).

In these terms, "individual person" and "community" are analytically
less interesting concepts than they were in modernist theologies. The way
"Israel" may refer equivocally to Jacob or to his children, both these concepts refer to fundamental relations, or "persons," known through their
works. Furthermore, in the same way that the community Israel would
number individuals among its *relata*, we may also assume that an individual member of Israel would include communities of Israel among its *relata*. Communities may function here as individuals, entering into relations with other individuals, and they may function as collections of
various sorts of parts. Finally, both communities and individuals remain
vaguely delimited, sharing sets of concrete *relata* with other persons. Fundamental relations overlap.27

Universality and Particularity. Overlapping relations are neither merely
particular nor non-particular. For PJT, relations have actual but indefinite identities. Displayed by way of an indefinite series of concrete *relata*,
the identity of any given relation may overlap to any degree with the
identify of any other relation. The overlapping does not diminish identity, but rather brings identities into intimate encounters with one another. Recall, for example, the role of Thomas Ogletree in the community of postmodern Jewish readers. We may assume that a set of *relata*
that we associate with his work—such as [offers critique of universality in
favor of critical recovery of traditions; describes personhood relationally
. . .]—could appear among the *relata* of a community of postmodern
Christian or postmodern Jewish thinkers. This means that the two communities encounter one another by way of his work. This is encounter,
rather than identification or assimilation, because Ogletree also brings

into each community *relata* that contrast, or even conflict, with other *relata*; for example, on the one side, his grounding in Christian sources; on the other side, his work with Jewish theologians. As discussed earlier, this may be the postmodern meaning of Ogletree's calling himself a "stranger" in the midst of the Jewish thinkers. In its "sameness yet difference," the series of *relata* he introduces into the postmodern Jewish community represents an "indwelling other," through which the community both expands its own inner dialogue and extends its dialogic encounters with other communities. This extension represents both a particular encounter (between these two communities) *and* an illustration of a indefinite capacity for encounters. Just as the Jewish community overlapped with this or that Christian community, so might it overlap with another, and so on. In the vocabulary of PJP, something like "the indefinite capacity for encounter or for overlapping" may function in place of "universality" in the modernist vocabulary.

One function of a postmodern study of readings, like this one, would then be to describe such "indefinite capacities" as they are articulated in readings of otherwise community-specific inquiries like *Renewing the Covenant*. Within a given inquiry, these capacities appear as claims, or symbols, that are neither strictly determinate ("particular," in modernist terms) nor indeterminate ("universal"), but, rather, *indefinite* or vague. The vagueness of a symbol is not immediately evident, but is displayed in the way the symbol is received by others. Vague symbols appear in locutions that seem determinate but in fact stimulate their recipients to define them further, which means to complete them in terms of other domains of meaning (other *relata*). In other words, they are symbols that say one thing but beckon another and, in this way, direct the recipient to move from what is determinate to something other. To observe an inquiry's "indefinite capacities," a reader therefore has to observe how the inquiry is received by other readers, as many as possible: in particular, to observe which symbols tend to be redefined by the readers and in which ways.

A study of Borowitz' readers suggests that the in-betweenness of his notions of "Covenant," "relation," and so on stimulated the most significant activities of redefinition, of which this study is another example. His postmodernism may therefore have a lot to do with the discovery of this in-betweenness itself within contemporary Judaism: the discovery that

Jews do not have to choose between the illusory alternatives of strict universality or strict particularity, because their Covenant itself designates a place in-between these two, in the indefinite capacity of God's word. Giving voice to this discovery, Borowitz writes that "the Hebrew Absolute . . . is relational," (p. 73) and he presents his argument as a review of the positions of the modern Jewish thinkers that have influenced him. His method, in other words, has been to observe how this Absolute has stimulated these others to display its capacity for indefiniteness.

EPILOGUE: POSTMODERN COMMUNITIES OF TEXTUAL REASONERS

Borowitz' covenantal theology is Jewish but with indefinite capacities to overlap with others forms of inquiry. In this way, it is an illustration of—but not a source of general claims about—the paths postmodern religious studies may take in the future. Abandoning what he considers modernist approaches to the study of "religion in general," Borowitz studies his particular religion as he sees it written and practiced and in its relation to his own writing and practice. If interpreted within the modernist terms generally available, Borowitz may appear on the one hand to have opted for a confessional and ethno-religiously particularistic approach, while retaining, on the other hand, universalistic ideals and methods of conceptualizing his discoveries. If interpreted in terms of a logic of vagueness, he appears, instead, to have examined some of his religion's "indefinite capacities," or what Kadushin would call its "value concepts." If so, we will be able to observe these capacities only in the ways Borowitz' readers are stimulated to define them. This brings us to a question asked by one of Borowitz' reviewers: "who are Borowitz' potential readers?"[28] This study suggests that they will be neither strict particularists (Jewish or other) nor universalists (Jewish or other) but, rather, Jews or others who are moved to examine the indefinite capacities of their religions or other religions. These readers would then represent at least one sub-set (abc . . .) of the community (R) of postmodern religious studies.[29]

The most likely place to find readers like this will be among those touched in some way by the academy, but only those whose rationality is informed by a logic of vagueness. This is, in part, the logic of thinkers who have not rejected modernism outright, but have sought to resituate

modernist criticism within the medieval/classical traditions of thought
and practice out of which it emerged and to which it is directed. Many of
these traditions are text-based, biblically text-based in particular, hermeneutical, oriented to communal practice and theological—that is, accustomed to discourse about God, the biblical God in particular. These
thinkers therefore tend to interpret texts and to talk about God. This is
not because they are confessional, nor because they have some dogmatic
argument to offer on behalf of textuality, narrativity or of theism. It is because, having dropped the taboos that separate modernity from its situation, they find themselves engaged with texts, with hermeneutics and with
God as much as they are engaged in criticism and dialogue and reason.

NOTES

1. For a detailed description, see the concluding section of the introduction to
   this book.
2. Peter Haas, "A Symposium on Borowitz' *Renewing the Covenant*" (paper de-
   livered to the Annual Meeting of the Association of Jewish Studies, Boston,
   1991).
3. Citing Eugene Borowitz, *Choices in Modern Jewish Thought, A Partisan Guide*
   (New York: Behrman House, 1983.)
4. Italics indicate the specific portion of the text cited by David Novak.
5. Novak adds: "It is not that the liberal Jewish religious community is devoid
   of *halakhah,* for *halakhah* simply means 'law,' and no human community
   can exist without law of some kind or other. But [the liberal Jewish relig-
   ious] community seems to have [*halakhah*] only in the area of interhuman
   relationships."
6. Julia Kristeva, "Revolution in Poetic Language," in *The Kristeva Reader,* ed.
   Toril Moi (New York: Columbia University Press, 1986), pp. 89–137. Orig.
   pub. 1974.
7. Max Kadushin, *The Rabbinic Mind.* 3rd Ed. (New York: Bloch, 1972), *passim.*
   See also Simon Greenberg, "Coherence and Change in the Rabbinic Universe of Discourse: Kadushin's Theory of the Value Concept," in *Understanding the Rabbinic Mind, Essays on the Hermeneutic of Max Kadushin,* ed. Peter
   Ochs (Atlanta: Scholars Press for South Florida Studies in the History of Judaism, 1990), pp. 19–43.
8. David Weiss Halivni, "On Man's Role in Revelation," in *From Ancient Israel
   to Modern Judaism, Intellect in Quest of Understanding: Essays in Honor of*

Marvin Fox, ed. Nahum Sarna. (Atlanta: Scholars Press for Brown Judaica, 1990), pp.29–52. Readers may appreciate the Talmudic illustrations Halivni brings for each position. For the maximalist position: the statement in JT *Peah* 17a that the revealed Torah included even "the comments that an astute student will someday make in the presence of his teacher." For the intermediary position: the statement from *Midrash Tehillim* 12:4, "R. Yannai said: The words of the Torah were not given with clear-cut decisions. For with every word which the Holy One, blessed be He, spoke to Moses, He offered him forty-nine arguments by which a thing may be proved unclean. When Moses asked, 'Master of the Universe, in what way shall we know the true sense of a law?' God replied, 'The majority is to be followed: when a majority says it is unclean, it is unclean; when a majority says it is clean, it is clean.'" For the minimalistic position: the statement from *Midrash Tanchuma Tisah* 16 that only principles were revealed to Moses, and not all of the details of the Oral Law.

9. Described this way, Borowitz may find support for his position from the Orthodox semiotician and Sephardic scholar Joseph Faur. Describing the influence of what he considers "Maimonidean skepticism" on Spanish Jewish thinkers, Faur writes that "paradoxically, the rise of secularism that followed the demise of religious *authoritas* allowed for the possibility of genuine religious life and experience: the discovery that religion need not be the effect of external compulsion, but of the purely subjective faith and free choice of the individual." José Faur, "Sanchez' Critique of *Authoritas*: Converso Skepticism and the Emergence of Radical Hermeneutics," in *The Return to Scripture in Judaism and Christianity: Essays in Postcritical Scriptural Interpretation*, ed. Peter Ochs (Mahwah: Paulist Press, 1993), pp. 256–76.

10. See Jean-François Lyotard, *La Condition Postmoderne, Rapport Sur Le Savoir* (Paris: Les Éditions de Minuit, 1979); *The Postmodern Condition: A Report on Knowledge.* trans. Geoff Bennington and Brian Massumi (Minneapolis: University of Minnesota Press,1984); and *Le Différend* (Paris: Les Éditions de Minuit, 1983).

11. Joan W. Scott puts the issue in these helpful terms: "When experience is taken as the origin of knowledge, the vision of the individual subject (the person who had the experience or the historian who recounts it) becomes the bedrock of evidence on which explanation is built. Questions about the constructed nature of experience . . . , about how one's vision is structured—about language (or discourse) and history—are left aside. . . . Experience is at once always already an interpretation *and* something that needs to be interpreted." Joan W. Scott, "The Evidence of Experience," *Critical Inquiry* 17 (1991), 773–97 (pp. 777, 797).

12. The best illustrations of this direction in Borowitz' recent work is a book he has co-authored with Frances Weinman Schwartz, *The Jewish Moral Virtues* (New York and Philadelphia, The Jewish Publication Society: 1999); and a work-in-progress on the *aggadah*.

13. In the concluding essay of this volume and in previous writings, Susan Handelman has introduced the form of direct address as a mode of scholarly exchange. In this volume, Gene Borowitz joins her, asking why we refer to each other in the third person and by last names. The claim of this paragraph of mine is more modest: While writing about some author, I am content to use the last name, breaking into a more familiar address only when I have reason to address a particular issue *to* this author. Of course, one may ask what it means to *do* this in the middle of a third-person account. This question belongs on the agenda of future discussions of writing in the context of postmodernism. One place for scholars of Judaism to begin would be the grammar of second and third person address in the rabbinical blessing formula ("Blessed are You . . . who has sanctified us . . ."). And one item to note is the indexical or demonstrative markers we tend to use for incursions of first and second persons into our discourse, as well as for incursions of the ineffable Other that or who displaces and interrupts us.

14. For illustrations of Jewish philosophies and literary theories that emerge out of dialogue with this tradition, consider the following: Marc-Alain Ouaknin, *Concerto pour quatre consonnes sans voyelles, Au-delà du principe d'identité.* (Paris: Éditions Balland, 1991); Jill Robbins, *Prodigal Son, Elder Brother: Interpretation and Alterity in Augustine, Petrarch, Kafka, Levinas* (Chicago: University of Chicago Press, 1991); Edith Wyschogrod, "Works that 'Faith': The Grammar of Ethics in Judaism." *Cross Currents* 40.2 (1990), 176–93; David Banon, *La Lecture infinie, Les Voies de l'interprétation midrachique.* (Paris: Éditions du Seuil, 1987); Betty Roitman "Sacred Language and Open Text," *Midrash and Literature.*, ed. Geoffrey Hartman and Sanford Budick (New Haven: Yale University Press, 1986); Edmond Jabès, *Le Livre des Questions* (Paris: Gallimard, 1963). See also Susan Handelman, *The Slayers of Moses, The Emergence of Rabbinic Interpretation in Modern Literary Theory* (Albany: State University of New York Press, 1982). For a semiological Jewish philosophy drawing on Derrida's roots in de Saussure, consider José Faur, *Golden Doves with Silver Dots, Semiotics and Textuality in Rabbinic Tradition* (Bloomington: Indiana University Press, 1986). A number of studies in rabbinic hermeneutics work in a border area between Continental hermeneutics and the "postcritical" approaches described below. Consider, for example, Steven Fraade, *From Tradition to Commentary, Torah and Its Interpretation in the Midrash Sifre to Deuteronomy* (Albany: State University of New York

Press, 1991); Daniel Boyarin, *Intertexuality and the Reading of Midrash* (Bloomington: Indiana University Press, 1990); and Michael Fishbane, *The Garments of Torah, Essays in Biblical Hermeneutics* (Bloomington: Indiana University Press, 1989).

15. See, for example, Hans Frei, "The 'Literal Reading' of Biblical Narrative in the Christian Tradition: Does It Stretch or Will It Break?" In *The Bible and the Narrative Tradition,* ed. Frank McConnell (New York: Oxford University Press, 1986); George Lindbeck, *The Nature of Doctrine, Religion and Theology In a Postliberal Age.* (Philadelphia: Westminster Press, 1984); Stanley Hauerwas, *Christian Existence Today, Essays on Church, World, and Living In Between* (Durham: The Labyrinth Press, 1988); Bruce Marshall, *Theology and Dialogue.* (Notre Dame, Ind.: University of Notre Dame Press, 1990). For a comparison of postmodern Jewish and "postliberal" approaches, see Peter Ochs, 1990 "A Rabbinic Pragmatism," in Marshall; and "Postcritical Scriptural Interpretation," in *Torah and Revelation,* ed. Dan Cohn-Sherbok (New York, Toronto: Edwin Mellen Press, 1992), pp. 51–73.

16. For a collection of postmodern Jewish process theologies, see David Ray Griffin and Sandra Lubarsky eds, *Jewish Theology and Process Thought* (Albany: State University of New York Press, 1996), pp. 195–231. For a comparison of process and rabbinic approaches, see Peter Ochs, 1991 "A Rabbinic Text Process Theology." *The Journal of Jewish Thought and Philosophy* 1.1 (1991), pp. 141–79 .

17. Michael Wyschogrod distinguishes the two kinds of thinking in this helpful way:
"It is best, at this point, to stop talking about reason and to begin talking about intelligence. Reason is a philosophical construct with definite theoretical implications. Intelligence is a working endowment rather than a theory and can be active in the absence of a philosophical theory about the rationality of the universe and the structures of mind that enables it to grasp the rationality inherent in the world. Intelligence is a quality of brightness that enables all normal human beings to some extent and some to an extraordinary extent to grasp relations and implications in complex situations." Michael Wyschogrod, *The Body of Faith, God in the People Israel* (San Francisco: Harper and Row, 1983), p. 5.

18. In *Textual Reasoning* (Journal of Postmodern Jewish Philosophy) vol. 2.1, Borowitz replies that he is fully willing to adopt a new non-modern paradigm of reason, once Samuelson comes up with one (he doubts one will appear too soon).

19. On Rosenzweig, see Robert Gibbs, *Correlations in Rosenzweig and Levinas.* (Princeton: Princeton University Press, 1992).

20. For discussion of a variety of postmodern philosophic approaches like these, see David Ray Griffin et al., *Founders of the Postmodern Vision*. (Albany: State University of New York Press, 1993); and see Peter Ochs, *Peirce, Pragmatism, and the Logic of Scripture* (Cambridge: Cambridge University Press, 1998).

21. See Max Kadushin, *The Rabbinic Mind*; Franz Rosenzweig *The Star of Redemption*, trans. William Hallo (Boston: Beacon Press, 1964); Norbert Samuelson, *Judaism and the Doctrine of Creation* (Cambridge: Cambridge University Press, 1994); and Gibbs, *Correlations*.

22. Radical deconstructors may charge that the series remains ideal, or else an hypostatization of "our attributions." For reasons I will not enter into here, this charge holds only if "S" is strictly defined; otherwise, the charge itself makes most sense if described in terms of some such series of *relata*. See Charles Peirce, *Collected Papers of Charles Sanders Peirce*, Vol. 5., ed. Charles Harteshorne and Paul Weiss (Cambridge: Harvard University Press, 1934), Par. 411–36; 464–96.

23. Peirce *Collected Papers*, Vol. 5. 448n1 and 5.447.

24. Ibid.

25. Ibid. For Peirce, the general represents the synthesis of a multitude of subjects: which is the character that *could* be shared by a collection of individuals.

26. Peirce, *Collected Papers*, Vol. 5.505. The *vague* represents the synthesis of a multitude of predicates: that is, an existent relation.

27. Within these formal terms, there are, of course, strategies for meaningfully distinguishing individuals and communities. One way to distinguish the two would be in terms of the specific characters of their *relata*: we could say, for example, that the constituent signs of individuals, alone, may include somatic or neurological events (comparable to what Kristeva calls "semiotic" as opposed to "symbolic" relations).

28. Peter Haas, "A Symposium on Borowitz."

29. Haas' answer is compatible with this: that Borowitz' readers are "academicians who need to place the spiritual crisis of Judaism in its broader modern and American context. . . . If the modern university becomes the vehicle for the creation of a postmodern form of Judaism, then the nature of Judaism after the rabbis can be seen already to be taking shape in the detailed study of how, in the postmodern world, we might renew our Covenant."

9

'Im ba'et, eyma—
Since You Object,
Let Me Put It This Way

EUGENE B. BOROWITZ

All authors hope someone reads them and finds their work engaging. And they dream of having insightful, accomplished people so taken with their effort that they will then want to write about it. Having learned and benefited for years from the work of the friends whose response to *Renewing the Covenant* is presented here, I am deeply touched by their kindness to me personally and by their searching responses to my ideas. May the Shekhinah long rest upon us all as we carry on this effort at contemporary Torah. Thank you, colleagues; thank you, God.

It will help me to respond to the specific issues raised by my colleagues if I first briefly indicate what I think I was doing in my book, for that is the conceptual context of what I now have to say. Some facts about me personally also have a bearing on my approach to these matters, so I will begin there.

I am a rabbi, a seminary professor, and my primary reference group is not the secular academy, but the believing, practicing community of non-Orthodox Jews, no matter which label they apply to themselves. That will help to explain why *Renewing the Covenant* is a work of apologetic theology. That is, it seeks to mediate between believers like myself and those who are inquirers, perhaps semi- or occasional-believers. Norbert—

following Susan's lead, I cannot, comfortably call a friend of nearly forty years "Samuelson" merely because a stuffy old academic convention thinks that's dignified—Norbert correctly indicates that I also seek to create a bridge between academic thinking about belief and the minority of believing non-Orthodox Jews who seriously want to think about their faith, a sub-community critical to the ethos of every group.[1] Apologetics seem inevitably to disappoint people in each of the communities addressed. Some outsiders always complain that you haven't properly accepted their truth. Some insiders feel you haven't been true enough to the faith (David and Susan) while others feel you might have used a more effective way of accomplishing the apologetic task (Edith, Tom and Norbert, with Yudit in both groups, and Peter trying to show what makes us all an intellectual family). Essentially, what we are debating in this book is what might constitute the most effective apologetic language for our time.

The apologetic argument of *Renewing the Covenant* proceeds in two unequal steps. The first describes the experiential basis for contemporary belief, chapters 1–3. In these pages, I do not analyze personal religious experience as has been the typical academic and prior non-Orthodox Jewish theological procedure. Rather, in keeping with my understanding of Judaism as the Covenant between God and the people Israel, I seek to lay bare the communal spiritual path of the Jewish people in the second half of the twentieth century, underground though most of it has been. In sum, the Jews, as part of Western civilization's turn from messianic modernism but particularly because of the Holocaust, came to a new openness to God (the contemporary search for "spirituality") and acknowledgment of the importance of Jewish peoplehood. These two pillars of renewed Jewish faith, God, and Israel (the people), derive from a root intuition: *"Regardless of what the world knows or cares, anything that mitigates the categorical distinction between the S.S. death camp operators and their Jewish victims violates our most fundamental contemporary experience and contravenes a central mandate of our tradition"* (The italics are in the original, one of only six sentences so distinguished in *Renewing the Covenant* (p. 43); all page references given in the body of this paper are to this book). This affirmation of a value inherent in the universe is the foundation of Jewish life today. Derridean postmodernism denies such a faith credence; that is the major reason I am not a Derridean postmodern.

The second, longer part of the apologetic case consists of an analysis and synthesis of the beliefs uncovered in our recent experience, God, chapters 4–10 and the people Israel, chapters 11–16. This consideration of God and Israel allows me to enunciate my radical recontextualization of the general self as the Jewish self. These foundations being set, I can move on to the classic task of a Jewish theology, creating a theory of sacred obligation, a meta-*halakhah*, in my case the delineation of what the contents page (vii) announces as "A Postliberal Theology of Jewish Duty." This is described in the section on Torah, chapters 17–20, with the last of these bringing all these strands together in a rare, systematic analysis of non-Orthodox Jewish decision-making. Its five integrated principles are presented in initial, italicized statements:

> *First, the Jewish self lives personally and primarily in involvement with the one God of the universe* (p. 289). . . . *Second, a Jewish relationship with God inextricably binds selfhood and ethnicity, with its multiple ties of land, language, history, traditions, fate, and faith* (pp. 289–90). . . . *Third, against the common self's concentration on immediacy, the Covenant renders the Jewish self radically historical* (p. 291). . . . *Fourth, though the Jewish self lives the present out of the past, it necessarily orients itself to the future* (p. 292). . . . *Fifth, yet despite the others with whom it is so intimately intertwined—God and the Jewish people, present, past, and future—it is as a single self in its full individuality that the Jewish self exists in Covenant* (p. 293).

Keeping this plan in mind will, I believe, lend greater coherence to my comments on the specific issues raised by my readers.

IN RESPONSE TO MY COLLEAGUES

Four words have proved troublesome in my communicating my meaning. The least disruptive of these may be "Absolute," which I use in one of my discussions of God. Far more contentious has been my applying the label "postmodern" to my thinking. Neither of them, however, has worked as much mischief as have the related terms "self" and "autonomy." Would that when I wrote this book I had known Peirce's logical category of "vagueness," so tellingly outlined for us by Peter, for I might have mitigated these difficulties by announcing that it guided me.[2] Despite the difficulties these terms have engendered I continue to find a certain justification for having employed them. What it means to be a "postmodern" and certain side-issues connected with the term are so significant for the rest of what I have to say that I shall begin with this broad-ranging topic.

The best justification for a taxonomy of thinkers in our time may be that philosophers who work by different methods (who are of different "schools") cannot easily talk to one another about fundamental matters without first indicating their philosophic "faith." That people are often seriously misled by these classificatory names has not made labeling obsolete because the information/opinion glut makes these shortcuts to understanding all the more useful. I begin, then, with the thinker's standard disclaimer: I am not my label(s); I am, of course, me, and so notorious a defender of thinking for oneself should surely be allowed even more than the usual distance from the reductionism of class-ification [*sic*].

I begin with a marginal matter, whether I am "a Reform Jewish" thinker. This comes to mind particularly because of a recent exchange of articles with Elliot Dorff whose recent review of *Renewing the Covenant* insisted that its true meaning could be discovered only in terms of the ideology of the Reform movement.[3] Since the (invidious) stereotyping of Reform Jews may lurk in the background of others' interpretation of what I wrote, I want to begin my response to my critics by citing a bit of what I said to Elliot: "I do not know how I can persuade you that 'I am not now and never have been a card-carrying Reform ideologue.' . . . I have always tried to think academically about Jewish belief and its consequences. None of my models—Cohen, Baeck, Kaplan, Buber, Rosenzweig and Heschel—ever did their thinking as part of a movement, or in the context of its ideology. They simply tried to think through the truth of Judaism in their day as best they could understand it, and I have spent my life trying to emulate them. I attempted to nail down my meaning in *Renewing the Covenant* by mostly speaking about 'non-Orthodox' Jews. When I mean Reform Jews there or anywhere, I say so."[4]

As to whether I am a "postmodern," a topic of considerable comment and difference of opinion among these readers, it depends, of course, on your taxonomic standards. Tom suggests that I'm probably better off thinking of myself as a "chastened modern," which description of me is certainly true. It was that cognitive and, in my case, Jewish "suffering" (to use Peter's term), that pushed me to go beyond modernity. Edith makes a strong case that my use of the term is intellectually inappropriate and will mislead thoughtful people as to my kind of thinking. She has such stature as thinker and leader in this area that she may well be right. Was it an unconscious ambivalence about this title that caused me not to utilize "postmodern" to refer to myself or my thought in my book's title but to refer in its subtitle to the cultural situation of my readers? The critical issue, of course, is whether it makes any sense to speak of a non-Derridean postmodern community of reflective communication. A number of the colleagues gathered here thinks it does and, emboldened by their agreement, I stand by my original self-identification and respectfully reject Edith's reproof.

Not long after *Renewing the Covenant* was published, I learned to specify what I thought entitled me to speak of myself as a (non-Derridean) postmodern. In two critical respects, I reject and radically revise modernist "doctrine." Modernists from Kant on made the individual human the independent basis for truth and thus, to validate religion, they had to seek ways of moving from their human certainties to God's possible reality and nature. But religious postmoderns like me know persons to be inseparable from God, their ground, and truth as what emerges between God and people (The fundamentalists say it comes almost entirely from God to humans, while the non-Orthodox say, in various balances, it is more two-sided than that). Modernists also knew that truth was necessarily universal and thus, if they wished to give some validity to a particular group, they had to demonstrate to what extent this particular group reflected universal truth. But postmoderns like me know that all truth begins in particularity and any universal one might affirm derives from that particular base. (Heretically enough, I also insisted that one premise of modernity was too true to be denied a place in the foundations of my—our—postmodernity: the close identification of human dignity with the exercise of a significant measure of self-determination. See below.)[5]

I must, however, confess that the issue of philosophic label is not very important to me. As Susan says, the critical term for us is "Jew" and we will use whatever intellectual language now least inadequately describes what we "know" that to be. So I was once a boy rationalist, evolved into a religious existentialist and, seeing its inadequacies, began to identify myself as a postmodern thinker. Let a more satisfactory way of talking about Jewish truth appear in our culture and I shall, I hope, have the intellectual courage to embrace it, temporarily, to be sure.

For me then, as for David and Susan, Torah truth, as best we understand it, is primary and it is the criterion for the apologetic language we will utilize—another radical break with the modernists. So again risking terminological static, I call myself a Jewish "theologian" in an effort to signal to my readers that my thinking is governed by my Jewish faith. Philosophy in recent decades has insisted that it alone was the rightful arbiter of truth. It therefore as good as dictated to modernist Jewish thinkers what might now properly be included in their Judaism, generally with radically reductionist results, *pace* Norbert, but I shall return to this theme again. I can understand how Jews of a critically philosophic bent might well become Derridean postmoderns and then see what Jewish sense that made possible, like Edith's stunningly creative use of Lyotard. But the image of Israel as silent victim straining for language to challenge its Accuser is one that says more about the hermeneut than about any significant reality I discern in the people Israel today. We are, however, still at the beginning of the Derridean evocation of Jewish meaning and, though my Jewish faith precludes my joining that interpretive enterprise, I look forward to the spiritual stimulation that the emerging Derridean description of Jewish faith and duty will provide.

Several of the non-Derrideans, who include me in the postmodern camp, wonder if I am not more residually modern than I realize. Two things must be said in that regard. First, I do not mean by the "post" in postmodern that everything modern must be put behind us. I, and the people Israel, continue to owe modernity too much to do such a thing. The process of modernization gave Jews freedom from the ghetto, equality of opportunity, and unparalleled security for our community. It taught us the extraordinary value of pluralism, the preciousness of individual rights, and the sacred dignity of substantial self-determination. Indeed, I proudly proclaim that the third premise in my kind of postmodernist thinking about Judaism is (a radically recontextualized understanding of) "autonomy." I do not seek to hide from my residual modernism but openly question whether postmodernity should really qualify as an independent, sixth stage in the long history of Jewish spiritual development (p.

4, pp. 49f. and the references cited in note 5). Nonetheless, my hybridized thinking is so fundamentally other-than-modern, that I think the term "postmodern" will usefully call to the attention of other "chastened moderns" the deep change of perspective and attitude now arising among us.

It seems to me that the appearance of a strong modern color to my thought is magnified because I am engaged in apologetics, a task which requires one to communicate with "suffering" moderns in the only language that still makes sense to them, despite their cognitive dissonance with it. This problem first forced itself upon me in 1967 when I was writing my book on Jewish sex ethics for college students. I could not hope to address them in my nascent language of Covenant faith and hope they would long continue reading, so I tried to find an idiom congenial to them that would also engage them in full seriousness. But I finally couldn't stand the self-repression and concluded the work by addressing them in the accents of Jewish faith.[6]

I did not have the systemic sophistication in 1967 to realize that the problem of standing at the boundary explained the curious logical break in the "argument" of *God in Search of Man* by Abraham Heschel.[7] Most of the first third of the book, on God, speaks the language of human experience with such eloquence that four decades plus later people find it speaks to their innermost being. But once Heschel draws his readers into the presence of the living God, he moves to the other side of the theological table and begins a continuing polemic against relying on human experience, rather than on the revelation of God he has led them to. That reversal, so crucial to his faith and his purpose in writing, regularly shocks readers who, snug in their modernity, anticipate that like other Jewish teachers he will indicate how radical amazement fits into their modernity and congenially modifies Jewish tradition. But he doesn't do so and that is why, though many quote Heschel's sentences, few Jews have adopted his theology as a whole.

In much of *Renewing the Covenant*, I speak to searching still-modernist Jews in their terms: those of "self," "autonomy" and "universalism." However, I do not concede the primacy of universalism and then try to validate particularity. I see no way one can do that and arrive at the primacy of particularity, which I take to be the Jewish and postmodern truth. My strategy is to undermine the three foundations of the universalizing modernist faith. I do this by arguing against the goodness of human nature, the discrete individuality of persons and the identification of truth with universals (chapters 11, 12, and 13 respectively). This allows me to ease them into my revision of "the self" as "the Jewish self." Perhaps I stay with my apologetic language too long, but I am hopeful that the cumulative transformation of my language will set the context of my getting there rather than vice versa, as often seems to me the experience of the reviewers in this book.

Norbert suggests that I should not equate modernity with a rationalism that Yudit nicely calls "linear." He speculates that I am really involved in an ongoing polemic against the thought of my late, lamented friend Steven S. Schwarzschild but have, in fact, misunderstood him. He then sketches in a picture of a Kantian probabilism which would yield a rationalism far more humane than the categorical one I so disdain. Passing quickly over the rational certainty of Kantian regulative ideals and emphasizing the imprecise judgments which necessarily ensue when the ideals are applied to real cases in the contingent world, Norbert argues that rationalism only claims that it is the best way of reaching our inevitably limited practical decisions. The Steven I knew would have quickly gone into one of his consciously self-indulgent tirades at the idea that he was a Kantian for essentially pragmatic reasons, namely, as Norbert puts it, that since no thinking can give us certainty, then "nothing is more likely to lead us to correct judgments (in science and ethics) than [Kantian] reasoning." Steven, like the creator of "pure" reason, and so forth, hated any hint of pragmatism. For him reason required or commanded us, and even in the realm of historical decisions, he, like most of my Germanic teachers, felt that a good measure of the "categorical imperative" passed over into his practical judgments. If there was a Cohenian neo-Kantian probabilist around in the heyday of modernism, I never ran into one. And if a biographical note is permitted, once Steven's brief, student-days' flirtation with Rosenzweig passed over, we never discussed the foundational clash between his rationalism and my non-rationalism, though an occasional loving barb on that divide did fly between us. To have done so would have destroyed our friendship since Steven insisted on being taken on his own terms, a position which he would have been happy to defend as rationally required, although he would have done so with a mischievous smile. I shall return to Norbert's explication of what I take to be a "chastened" rationalism when I respond to the questions about my discussion of Israel.

THAT TROUBLESOME TERM, "THE SELF"

David and Susan are only more emphatic than Yudit and Peter in charging that I give the individual too much freedom in relation to God. A good deal of their unease arises from my frequent references to "autonomy," a term their philosophical sophistication necessarily connects with Kant and its meaning in his thought. For Kantians "autonomy" indicates that the self alone gives the (moral) law, not God or anyone else, though Cohenian neo-Kantianism rushes in to show how God, as the most foundational idea in the rational worldview, undergirds the moral law and is closely identified with it. My postmodern thinking asserts something quite different. I claim that people are, on their own, incompetent to legislate the basic laws by which they ought to live. They are similarly ill-equipped to bring the Messiah by their own action, as the Kantian liberal Jews grandly professed. I speak of a God who is real in His / Her own right and is not merely the grandest of my rational ideas. I further insist this God commands people, albeit nonverbally, and, as best we can put it, has input into our lives by coming into relationship with us. How, then, as David warned me years ago, can I use the term "autonomy" to describe an aspect of my God-humans relationship and not expect to be taken as a neo-Kantian semi-secularist masquerading as something else?

Perhaps my difficulty in this respect is that I suffer from a failure of imagination. I have not been able to find another term which succinctly points to the truth which almost all modernized Jews take to be the core of their existence: that their humanity demands that, in some significant measure, they think for themselves. They have learned this from modern social life, and its telling symbol for them is the right to vote. Most of these Jews have never seriously heard of Kant, and they will glaze over if you try discussing heteronomy and autonomy, suggesting theonomy as the way to resolve the ethical dilemma this contrast poses. And, having heard of religious frauds, who in the name of God have gotten people to do terrible things, they reserve the right to judge for themselves any religious claim to having the truth to which they should accede. In short, they believe God gave them freedom to think, and wants them to use it in determining their Jewish duty in a more proactive way than traditional Judaism allowed / allows.

Against Buber's championing of the "I" in determining the law, Susan calls on us to follow Rosenzweig's recommended response to God, *"Hineni,"* "Here I am." Rosenzweig declares that the Law as a whole is binding upon us. The semi-believers I am addressing, Susan, may be able to join Rosenzweig in acknowledging God's "authority," but they will cherish that Rosenzweig who also taught, as you know, that the self retains some rights even in its acquiescence to God. For he gave sufficient credence to the nomos-making dignity of the self that he found it necessary to validate the Law by calling on us to turn what came to us as *Gesetz,* an objective statement of law, into *Gebot,* a command addressed to each of us personally. And he famously, if cryptically, indicated that one need not do what, at the most serious level, one was not "able" to do.

Even the modestly "liberal" Rosenzweig, I suggest, grants too much to the Law and to little to us for most of us to follow him. If the law the sages are teaching is entirely binding upon us in principle, then, to give a telling example, God does not want women to be full members of a *minyan.* An increasing majority of modernized Jews know, by their own judgment, that such discriminatory rulings are better charged to human invention than to God's revelation via the sages. It is this authority of the self—which I limit by the recontextualization Covenant selfhood lays upon it—for which I need a term (I shall later return to the topic of the law in my comments on Torah).

My apologetic problem, then, is finding a word for the significant, but not exclusive, enfranchisement of persons in determining their/our Jewish duty.[8] Yes, the Kantian associations of "autonomy" give too much power to the "autos," the single self, but I can think of no better word to protect the self's legitimate role in law-making. It would be tedious to regularly put quotation marks around it, "autonomy," and eccentric to write it ?auto?nomy, or with dashes through the "auto," ~~auto~~nomy, though this might qualify as a visual postmodern doubling. So I risked retaining the term, hoping that people would see how differently it functions when Covenantalized. I consider the reinterpretation of selfhood—which still has a measure of legislative authority for us—as Jewish selfhood in which individuality cannot be separated from its relation to God as one of the people of Israel's Covenant relationship with God—to be the most creative and important thing I accomplished in *Renewing the Covenant.* That is to say, I do not see how we can have a Jewishly satisfactory "Theology of

Postliberal Duty" with the old "autonomy," yet we need to make some place in such a new understanding for our sense of the sacredness of our ability to think/choose for ourselves. So I crafted a system which did that.

Let me be specific by pointing again to my epitome of my theory of how non-Orthodox Jews today ought to determine their Jewish obligations. I prefaced these on page 288 with a general statement of why the modernist, Kantian, or Buberian ideal of a universalized self needed to be replaced by the ideal of a "Jewish self." Because of its Jewishness, that self was not an isolate, but was necessarily involved as one of five, co-functioning factors involved in the "law"-making process. Of these, the real God I had previously delineated, was the first and dominant participant (p. 289). Fully three of the five factors were devoted to the people of Israel's significance in the process: as contemporary reference community; as bearer of a vast repository of prior Covenant-duty deliberations; and as a people pointing toward the Messiah. Only then, fifth, do I speak of the continuing place of the self. "Fifth, yet despite the others with whom it is so intimately intertwined—God and the Jewish people, past present and future—it is as a single soul in its full individuality that the Jewish self exists in Covenant" (p. 293, italicized in the original). When I said "a single soul in its full individuality," I was thinking not just of the remnant of ?auto?nomy we still rightly insist upon, but of the precious individuality of all those historical Jewish "characters" whose very idiosyncrasy Jews have long cherished. It did not occur to me after all I had written about the Jewish self and what that very sentence says about the soul "intimately intertwined" with God and the Jewish people, that readers could still think I meant by it something like that notorious caricature of a Reform Jew, a person who did what they personally pleased. And how any philosopher reading these words could find this a heavily Kantian "autonomy" is a tribute to the way the past impedes the creative present.[9]

Again, let me note my surprise that my early statements (in the chapters on God) seeking to clarify what remained of individual human power in the presence of the transcendent God determined what some readers thought I was doing in my later transformation of selfhood into Jewish selfhood. The people I was addressing would have been uncomprehending had I tried from the first to talk to them about the Jewish self, and I would have lost them. I needed first to develop my argument for particularity, and then clarify what I meant by Israel before I could begin trying to wean them away from a central idea of contemporary culture, that there is a general selfhood. I thought that my crowning, final statement of my theology would put the prior pieces transformingly into place. I am now chastened by the fact that my strategy has not worked out well with a good number of these sophisticated readers. Such are the perils of apologetics.

The selfhood issue particularly troubles Tom. He feels that despite my devoting a chapter to "The Social Side of Selfhood" (chapter 12), and my giving the community three places of the five in my calculus of decision-making, that I do not seem to appreciate how socially determined the self is. "The central point is that I cannot simply opt out of the formative bonds that figure in my moral identity and still hold onto my moral autonomy. I can exercise my free conscience in opposition to the teachings of my formative community only by means of resources also supplied by that community. . . . When I become alienated from the community that formed me, my moral autonomy is itself at risk. . . . In fact, my alienation from my primary community of reference is, more than likely, a reflection of the fact that other attachments . . . have already gained preeminent importance in my life." So he believes that I ought to spend more time on "the critical retrieval and mediation of the normative traditions that constitute Jewish particularity."

To a considerable extent I agree with Tom, and clarifying this will also allow me to highlight our differences. I agree that in the usual case one's morality is substantially formed by one's "primary" community, and that one cannot "simply" leave it and still easily hold on to one's moral self. Yet that, as I read Jewish history, is just about what the mass of modernizing Jews did when they left their essentially inner-oriented ghetto or *shtetl* identities and opted for the world of urban, educated, secularized Western culture as their primary "moralizing" community. Of course this involved a good deal of boundary-crossing pain, but this was not undertaken and endured on the basis of anything previously visible in the pre-modern Jewish community, but because something deep in their human nature indicated its value. Something vaguely similar occurred when they gave up their formative national environments and immigrated to countries with a rather different ethos, and then when they gladly gave up the formative powers of the lower class for the middle class and beyond. Anyone who has tried to work in the Jewish community in recent generations knows that, until recently, the only hope of promoting Jewish life was to show how Judaism fit in with its primary values—those of a humanizing slice of secular Western society.

I derive two lessons from this applicable to Tom's critique. First, that for all the sociality of selves, they also have an inner power to transcend their group—a rather phenomenal one in the rare cases of prophets and saints. In the more common case, they can radically shift groups and transform their "selves." Let me call attention to a term in Tom's tradition which points to a special case of this, "conversion," that human/divine power which makes it possible for pagans to find a radically "new being" by becoming Christians. Something human vaguely similar to that happened when Jews, utterly uncoerced, opted to transform their lives in societies with radically different value concerns against what their traditional communities taught them, and their communal leaders advised. I should add that I am unacquainted with Tom's theology of conversion, and look forward to learning how it relates to this discussion.

Second, the primary value-forming community of the Jews whom I am addressing is neither that of traditional Judaism nor that of one of its modern reinterpretations. The non-Orthodox communities—and to a considerable extent people who affiliate with "centrist" Orthodox communities—almost always keep their Jewishness secondary to the larger social worlds to which their parents adapted. So when I am speaking to the Jewish public in terms of "self" and autonomy," I am doing so in the accents of their primary moral community, "chastened" though they have been by their affiliation with humanizing American secularity. Nor do I see this secondariness of Jewishness in the free countries soon disappearing. No new "hot" intellectual or spiritual movement breaks out in America these days without our soon hearing of the large number of Jews who have become its devotees. So my modest "attention to the critical retrieval and mediation of the normative traditions that constitute Jewish particularity" is, as I understand it, in keeping with Tom's sense of the power of the social in individual life.

However, Tom's positive project intrigues me sufficiently that I should like to take a lightning stab at it. To begin with, I think this task of the retrieval of "normative traditions" would be rather easier for Christians than for Jews, since the church has a tradition of creeds and of classic doctrinal statements to draw on. Jews have nothing truly similar. But let me hazard an informed guess about our "normative traditions of particularity." Positively, they are God's choosing us from among all peoples to receive God's Torah and the resulting *halakhic* structure which expressed its mandates in Jewish life. But to these shaping beliefs we must add the ongoing, negative experience of anti-Semitism, the social experience which long made and kept Jews Jewish. None of these "traditions" is highly effective among us today. Most modernized Jews do not believe in Jewish chosenness, and they do not observe Jewish law as law, but only as a resource from which they select those practices they think will enhance their American lives. Fortunately, anti-Semitism continues to decline in the Western world, though only a dreamer would suggest that it no longer exists. But Jew-hatred is less a threat to our continuity these days than is the general acceptance of Jews which makes intermarriage and its assimilation so rife.

Renewing the Covenant is faithful to its title. It seeks to reinstate God's reality (chapters 3–10), to substitute Covenant for chosenness (so after the preparation of chapters 11–13 the delineations of chapters 14–16), and thence create a structure of duty-making that can replace the abandoned legal system (chapters 17–20). It hopes to so establish the cogency of these beliefs that a growing, eventually critical minority of Jews will want to live by them because of their truth, and not because some enemy will not let them be anything else.

SOME WORDS ABOUT THE INEFFABLE ONE

My terminological *teshuvah*, repentance, must now proceed to my calling God an / the Absolute, albeit a Weak Absolute. My philosophic colleagues are aghast at my oxymoron and would like me to provide some conceptual clarity of the description of God as Absolute. Alas, I was being midrashic / heuristic, not spinning out tightly cognitive claims. I had argued in the experiential section that revulsion against the immorality of our times had sparked a new search for the Ground of our values. I wanted a term that, as an old *aggadah* put the need to penetrate the usual complacency, would "smash into the ear" of the hearer. If relativism is the evil to be opposed, then we needed to find its opposite, or at least the ground of non-relativism, what is termed in common parlance an "absolute." Used figuratively, "absolute" usefully marks the rather desperate search of people these days to find something stable to hold on to: to hold on to, no matter how bizarre it may be and no matter how costly (in dollars and cents, too). Jews, those fervent modernizers, show the same phenomenon. By calling God an absolute I only meant to call attention to the importance of the anchoring function of God in our lives. Any postmodern Jewish view of God, in my view, would have to provide for God's effectively exercising this role.

However, to connect God with a reasonably stable commandingness opens God to the modernist fear that God's grounding greatness will as good as wipe out persons. To refute this, I sought to call attention to biblical and rabbinic Judaism's unselfconscious paradoxical insistence that the One Ruler-God of all the universes nonetheless created a real world, and in it gave people the astonishing freedom to obey or to defy God. So borrowing a philosophic usage, I added "weak," in the sense of "don't push the substantive term too far," to the term "Absolute." That makes good Jewish theological sense and seemed to me sufficiently evocative that it might "shatter the ear" of my readers, but for philosophers it makes no sense. It is, I believe, a good instance of the translation problem we have when we seek to move between these related but disparate disciplines.

A somewhat similar problem arose in relation to my suggestion that God's redemptive power is sometimes seen in historical events in our time. Yudit and Edith particularly are troubled by this (as I think many in the Jewish community are). They want to know how I can say that God is involved with particularly beneficent events, and then not also involve God in the terrible things that happen in history. Classically, Judaism has said that God is involved in both, and that creates the problem: the incompatibility of the good God and horrible evils. The Bible already knew that justice was a limited answer indeed, and the rabbis taught that the life of the world to come would compensate for the lack of justice in this world. But, overwhelmingly, believing Jews were able to accept the fact that there are some things that we just cannot understand, probably because they were grateful for all the goodness they did in fact receive, beginning with life. The pious live, not always easily, with God's inscrutability. Philosophers care too much about rationality to accept that "answer." And they cannot easily accommodate the insight of believers old and current suggestion that, if the clumsy locution is permitted, history is "lumpy" and God's saving acts are sporadic. In several places in *Renewing the Covenant*,

I have tried to explain why, after considerable reflection, I take this stand.[10] Now the gap between what philosophers consider intelligible speech and what religionists know must truthfully be said, widens to the point where discussion is difficult indeed.

This necessarily brings us to a discussion of the place of the Holocaust in contemporary Jewish theology. A number of my critics believe that since those terrible days we must operate with "a displaced and decentered faith." This phrase and its equivalents are frequently repeated by thinkers today, and they convey the understanding that since the Holocaust, we cannot believe in God as we once did. I demur from this position. I do not believe God is the central problem of post-Holocaust theology—a radical revisionism which I sought to justify in chapter 3 of *Renewing the Covenant*. None of my critics represented here have found this interpretation worthy of comment or refutation. Nonetheless, the matter is so important to assessing how the Holocaust should influence our religious thinking, I think it important to restate my case, even briefly.

Belief in God cannot die for people who don't really believe in God's existence to begin with, and who had already given up the idea of God's retribution as far back as the Kishniev pogroms of 1903 and 1905. By mid-century, the overwhelming majority of modernized Jews were agnostic if not atheist. What they believed in, what functioned as their "god," was not *Adonai* but humankind and its capacities. They built their lives on education, politics, business and culture—not the God of the 613 commandments. As the century drew toward an end they began to realize, in a subterranean, postmodern way, that their secular "god" had failed them and that a messianic faith in humankind is ludicrous. What was "displaced and decentered" in our effective faith was not God, but human power, that is, the ethos of modernity—and out of that recognition, the widespread religious search and postmodern spiritual longings of our time emerged. That is why I do not make the Holocaust, or the problem of theodicy, central to my thinking about God, though it is fundamental to my teaching about human nature and our need for God's help. I urge anyone reading these lines to make their own judgment of the case I have presented in chapter 3 of my book.

I could have as good as written the previous paragraph nearly a decade ago, when I was completing the manuscript of *Renewing the Covenant*. The intervening years have only confirmed my view. The Holocaust, once at the forefront of Jewish writing, is rarely a living theological issue today. As the second edition of some of the old radical books appear, their authors now share their second thoughts about what they once proclaimed and that, if nothing else, should give us pause in our continuing to mouth the old slogans about the Holocaust.[11] It is not that we are forgetting the Holocaust, but simply that we have begun to do what Jews have always done with a great historic event: we have begun to ritualize it. And I include in that ritualization the rhetoric we still use when we do discuss it. Old phrases and images reappear, old emotions are evoked and relived, the past and present are momentarily joined, and, having heeded the command "to remember," we go back to what are now the living questions of our existence. And among caring Jews of diverse temperaments and labels, that live agenda often centers on building a personal relationship with God, as incredible as that would have sounded in the heyday of the death-of-God movement.

THE PEOPLE ISRAEL

Yudit asks why I do not give more attention to the State of Israel and its ongoing place in covenanted lives. Since I am a religious rather than a secular Zionist, I devote myself to the primary task: determining what Jewish faith is in our times. Only with that in place can one hope to know what our relationship might be to the Land of Israel, to the State of Israel, and to the community living upon it. This not being a book in which I move very far from theoretical issues to practical ones, I limited myself to one paragraph on the State of Israel which I hope readers will find as rich in meaning as I do (p. 290). Some time after the book appeared I was asked to give my views on "What is Reform Religious Zionism?" And that paper connects my theology with our immediate obligations theoretical and practical.[12]

Yudit also wondered why I do not explain why exactly a general self, who happens to be Jewish, should strive to become a Jewish self. Once one grants the premises of Enlightenment rationality—the individualistic self and truth as universals—I do not see how it is ever possible to make a case for the value of the particular that does not relegate it to second best. Why detour through an old, self-serving particular, when one can find groups that try to move as directly as they can to the universal goal? And why then also take on the oddity and disability of Jewishness in Western culture? Those assimilationist questions have bedeviled Jewish thinkers in this century who have accepted the supremacy of modernity, and attempted to build a robust Judaism from the foundations of universal human reason or experience. That is why I framed my case first as an attack on the universalist counter faith (chapters 11–13), and only then tried to show the admirable character of the Jewish people in relationship to God, each other and humankind (chapters 14–16).

Norbert suggests that there is now a rationalism that no longer atomizes individuals, but sees them relationally. It therefore gives rational credence to collectivities, and not merely to individuals. That certainly would provide us with an argument for the validity of particular groups, such as the people Israel. But, in typical philosophic fashion, it would do this for all groups universally. So the particular Jewish group would again be only another possibility for satisfying that rational need. Any other collective that satisfied the rational standards for relationality would, in that sense, be similarly commended. We are left again, though on a new level, with the problem of getting from philosophy's universalism to the unique significance of Jewishness.

This matter is critical to my determination not to be a philosopher in the present philosophic climate. In some bedrock, primal fashion, I and others like me know that the existence of the Jewish people in Covenant with God is a matter of unique cosmic significance. Any way of thinking that doesn't readily allow me to express and validate that truth cannot be the medium by which I will explain Judaism to others. Until someone creates a rationalism that can give particularity a primacy Jewishness has in my life, I cannot be a first-level rationalist. (But as my writing makes clear, I am a devoted second-level rationalizer, trying to think as hard and as clearly as I can about my first-level experience. Philosophers, of course, deny there can be "experience" without it's already containing some mental structuring that can make something into my "experience." In effect, then, everything must begin with philosophy. For my rejoinder, see chapter 19 of *Renewing*.)

Let me only briefly add to this that most rationalism is resolutely secular and so constructed that the *Covenanting* God of Israel is as good as ruled out *ab initio*. I also cannot accept a system of thought which will devalue, if not rule out, what I and others like me know to be the ultimate ground of our existence. So I practice theology but, in the present intellectual situation, not philosophical theology.

TORAH, GOD'S INSTRUCTION

If Judaism values *praxis*, what we do, more than it values *doxis*, what we say about what we believe, then the questions David, Yudit, and others have raised about relationship's ability to command and, in addition, to generate law, are central ones for my enterprise. The topics are closely related but it will be necessary for me to focus on them somewhat separately.

Anyone who has long been in a relationship with another—neighboring, friendship, work—will surely have realized that involvement generates responsibility and that the more intimate and long-standing the relationship, the more it commands me. The paradigm case is marriage. The spouse commands simply by being spouse rather than stranger, and does so more compellingly than does a neighbor, friend or coworker with whom I have a relationship. When the demand is put into words, its specificity and the fact of its being spoken to me gives it great urgency. But even when no word is spoken, one knows that there are things one must, and others one must not do. In that situation, you may be uncertain what exactly you ought to do or how best to go about it—the advantages of the verbal—but you know that you must respond to the unverbalized command. Often, we discover, such unarticulated demands have a greater power than the spoken ones, for there is something particularly reproachful about the spouse's cries, "You should have known what to do," or, "If I had to tell you it wouldn't be the same thing," or "If you really loved me, you would have known."

This telling experience furnishes us with a metaphor for what happens between us and God in the Covenant. No wonder Rosenzweig spoke of revelation as love. When through the religious life one builds an intense and long-lasting intimacy with God, one knows one "must" not stain the relationship by one's behavior, but one "must" rather dedicate oneself to acting as the loved One would want us to. (That is the general case—but we should not forget, as Yehudah Hanasi once wailed, "Some people win the life of the world to come in an instant while others must spend their whole lives striving to attain it and never know whether they have.")

I suppose that is another reason that I am a theologian. I want to clear away the intellectual rubbish that so often keeps us from allowing a budding relationship with God to mature. And I want to provide as fine an understanding of the Covenant as a relationship as I can so that people will not only be attracted to it in theory, but enter into it as a bond which directs their lives. Ideas are not the only, or often even the best way of carrying on this "dating service" but, without them, I think a community as educated and critical as ours is will not be willing to "commit."

Relationship commands, but it is too personalistic to yield what we normally think of as law, the enduring-evolving, clearly specified norms of what we must regularly do or else carry a burden of guilt and/or punishment. What is at stake between the two views is not merely the vagueness of relationship and the specificity and objectivity of law, but the intensity of the urgency to act connected with each kind of command. In fact, can relationship get people to act as well as law can? We cannot answer that question by dismissing the former as too easy to subvert, for no system is people proof and the law, too, is regularly subverted by literalists, positivists, and other less elegant sinners. We will, I believe, get a better picture of what each viewpoint can and cannot do by leaving off comparisons of who fails in each, and turning to a case to illuminate this difference of approach.

Assume, that after a reasonably energetic effort, a tenth man is not forthcoming to complete a *minyan* and people will start to leave if we delay any further. What shall we do about the person who came to say *kaddish*? The Law is clear. For all our concern for the mourner, he cannot say the mourner's *kaddish* as part of the service. That is what Susan and Soloveitchik mean when they refer to "sacrifice" as an ingredient of Jewish duty. There are things which have long been difficult to understand in Jewish Law, but God's behests have such an urgency to them that we set aside our qualms and do them. Thus, while I do not know how Susan feels about sitting behind the *mehitzah*, which divides the sexes in her centrist Orthodox *shul*, when she comes to the synagogue that is where she will sit; it is the Law. Thus, too, the mourner will understand why he could not say *kaddish* in this unfortunate circumstance, but he and the rest of the people there will know they have fulfilled the centuries-old ruling and acted with a Jewish authenticity any observant Jew will admire. In a society as shifting and unstable as ours, these are virtues to cherish.

Yet if I recall David's position of some years ago correctly, there are rare occasions when he, who like Susan gladly wears the "yoke of the Kingdom of Heaven," might break with the Law. Say that, as in cases of *mamzerut, halakhic* illegitimacy, the Law is blatantly unethical, punishing the innocent offspring for the sin of the parents, and no classic *halakhic* device avails to declare that there really is no case. In such an extreme case, David, most reluctantly to be sure, would not follow the classic *halakhah*. But he would be most stringent in limiting what qualified as a case of "blatantly unethical" Jewish law. It does not include allowing a gathering of nine men to carry on a service with the mourner's *kaddish.* I raise this matter only to indicate that so redoubtable a champion of Jewish law as David, once acknowledged that in quite exceptional circumstances it might be necessary to exercise extra-halakhic moral authority.

For a large and, in my view, increasing majority of modernized Jews, feminism is the issue that mandates the need to revise or even break with the Law as it is understood by the sages of that community of Jews who are most devoted to its study and practice. To these Jews who insist on thinking about the Law's purposes, it seems plain that, in the case given above, should a woman be available to join the prayers she should be counted in the *minyan* so that *kaddish* could be said. Indeed, women should be counted in *minyanim* regularly, and be as required to say *kaddish* as men now are. All such changes would act to strengthen the living Covenant relationship. Many believe that they can use the term *"halakhah"* for these revisionist rulings; others believe that co-opting a traditional title obscures the contemporary relational authority behind them, and does violence to what the term *"halakhah"* traditionally meant. In any case, to ask all women to accept the lesser status that traditional law effectively assigns to women, is to demand more of a "sacrifice" than seems compatible with Covenant as the relationship between God and the entire Jewish people.

I find that Peter's suggestion that we think of our duties in terms of Kadushin's "value concepts" pushes us too far to the permissive pole of the duty spectrum. Kadushin, after all, was working with *aggadah*, lore, rather than *halakhah*, law and, while *aggadic* statements do have a certain limited authority for believing Jews, they do not come with anything like the rigor associated with the notion of command. Moreover, thinking of *praxis* in terms of value concepts is made more troubling by Kadushin's insistence that their meaning is always indeterminate. I may be reading too little into Peter's suggestion, but I am sensitive to this issue because of our spate of writers who, in their eagerness to co-opt the term *halakhah* for their non-Orthodoxy, regularly so empty it of legal forcefulness that their *"halakhah"* effectively retains only *aggadic* authority, despite its more stringent sounding label.

Were I the rabbi of the nine person [*sic*] non-*minyan*, and the mourner asked if we could have the service anyway so she/he could recite the mourner's *kaddish*, I would think of the Law in order to see if it reasonably clarified the present Covenantal imperative. Clearly tradition would prohibit it, but a great many caring Jews in our community today would think it a shame that a mourner who came to synagogue to say *kaddish* was denied that possibility because of what they would call "a technicality." They, like me personally, could not imagine God frowning on us because of our untraditional effort to have nine people, not ten, symbolize the Jewish community seeking liturgically to renew its ancient Covenant, as well as allow our neighbor to fulfill her/his special responsibility in that regard. But if the group present, understanding the situation, was willing to go ahead, I would lead that service. Someone else utilizing the same Covenantal calculus might rule differently, but that is the pluralism that this kind of goal-oriented reasoning encourages.

If *keva*, the regularity, of Jewish law is critical to us, I do not see how we can ever achieve that without a firm belief that God stands behind just these words, this ruling and the dialectical system which gave birth to it— ten men, not nine, or not nine and a woman. Without that dogmatic faith, other rationales for the Law will produce only tepid results. Most Jews are too critical and questioning to accept classic Jewish law as binding because they are told it is, if not God's revelation, the established historic structure of Jewish living. This position and its corollaries have thus far failed to produce communities who live by even a modernized Jewish law, as Conservative Jewish leaders regularly ruefully acknowledge. In my opinion, the theological root of the difficulty for the non-dogmatic theories is the depth of our commitment to the religious validity of the self's rightful part in any rule-making. Only a living relationship with God, I insist, can hope to demand that we work out our individuality as part of the Jewish people's Covenant with God.

The great contribution of Covenantalized decision-making will not be *keva*, but its emphasis on *kavannah*, intention. What transpires between us—God-Israel-me—is here a matter of consciousness as well as of act. When our doing grows out of a consciousness of self-in-relation, that inwardness will shape our persons as well as be a commanding power in our doing. At the moment, Covenant relatedness is largely a matter individual Jews feel privately. Yet I would hope that we will soon see the day when there are communities of Jews who share enough of this Covenantal sensibility that they will want to move beyond the isolation that many Jewish selves feel in our time, to the formulation of communal norms for Covenanted Jewish living (p. 294). I do not think that will ever likely become "law" but it would flesh out the communal aspect of Covenantal existence, and add another layer of urgency to being a *praxis* Jew.

RENEWING THIS CONVERSATION

Several of the colleagues have commented on my book's failure to show the Jewish textual basis on which my thought rests, while others wish I had indicated more clearly what sort of practice this theology entails and how Covenantal reasoning leads to it.

As to the missing texts, I am unable to resolve the methodological problem which besets us all with regard to texts and contemporary thought. No matter how many citations one adduces, they can merely illustrate a possible relation of some aspects of our tradition to the new thinking. That is because we have no way of determining what they all say, or how to give a representative sample of them or indicate their essence. None of these possibilities carries much credence, so all textual citation remains a thinker's selection of what she/he finds relevant in the tradition, and testify more to the thinker's hermeneutic than to "the normative" ideas in the tradition (whose existence is another hotly debated notion among us). In this situation I have thought it wiser to clarify my hermeneutic than to gather texts to demonstrate its putative Jewishness. I also hoped that various of my briefer writings would indicate my roots in rabbinic literature, and my way of learning from it. In the winter of 1999, the Jewish Publication Society will publish my and Francie Schwartz's book, *The Jewish Moral Virtues*, which, in typical *musar* fashion, is highly textual and ranges across the entire Jewish tradition. That will give my readers some greater indication of my relationship to the Jewish sources. And as I indicate in the preface to *Renewing the Covenant* (pp. x-xi), I hope that one day my decades long study of *aggadic* discourse will see the light.

As my theological work was coming to systematic fruition, I began testing out various of its notions in one area of *praxis*, Jewish ethics. A collection of many of my papers in this area was published in 1990 by Wayne State University Press under the title, *Exploring Jewish Ethics*. A better indication of how my mature theology relates to decision-making may be found in the results of a seminar I conducted for a number of years, in which students rendered a decision on a current ethical issue of concern to them, based on the five point schema I had outlined in the last chapter of *Renewing the Covenant*. Fourteen publishable student studies resulted from that course, and these were published by Behrman House in 1994 as *Reform Jewish Ethics and the Halakhah, An Experiment in Decision Making*. While these are my students' papers, not my own, the approach to reading *halakhic* (mostly) texts is strongly guided, occasionally in dissent, by my viewpoint. Thus, this volume may be said to open a window on how my theology would work in practice.

God, rain blessing on Peter Ochs for his dedication to furthering Jewish thought in our time, and for his imaginative effort here to push postmodern thinking about Judaism another step ahead.

And to You, dear God, I say "Blessed are You" for all you have done to sustain me to this day.

NOTES

1. On the notion of a Liberal Jewish elite, see the chapter on "Jews Who Do; Jews Who Don't" in my *Liberal Judaism* (New York: UAHC, 1984), pp. 459–67.
2. Not long after the publication of *Renewing the Covenant*, when giving some lectures at the University of San Francisco, I gave as one reason for my finding postmodernism congenial: "I am grateful to postmodern discourse for authorizing those who admit they cannot give reasonably unambiguous voice to the *logos* to speak their truth, sloppy in structure as it may seem to some. This structural untidiness is abetted by my writing with conscious imprecision, a

choice designed to warn my reader that my theology does not allow for geometric clarity." *Our Way to a Postmodern Judaism: Three Lectures* (San Francisco: University of San Francisco, Swig Dept. of Jewish Studies, 1992), p. 38.

3. Elliot insisted that, regardless of what I said in *Renewing the Covenant*, it must be understood as a statement of Reform Jewish ideology. Note his subtitle: "Autonomy *vs.* Community, The Ongoing Reform/Conservative Difference," *Conservative Judaism*, Vol. XLVIII, No. 2 (Winter 1996): 64–68. My response and Elliot's rejoinder appeared as "The Reform Judaism of *Renewing the Covenant*" and "Matters of Degree and Kind" in *Conservative Judaism*, Vol. L, No. 1 (Fall 1997). (The issues were dated to maintain the consecutive publication of the journal but they actually appeared at a considerably later date.)

4. Ibid., p.62.

5. This torah self-understanding appeared about the same time in two publications in slightly different form: *Choices in Modern Jewish Thought*, 2nd ed. (W. Orange, N.J.: Behrman House, 1995), pp. 288ff. and *The Human Condition, the Alexander Schindler Festschrift*, ed. Aaron Hirt-Mannheimer (New York: UAHC, 1995) as part of my paper, "Reform: Modern Movement in a Postmodern Era?"

6. See Eugene B. Borowitz, *Choosing a Sex Ethic, a Jewish Inquiry* (New York: Schocken Books, 1968), pp. 116–20.

7. Abraham Heschel, *God in Search of Man* (Philadelphia: Jewish Publication Society, 1956).

8. The issue cannot be that individuality has no place at all in traditional Judaism. Even Heschel, the defender of the accuracy and empathic passivity of the prophets, acknowledges that they express God's truth in terms of their individual personalities and styles. *Halakhic* decisors are regularly described as having *shitot*, individualized systems of reading the tradition. I discussed how this functions in Conservative Judaism in my response to Elliot Dorff, "Autonomy *vs.* Community, the ongoing Reform/Conservative difference." *Conservative Jusaism*, pp. 64–65.

9. The most egregious misreading of that sentence was Ellen Umansky's. Because I spoke of the self in its full individuality, she accused me of not having progressed beyond classic Reform Judaism. Her astonishing misreading was compounded by her gerrymandering of my statement. She omitted its first word, "Fifth," the one which indicated how I had recontextualized selfhood to give it a properly postmodern, Jewish relational situation and made it the Jewish Covenant self. My appreciation of her ideas was not enhanced by her suggestion that we now ought to move on to a theology where selves and religion were thought of relationally, a matter central to my writing for some

decades. "Zionism and Reform Judaism: a Theological Reassessment," *Journal of Reform Zionism*, vol. 1, no. 1 (March 1993): 44–50. My response appeared as a lengthy endnote, no. 4, in my own contribution to these discussions, "What Is Reform Religious Zionism?" *Journal of Reform Zionism*, vol. II (March 1995): 24–30.

10. See Borowitz, *Renewing the Covenant,* pp. 123–25, 128, and 131 on the limited God; and pp. 148–50 on retribution.

11. Most notable is Richard L. Rubenstein's preface to the second edition of *After Auschwitz*, 2nd ed. (Baltimore: Johns Hopkins University Press, 1992), pp. xi–xiii; see also the quite different tone of the preface to the second edition of Emil Fackenheim's *To Mend the World* (Bloomington: Indiana University Press, 1994), pp. xi–xxv.

12. Eugene B. Borowitz, *Journal of Reform Zionism*, vol. II (March 1995): 24–30.

Postmodern Theological Renewal:
A Meditation

10

"Crossing and Recrossing the Void": A Letter to Gene

SUSAN HANDELMAN

Dear Gene:

I write this in the form of a letter to you for many reasons. I struggled through many drafts of this essay until I finally realized that it should be a direct address. For one thing, only that form would enact and embody the direct I-thou encounter between persons which is at the cornerstone of your theology of Covenant, community, and revelation. For another, this collection comes to honor you. So far you have been addressed here in the third person, as "Borowitz," a thinker who put forth a set of ideas open to critique by your colleagues in traditional academic fashion. Taking your ideas so seriously is indeed one way to honor you. And it fits your own credo of engaging in continuous, rational, collective scrutiny of the personal, nonrational sources of your faith, a dialectic that you so eloquently describe in your book. This collective critique also reflects that characteristically generous Borowitzian personal style that those of us who know you have come to cherish: your encouragement of all varieties of Jewish expression, even those that differ radically from your own. So, too, we honor you by wrestling with you, as Jacob wrestled with his angel, wrestled towards a blessing, a wrestle that was also an embrace.

Yet these words of critique and debate which you have sparked still do not seem to me enough. So I would like also to honor you, Gene, with a few words of praise, appreciation, and gratitude: you are, as you describe in the moving epilogue to your book, well named *Yehiel*, meaning "God will live": "a prophetic name for an American boy who would grow up wanting to be a Jewish theologian and would spend much of his time explaining that God was not dead."[1] You have spent your entire career making God live, and so you do also in this book.

Another reason that I am writing in letter form is that unlike the other writers who preceded me here, the task assigned me was not to present another analytical, academic response to your ideas. My mandate was to "meditate" on this entire collective dialogue as it relates to "postmodern Jewish renewal," on the living consequences for us as Jews, for where we may be going, for what our possibilities are. What kind of style, I asked myself again and again, should this "meditation" be written in? And this question of my own style intersects a larger one: How does the postmodern critique of Enlightenment rationalism that you so persuasively describe also require us to speak and write and teach differently? Many in the field of literary and cultural theory have argued that a postmodern discourse is also a "post-critical" discourse that necessarily reveals its personal commitments and passions. So what models should I look to? Autobiography? Testimony? Midrash? Commentary? Confession? Talmudic pilpul? A collage of quotations?

In the end, I think I incorporated a bit of each. But as I began to meditate on my "meditation," I was led astray by the connotations this word has in English, which I associated with an act of solitary and silent reflection. Yet one of the main tenets of postmodernism has been called "the linguistic turn " from Wittgenstein to Derrida, the recognition that language mediates our knowledge and experience of the world. Although you, Gene, write that you are ultimately more comfortable with nonverbal experience, and that a notion of a Divine Verbal revelation constrains you, both you and I are searching for ways to construct and protect a specifically Jewish voice in the cacophony of postmodern culture. In writing an academic essay or book, in engaging with the thought and philosophy of the West, how do we do that?

For me, one of the ways is to speak "Hebrew." That is, to speak through the sanctified voices from our classical Jewish texts in all their stubborn particularity. And also, to speak Hebrew literally: to tease out the subtle psychological, philosophical, and cultural resonances in the language. For the language is itself a form of thought, or to use Rosenzweig's term, "speech-thinking." Yet, at the same time, we also speak the languages of Western thought, and that is an important task.

MEDITATING AS *HAGUT*

Let me begin with the Hebrew word for "meditation," *hagut*, which comes from the root *hagah*.

הגה In the Bible, the verb *hagah, la-hagot*, encompasses several meanings: "to pronounce, speak, utter, articulate, to study, meditate, moan, murmur, coo."[2] And interesting enough, *hogeh deot* means " thinker, philosopher." From the root *hagah* also comes the word *higayon* meaning "logic," "rationality," and "common sense." So in a sense, *hagut* already implies a "postmodern" notion of thought: To think, to meditate is not to conduct a silent, solitary set of rational deliberations in the Cartesian sense, but to enact a relation to an other. To meditate also means to study a text and, as Jewish law prescribes, study and prayer must be oral, the words must be vocalized, given body, sung out in these matters: *hirhur c'dibbur lo damei*, [הרהור כדבור לא דמא], "thought is not counted as speech." That is, one does not fulfill one's duty of Torah study or prayer unless she/he actually utters the words with the lips.[3] "Reading," as the Hebrew word *kriyah* instructs us, should be a "calling out." It has been noted that each of Rashi's first commentaries on the first line of each of the first five books of the Bible expresses the love of God for Israel: and so it is in Rashi's first comment on the word *va-ikra*, "and He called" which is the first word of the Book of Leviticus. Rashi says, "Before all instances of 'speak' [i.e. when God speaks], and before all instances of 'say,' and before all instances of 'command,' the terms 'call' [*kriyah*] preceded; it is an expression of endearment." *Kriyah*: reading as calling out, as endearment: I want to bear this in mind, for I think we often forget in all our postmodern academic "theories of reading" ("intertextualities," "semiotic systems," and "discursive practices") that our readings should be callings out to God and to each other. So much of postmodern discourse in the humanities is a hermeneutics of suspicion, an attempt to "overcome oppression" by unmasking hidden ideologies, unconscious desires, and unjust power relations. One of the tasks of a *Jewish* postmodernism is to give a soul back to postmodernism. It is here, Gene, that you and I are allies, that we have a common project.

THE SOUL OF POSTMODERNISM

At its best, I would say, postmodernism can be a way for Jews who have passed through the fragmentation and secularization wrought by modernity to renew themselves Jewishly. This is the focus of your book and my central concern here. How can the search for postmodern or postsecular "spirituality" cross the void that modernity opened up? In what ways does it reconnect to and reconfigure a "pre-modern" faith, but one which does not deny or suppress all that we have learned and experienced in modernity? Yet, on the other hand, isn't renewal and return, *teshuva*, the eternal task of the Jewish people? *Teshuva*, as the ancient rabbis said, preceded even the creation of the world. And we are, as Simon Rawidowicz so aptly characterized us, the "ever-dying people." Constantly confronting disasters, catastrophes, the undermining of our foundations: then reconstructing them and renewing ourselves. Even the book of Genesis, from a certain point of view, is a book of collapse, destruction, concealment of God and fragile survival. Let alone the book of Job.

I believe we also need to overcome a certain *hubris* about our generation and its challenges. Indeed, whereas the ideologies of modernism had apocalyptic overtones, there is an ironic self-awareness in postmodernism, a deflation of the self and its pretensions to final understandings, revolutionary upheaval, or what you so aptly call the "human *tzimtzum*." Peter Ochs in his essay "Compassionate Postmodernism" has also characterized postmodernism as "redemptive" of modernity, and that is a distinctively Jewish perspective without which secular postmodernism can degenerate into another form of radical skepticism and irony.[4]

I must pause here, though, and express my discomfort with large categorical statements about what postmodern "is." There are many kinds of postmodernism, from the philosophical intricacies of Deconstruction, to complex global political developments, to certain artistic and cultural practices, down to "MTV." I certainly do not want to engage here in another abstract debate about what is and isn't postmodernism. It is a mixed genre, as is your own book, which is an unusual combination of personal confession, social observation, and dialogue with thinkers such as Buber, Heschel, Cohen, Kaplan. Since one of your main goals is to safeguard the "freedom and autonomy" of the individual self, Edith Wyschogrod argues that yours is really an existentialist response to modernity rather than one grounded in the work of preeminent postmodern thinkers such as Foucault, Derrida, Lacan, Levinas. For these thinkers, postmodernism is defined precisely in opposition to the notion of some personal, coherent, inner individual essence. She is theoretically correct. But I think you also justly reply that none of these thinkers should be given any dogmatic rights to speak of and for what is postmodern.

Nevertheless, the thinkers whom you rely on, and those whom Edith and Yudit Greenberg and I are inspired by—such as Levinas and Rosenzweig—all follow that path of return to Judaism, of "post-assimilation." It is also the path you autobiographically describe, and it is my path too. However we define the self, postmodernism requires us to delineate the location of that self and how it came to be "constructed," to trace the intersection of forces, cultures, languages that give rise to it. In your epilogue, you write of your grandparents, and parents, being a mix of rationalist Litvaks and Hungarian Hasidim. As a native American, your formative Jewish experiences came from an upbringing in Columbus, Ohio in the 1930s, in a very small Jewish community with inadequate institutions. In your studies for the rabbinate at Hebrew Union College in Cincinnati, you were trained in modern "scientific" historical and philological criticism and imbued with a faith in the university as a redemptive, civilizing force. Now, at the end of a century of barbarous slaughter, you write movingly of your "loss of faith in the intellectual and cultural pretensions of modernity" and in the power of the university. You have become, as you aptly phrase it, "skeptical of skepticism."

Like you, my ancestors were also Litvaks. I am a product of highly assimilated suburban Chicago of the 1950s and 1960s. In one sense, our generational differences are strong. But, in another sense, we are both Jews who keenly feel effects of the Shoah, the failures of modernity, and are skeptical of the university as an arbiter of value and ideals. We both seek a return to the particular Jewish self defined in a binding relation to God, other Jews, and community. We are both engaged in a kind of *teshuvah*.

HALAKHAH

Unlike you, however, I have chosen to be a *halakhic* Jew, and I believe that one of the key unmet tasks of postmodern Jewish thought is to overcome what I would call—forgive me—a secularized theological antinomianism. That is partially a legacy from the German philosophers who also inspired the Jewish *haskalah* and modernist thought. Especially Kant, that great proponent of morality. Kant defined morality as duty observed out of inner conviction through reason and autonomy in contrast to duty observed due to externally commanded law (that is, through authority and heteronomy). In his schema, Judaism becomes an inferior religion of heteronomous law, rightly superseded by a higher Christian religion of inner freedom. Kantian autonomous reason, as Natan Rotenstreich once put it, is an equivalent or transformed version of Protestant grace or "inner illumination."

When I say that postmodern Jewish thought needs to recover the meaning of law in Judaism, I should insist on using the word *halakhah*, originating in the Hebrew root for "path, or walking." But I don't want to rehash worn old arguments between "Orthodox" and "Reform" Judaism—terms I am not comfortable with in any case. I want rather to emphasize here that *halakhah* cannot be understood in terms of modernist categories of "autonomy" and "heteronomy." As Emile Fackenheim once wrote in *Encounters Between Judaism and Modern Philosophy*, Kant did not understand the nature of revealed morality in Judaism because it is outside the realm of both autonomous and heteronomous morality. Its source and life "lies precisely in the togetherness of a divine commanding Presence that never dissipates itself into irrelevance, and a human response that freely appropriates what it receives."5

Postmodernism can help move us beyond the sterile antinomy of autonomy/heteronomy. For one thing, the autonomy/heteronomy dualism presupposes an independent isolated self, a notion which is heavily criticized in postmodern thought. For another, it is a mistake to identify the obligation, the "must" of a *mitzvah* with the "must" of rational propositions and deductive logic. Rosenzweig and Levinas well understood the need for this "third term" beyond the heteronomy/autonomy dualism. The paradigm for their construction of the self is the biblical cry of *hineni*, *"Here I am."* These are the words with which Abraham responds to God before the *akedah*. And with which Moses responds at the burning bush, and which the prophets use when they are called by God. Rosenzweig writes that when God calls out to Abraham in direct address, in all his particularity, then Abraham answers, "all unlocked, all spread-apart, all ready, all-soul: 'Here I am.' Here is the I, the individual human I, as yet wholly receptive, as yet only unlocked, only empty, without content, without nature, pure readiness, pure obedience, all ears."6

Or let me quote Peter Pitzele, who eloquently describes what is so difficult for us moderns to understand about Abraham's "obedience": "History has given obedience a bad name; too many docile lambs led to the slaughter; too many obedient functionaries murdering the lambs. Whenever we hear of talk of obedience, we are likely to feel ambivalence and fear. And a personal revulsion curdles the word as well. . . . Obedience is a giving over of one's personal power; it is a loss of control." But there is another kind of obedience, Pitzele notes:

> The word *obey* in English comes from the Latin word meaning "to listen, to hear." Abram *listens* to the call to leave his native land. And his father's house. He obeys. He experiences the call as something coming from a God who is felt to be Other and outside him. But this God is also inside him. Deep speaks to deep. . . . Abram is not being obedient to some external dictate, to some chain of command. On the contrary, he breaks with customary conventions. . . . What Abram obeys flashes upon him like a beacon, points a way, then disappears. . . . On each step of his journey he must renew his commitment to his task, for his obedience is voluntary, not compelled.7

So often you reiterate that central to your project is the need to protect our integrity in the face of the God who commands. But this is what the interpretive tradition of Oral Torah has always done. The Talmud already voices your concern about an external compulsion which invalidates the revelation at Sinai in the famous passage in *Shabbat* 88a. I want to quote at some length from the Talmud here, for as much as I cherish the personal moments in *Renewing the Covenant*, I also sorely miss in it the embodied texture of classical Jewish discourse—the cacophonous yet melodic weave of voices from different eras and times in the commentaries and super-commentaries, the dialogic voices of Talmud and *midrash*.

The biblical text[8] tells us that the Israelites stood *b'tachit ha har*— translated idiomatically "at the foot of the mountain," but having a more literal sense of "at the underside." Here the Talmud comments:

> Rav Avdimi bar Hama bar Hasa said: this teaches us that the Holy One Blessed be He turned the mountain over on them like a cask and said; "If you accept the Torah, all is well; if not, here will be your grave." Rav Aha bar Jacob said: "Based on this, a major complaint can be lodged against the Torah." Rava said. "Nevertheless they reaccepted it willingly in the days of Ahaseurus, for it is written,[9] "the Jews [*kimu v'kiblu,*] confirmed and accepted." They confirmed what they had accepted previously.

Rashi explains the nature of this complaint: "for if they were brought to judgment about why they had not fulfilled what they had accepted upon themselves, they could answer that they were compelled by force to accept it." In other words, it was not of their own free will. Nevertheless, they re-accepted it a thousand years later in their exile in the Persian Kingdom of Ahaseurus—"from," says Rashi, "the love of the miracle that was done for them."

In other words, what the book of Esther is referring to in verses 9:27 ("the Jews confirmed and accepted upon them and upon all their seed . . . to observe these two days of Purim.")[9] is not just the Jews' confirmation and acceptance of Mordecai's instructions about how to commemorate their miraculous rescue. On a deeper level, they confirmed and accepted what had previously been "forced" upon them a thousand years earlier at Sinai; only *now* they did it out of free will. In "The Temptation of Temptation," Levinas' commentary on this passage, he understands this *midrash* on the relation of Sinai and Purim as indicating a "third way" beyond the dualistic alternative freedom/violence or autonomy/heteronomy.[10] It signifies that there is a certain "non-freedom" prior to freedom, one which makes freedom possible—a prior saying of *Na'aseh Ve-Nishma*[11] "we will do and we will hear/obey/understand," a prior calling to responsibility which is what in fact constructs the self. The self is defined by saying *hineni*, "Here I am for you." Moreover, Levinas notes, the thousand years of history between Sinai and the Persian exile were filled with the difficult consequences and suffering resulting *from* that first acceptance of the Torah. In re-accepting it at Purim, we do so in full cognizance of its price.

In this light, I also find Rashi's comment even more poignant: the motivation for reaccepting the Torah was "from love of the miracle." Acceptance out of love, and in a time of threatened mass annihilation. For Purim is, in its own way, a holiday made for a postmodern sensibility: a holiday of masks, inversions, comic mockery, concealment of God whose name is never even mentioned in the *Megillah*. For the rabbis to make out of this a second Sinai is an act of hermeneutical genius and profound theology.

This is the continuing task of any Jewish theology, of course, to continue Sinai. The great climactic scene at Sinai filled with thunder, lightning, and the Voice from heaven, is followed in the biblical narrative by a seeming let down: the minutiae of law regarding goring oxen, Hebrew bondmen, and so forth. Then come the long seemingly tedious narratives of the building of the *mishkan*, the Tabernacle, descriptions of its boards and nails, the dress of the high priests; and then we proceed on into the book of *VaYikra* (Leviticus) and its elaborate descriptions of the sacrificial system. These are the parts I usually skip when I teach "The Bible as Literature" to my mostly non-Jewish undergraduates. But perhaps this is a mistake. For these are also the parts that are so distinctly Jewish, ways in which the elevated abstractions are brought into the concrete world. This is what *halakhah* is: Second Sinai, the continuation of the voice of God echoing through the voice of human interpretation, and the extension of the revelation into the seemingly most mundane aspects of human life.

For revelation cannot remain an awesome inchoate Presence. It needs to be concretized and brought into the realm of the everyday. A student of mine once made a startling comment about the prosaic ending of the book of Job. After the voice from the Whirlwind, the text returns to a strange, prose episode which matter-of-factly recounts that God restored to Job double what he had lost; Job became wealthy, Job remarried, had many new sons and daughters, lived to a ripe old age and "died, old and full of days." My students are often offended by this ending. After God has taken everything away and tormented Job unfairly and then made a thundering speech from the Whirlwind, what is this, they ask indignantly? Some kind of attempt at recompense? How could that ever make up for all his suffering? But this one student said: No. One cannot continue to exist on the level of the Voice from the whirlwind. One has to come back into daily life. Remember the Voice, be transformed by it, but come back to living day-to-day in the prosaic rounds of family life. A more "orthodox" way of saying all this would be to characterize it as the "Will of God." The divine will must manifest itself and be reflected in the minutiae of daily life. Where else should it manifest itself? Where else do we make a *mishkan*, a holy dwelling for God, if not in those areas of life most central to human finite existence: food, dwelling, clothes, sex, economics?

Our Jewish postmodern world is a post-*shoah*, post-Whirlwind world as well. And the hermeneutic theories of postmodernism have helped us gain a new appreciation of the radicality of rabbinic ways of reading and rereading. These insights fortify me on my own path of *teshuva*. But it is not just in the realm of *aggadah* that humans are partners with God; that partnership has always been part of the traditional *halakhic* imperative. That is the whole notion of the Oral Torah. It is a caricature to describe the classical notion of *"Torah Mi Sinai"* as something handed down by a dictatorial God who takes away autonomy.

THE PROBLEM OF AUTHORITY: THE SERMON

But somehow, I do not think I have persuaded you. The problem is not so much with these general ideas. It is really, I have a hunch, the notion of authority that bothers you. "Why," you ask "should thinking Jews consider giving up their self-determination to follow the rulings of decisors who have Jewish learning, but otherwise no greater access to God's present will than the rest of us posses?"12

I may have been sounding as if I were giving a sermon, and as a rabbinical practitioner of that genre yourself, allow me to indulge that impulse even further. (Although I could also justify myself by saying, along with the rhetorical theorist Richard Weaver, that all language, is in a way, sermonic . . . or with Levinas that all language is apologetic . . . an address to the other which attempts to persuade and justify.)

So here is a sermon that comes from my own particularly located Jewish life in Washington, D.C. from my own Rabbi, Barry Freundel of Kesher Israel, the Georgetown Synagogue. One Shabbat, he made an intriguing distinction between "power" and "authority" during one of the winter weeks when we were reading the early parts of Exodus in the cycle of Torah readings. Pharaoh has "power," he claimed, but no "authority"; Moses has "authority" but not " power." What does this mean? Pharaoh, the paradigmatic political authoritarian, speaks the language of "power." Like contemporary anti-Semites, he has an exaggerated fear of "Jewish power," far in excess of the reality of Jewish social position and influence. In coming to Pharaoh, Moses does not speak the language of "power," but asks instead that the Jews be allowed to go to the desert to sacrifice to their God. Rabbi Freundel preached:

> It must be understood that the Bible does not take an anti-power stance, nor is it a "meek shall inherit the earth morality," but it is a recognition that power is not the ultimate good and that when used, power is to be used in service to the true *summum bonum*—a proper relationship to God.

Jewish literature challenges a power-centered ethos—as we are often reminded in the prophetic literature: "not by power, nor by might, but by my Spirit," says God. As a people, we survived for thousands of years without land and traditional kinds of power, and this makes us seem inversely magically powerful to those who only worship power. (Needless to say, I must add that, with the rise of the State of Israel, one of the primary challenges for Jews today is how to deal with power. Some of our postmodern Jewish disorientation is caused by the loss of the image of Israel as vulnerable, agricultural, pioneer state, and the disintegration of the 100 year-old ideology of pioneer Zionism. Israeli culture today is undergoing its own radical questioning of all its traditional norms. And the Israel of 1996 is a highly industrialized, high-tech, global competitor. That old icon of the kibbutznik in shorts and peaked cap should be updated by sticking a cellular phone in his ear.)

But the key part of Rabbi Freundel's drasha related to the redefinition of power and authority: "Today in many circles," he said, "everything—politics, religion, literature, the family—is discussed only in terms of the power relationships involved. Hierarchy, patriarchy, racism, sexism, and so forth, . . . is all about the language of power. . . . What has been lost is, first, the Jewish opposition to seeing the world only in terms of the dynamics of power. Second we have lost the distinction between power and authority." Citing Eric Fromm, he defined authority not as a quality one has, but "an interpersonal relationship in which one person looks upon another as somebody superior to him. Put another way, while power is a quality that flows from the top down and carries with it coercion and tyranny, authority comes from the bottom up and begins with the acceptance of something larger and better." This dynamic is modeled in the relation between Sinai and Purim: When the Jews at Mt. Sinai say "We will do and we will obey" and re-confirm their acceptance of it in the days of Esther, they establish God's authority. In other words, "God's authority begins from those in a position of less authority accepting that something special exists in the higher authority. That legitimacy does not depend on power as superior strength but conveying of authority." I move from my modern Orthodox rabbi to the contemporary Quaker educational theorist Parker Palmer, who has some eloquent and strikingly similar things to say about the relations among knowing, freedom, and obeying—and what it means to teach and to learn. Noting that the English word "obedience" does not mean slavish adherence, but comes from the Latin root *audire* which means to "listen," Palmer writes:

> At its root, the word "obedience" means not only "to listen" but "to listen from below." How fascinating that this is also the common sense meaning of the word "understand," which suggests that we know something by "standing under" it. Both obedience and understanding imply submitting ourselves to something larger than any one of us, something on which we all depend. Both imply subjecting us to the communal bonds of truth. The objectivist will doubtless argue that the personalist mode of knowing is dangerously subjective. But the complex of word and images I am exploring here opens up a new sense of what "subjective" knowledge might mean—for that word also means "to place under." In that sense of the words, I *am* arguing for a subjective conception of truth, a truth to which we must subject our selves. Truth calls us to submit ourselves, to the community of which we are a part, to fidelity to those bonds of troth in which our truth resides.13

In other words, "truth is troth," and Palmer uses the image of covenant to express this:

> The English word " truth" comes from a Germanic root that also gives rise to our word "troth," as in the ancient vow, "I pledge thee my troth." With this word, one person enters a covenant with another, a pledge to engage in a mutually accountable and transforming relationship, a relationship forged of trust and faith in the face of unknowable risks. To know something or someone in truth is to enter troth with the known, to rejoin the new knowing what our minds have put asunder. To know in truth is to become betrothed . . .14

I find in these words a wonderful "Quaker" dash on the rabbinic interpretation in *Shabbat 88a* of the Jews standing "at the underside of the mountain." And they are words which echo your concern for Covenant. But I do not think that Covenant, as a binding over to the other, and the kind of "sacrificial ethic" you want to construct can find a firm basis in your model as you describe it in a crucial passage:

> Here the "law" *(nomos)* arises from what freely passes between two fully dignified selves, neither subordinate to the other, each making its claim on the other simply by the act of relating. . . . What, then does God "reveal" if not a detailed teaching that legend says has been kept in Heaven since before the creation? God makes known just what we make known in a relationship: self, or more familiarly, presence.[15]

Yes, as you say, the parameters of the Covenant have to emerge out of the relationship. But there are symmetrical and asymmetrical relationships. This was part of Levinas' dispute with Buber over the nature of the "I-Thou" relation. For Levinas, the primary relation to the other is asymmetrical and modeled on the Jews' proclamation at Sinai, *na'aseh ve-nishmah*, "We will do and we will hear."[16] In other words, I am *first* called by and bound over to the other; only after (and as a result) of that primary binding do I then become the "equal" of the other, in a symmetrical relation. Otherwise, there's ultimately an eternal war of competing "I"s, of power interests. The other is not just my friend, lover, partner, but also my Teacher. One who calls to me from a height. Or as, Parker Palmer says "to teach is to create a space in which obedience to truth is practiced."[17] Which leads me to my next section.

RAV-TALMID

Let me restate your question again: "Why," you ask "should thinking Jews consider giving up their self-determination to follow the rulings of decisors who have Jewish learning but otherwise no greater access to God's present will than the rest of us possess?"[18] What, indeed, is Jewish learning? "This book of the law shall not depart out of thy mouth, but you should meditate on it day and night"[19] *Ve-hagita bo yomam VaLila.*

[והגיטה בו יומם ולילה]. Jewish learning is also the Jewish path to God. As Levinas notes, the end of the *aggadic* discussion of the scene at Sinai and the *na'aseh ve-nishma* in *Shabbat 88a* has a sectarian mocking the sage Rava whom he observes buried in study, holding his fingers beneath his foot so tightly that blood spurted from it. The sectarian mocks the sage for belonging to a people whose mouth was too quick to speak and accept the Torah: first, he says, you should have listened to see if you could accept and fulfill, not the obverse. As Levinas interprets it, study, the forceful exercise of intellect—so forceful that blood is spurting from Rava's fingers in his intense concentration—comes after and as result of the *na'aseh*, the "we will do," the primary acceptance of obligation.20

But true Jewish "learning" is not something one possesses like an exterior piece of property. Not a list of publications on a CV. The true teacher is not simply a repository of knowledge, but an embodiment and performer of that knowledge (and this parallels a postmodern definition of knowledge as performative relation). Perhaps this is why the rabbis talk about the importance of *shimush hakham* [שמוש חכם]—attending to, or serving one's teacher: "Who is ignorant *[am ha-aretz]*. He who has studied scriptures and mishna, but has not attended or served the scholars."21 This is not a slavish, mindless act, but a way of learning by attending to the personhood of the Rav. Torah cannot be obtained only from books or by oneself or through one's "inner light." It is not a "knowledge" in that sense, as I have argued elsewhere. "Greater than the learning of Torah is the attending upon Torah scholar" *Gdolah shimush ha Torah yoter mi-limudah* [גדולה שמוש התורה יותר מלמודה].22

And, of course, there is the famous talmudic story of R. Akiva who followed his teacher Rav Yehoshua into the bathroom, and Rav Kahana who hid under the bed of his teacher Rav. Asked how they dared to observe such private activities, they answered, "It [his deeds] are Torah, and I must learn."23

In all our academic discussions of the hermeneutics of Oral Torah, we tend to forget that ultimately it is also the word made personal by being mediated through another: through the living voice, face, and being of the teacher. Not the assertion of absolutist authority, but the recognition that knowledge has a face. We are not the People of the Book; we are the People of the *mouth*. It was the Muslems who dubbed us the "People of the Book." That is a mistake and misnomer. Books are fixed, rigid. For us, The Oral Torah illumines, breathes voice and life and personal presence into the Written Torah through the collective voices of the teachers and their students through the generations whose dialogues and debates it records. And with whom we converse and add our voice every time we pick up a Talmud or Mishna or Mikraot Gedolot and study. (I often feel that the most appropriate rhetorical form for my "Jewish voice" would be as commentary on classical Jewish texts, commentary which retains its orality.) After all, the root meaning of Torah is "teaching." In the *Sefat Emet*, Yehuda Arieh Leib, the Rebbe of Ger, comments as follows on the phrase from the "Woman of Valor" hymn in Proverbs 31:13: "She seeks out wool and flax to work willingly with her hands": the image of the woman creating a great tapestry out of simple materials parallels the Jewish people who are like a silk-worm that spins exquisite strands of silk from its mouth. That is the Torah *she b'al peh*—the Torah "of the mouth"—the thoughts that Jewish scholars of all generations will generate from their mouth.

I think one of the paradigms we need to develop further for a Jewish postmodernism is not the Buberian "I-Thou" but rather the Rav-Talmid (Teacher-Disciple) relation. This constructs the kind of "authority" that is granted by those "below" to those "above" in recognition of some superior quality. Moses, after all is not referred to as "Moses our Prophet," but "Moses, our Teacher," Moshe Rabbeinu. The Rav-Talmid relation is also a bond of love. Thus do Maimonides and Bertinoro comment on the famous line from *Pirke Avot*, 5:16; "Any love that depends on a specific consideration, when the consideration vanishes, the love ceases; but if it is not dependent on a specific consideration—it will never cease." What love is that?—the love between student and teacher because it is based on the wisdom of Torah. It is striking that the great Torah teachers do not seem to be solitary monologists. They come paired with disciples. There is always a Rav and Talmid together: Moses and Joshua; Elijah and Elisha; the Ari and Rav Chaim Vital; Rabbi Nachman and Rav Nosson (maybe even Ruth and Naomi). They are defined by the one they are bound to. There is here a mutuality, there is a co-creation. Teacher and disciple, as Rabbi Nachman said, are like the form of the letter aleph [א]—two *yuds*, one above and one below connected by a *vav*. And teacher and disciple are shifting roles into which every Jew is constantly cycling. Again *Pirke Avot* 6:3: "He who learns from his companion even one chapter, one rule, one verse, one word, or even one letter is obliged to treat him with respect. David, the king of Israel, only learned two things from Achitophel and yet called him master, guide, friend."

But somehow I feel as if we are still going over old issues. You will probably say that I have given a very idealized description. You could easily point to rigid notions of authority and *halakhah* that have led to oppressive and mindless fundamentalisms. So could I. And, of course, there is the difficult experience of Jews in Israel where rabbinic authority has become allied to power politics and created a kind of religious coercion from which we Diaspora Jews do not suffer.

But perhaps we can understand this fundamentalist reaction as itself a shadow creature of modernity, part of that old "modernist" debate between heteronomy and autonomy that we need desperately to move beyond. Let me try to explain. The kinds of scholarly tools your seminary teachers taught to you to apply to Jewish texts, with all their emphasis on "empirical fact," "critical-scientific approaches," "accurate historical reconstruction" of religious texts: all that is itself a kind of literalist mentality which sparks a flip side—an equally literalist fundamentalist, defensive response.

As the brilliant rhetorical theorist Chaim Perelman has observed, the skeptic and fanatic are flip sides of the same coin; they both hold that the only criteria for truth are those which are "absolute and indubitable." The skeptic thinks that no one can fulfill the criteria: whereas the fanatic thinks he or she indeed has done so. When truth is defined differently— postmoderns might say "contextually" or "rhetorically," or as a function of the dynamic between community, text, and interpreter, or perhaps kabbalistically as beyond all ontologies of presence and absence—then one can begin to escape that dire binary opposition and come to new affirmations. Or as you put it so well, being postmodern means to become "skeptical of skepticism." And this is the path some of the most interesting twentieth-century Jewish thinkers have taken. For example, the extraordinary first chief rabbi of Israel, mystic, poet, and theologian, Rav Avraham Yitzhak Kook, who wrote that all the forces of secular modernity have a holy source and come to purify the crude materialization of faith:

The fact that we conceive of religious faith in a distorted form, petty and dark, is responsible for atheism's rise to influence. This is the reason that the providential pattern of building the world includes a place for atheism, and its related notions. It is to stir to life the vitality of faith in every heart, so that religious faith be brought to its highest levels . . . by including the good that is embraced in the theoretical conceptions of atheism, religious faith reaches its fullest perfection.[24]

TZIMTZUM — CROSSING THE VOID

I reread what I have written. From the confusion of my beginnings, I see a pattern has emerged, and that I have been more or less following the traditional Jewish exegetical path of the four levels of interpretation: *peshat, remez, drash, sod*—from the literal, to the intertextual, to the homiletic. Rav Kook now leads me to the last level, *sod*, the *mystical*.

For is it only postmodernism that has taught us about ruptures, radical reinterpretation, alternative epistemologies and ontologies, the need for revealing a new face to the Torah? Wasn't that also the project of Kabbalah and Chassidut? As Arthur Green has argued, we err greatly by restricting study of Jewish responses to modernity only to the line of thinkers who came from and reacted to the heritage of German philosophy — figures such as Cohen, Buber, Rosenzweig, Levinas, Scholem, and others. Of course, Kabbalah and Chassidism played a key role in modernist Jewish revival — in Buber's retellings of the Chassidic tales, in Scholem's academic investigations of Jewish mysticism, and so forth. But as Edith Wyschogrod has pointed out, this was a Chassidism formed in the image of German romantic reaction to modernity. And it is time for a "postmodern reappropriation of Chassidic texts. One which understands their deep roots in kabalistic ways of thinking about God's withdrawals and absences, about fragmentation, shattering of the vessels, exile and repair."[25] For these are indeed tales and teachings which speak to a post-*shoah* world. Yet the discourse of Chassidism is all too often characterized as "pre-modern." Yehuda Mirsky makes a fine distinction when he says that thinkers like Rav Kook and the author of the *Sefat Emet*, spoke to the felt "experience of" modernity, although they did not speak the "language of" modernity.

It is interesting to me, Gene, that you use one of the fundamental kabbalistic metaphors, that of the *tzimtzum*, to describe one of your central "postmodern" moves:

I am setting forth the postmodern, yet rabbinic position that a determinedly self-reliant self can never become properly human. We need to have a certain realism about our limits if only so that we can appreciate how individuality implies community, not only with other people but with G-d. Acknowledging this would allow for a reverse *tzimtzum*, a sufficient contraction of our human self-importance that would leave room in our lives for our community and for God's presence.26

The *tzimtzum* is the kabbalistic notion of God's primordial self-contraction in order to open up a space, a void, *halal panui*, in which the finite universe could be created. (I find it interesting that the "Ari," Rav Isaac Luria developed this notion in sixteenth century Tzfat coincident with the rise of early modern Europe. The modernist focus on the self seems to here already have its postmodern counter-echo in the Ari.) I am using "postmodernism" here not only to specify a certain historical or cultural moment—which it is—but also a certain sensibility. The Vacated space of Kabbalah becomes for me another metaphor for modernity's shattering of the vessels, absence of God, withdrawal, fragmentation. A Jewish postmodernism would come to help repair those vessels, but recognize that can only be done by first inhabiting the cracks, ruptures, fissures. And that ultimate repair belongs to a horizon beyond all our conceptual systems.

You, too, propose a "reverse *tzimtzum*" as a necessary step for that *tikkun*, an emptying out of the self on the model of God's emptying out of himself in order to create a world. What, then, is the content of that self? Or as we might ask in contemporary literary theory, "How is subjectivity constructed?" A Chassidic interpretation notes that the letters that compose the Hebrew word for "I" [אני] *aleph, nun, yud*, when rearranged, spell "nothingness" [עין] *ayin, yud, nun*. If modernism gazes into the self and finds an abyss that terrifies, postmodernism accepts with equanimity that lack and seeks to turn that void inside out, so to speak. To cross and recross it. Without the voice of God, though, that emptied, contracted self can become the cynical laugh of a character from Beckett or a self trying to fill itself through games of power and sexuality as in Foucault. But if Divine selfhood is itself manifested in *tzimtzum*, self-contraction, then the void becomes the source of ethics, an emptying out of self to give to the other.

Among those Chassidic masters who knew how to inhabit that void, spoke from it, and tried to cross and recross, was the inimitable Rabbi Nachman of Breslov. As I move here to the level of *sod*, the "mystical" meaning, I find myself again dealing with those same texts about Exodus and Sinai that have been presenting themselves to me throughout my meditation. Rabbi Nachman has an extraordinary teaching in his *Likktuei Moharan*, #64 on *"Bo el Paroah."* God tells Moses in Exodus 10:1–3, 24: "Come to Pharaoh, for I have hardened his heart and his servants' hearts, so that I may place these, my signs, in their midst; and that you may tell your son and your son's son how I made sport of Egypt, and my signs that I performed among them; that you may know that I am God." Rabbi Nachman's exposition is quite complex, and I can here give only a small piece of it. He interprets the word "Pharaoh" to refer precisely to the Vacated space, the *halal* created by the *tzimtzum*. The word *paroh* [פרעה], he says, comes a from a root meaning "annihilation" and "removal" as in Exodus 5:4, where the Pharaoh says to Moses "You have removed *(tafriu)* the people from their work." And it is also related to the root meaning "uncovering and revealing."

So, says Rabbi Nachman, in the Vacated space, from which God has withdrawn, there arise all the philosophical questions which have no answer, which pain, and confuse us . . . and in which our hearts become hardened. But Rabbi Nachman then interprets the name *"Hebrew"* [עברי]—*ivri*—in a reparative sense as coming from the root *iver* [עבר]. In this sense, it means "to cross over, or ford some space," thus signifying that the Jews, the Hebrews—*ivri'im*—have the task and power to cross the void created by the *tzimtzum*, the empty space where God is absent. And that is also why God is called in Exodus 5:3. "God of the Hebrews." The root also yields the word *ever* [עבר] meaning the "sides" of a river. In the Lurianic notion of the *tzimtzum*, the empty space is created by the image of God contracting his light to the "sides."

The notion of this Vacated space, an absence where there is also yet a presence of God, is an epistemological and ontological paradox, unsolvable in terms of human intellect. Needless to say, a postmodern world, a post-Shoah world, is one in which we seem to be in an empty place from which God is withdrawn and absent. Postmodernism in its deconstructive modes leads us right into this emptiness: this undoing of the notion of solid being, this vision of flickering presence in absence. The key question is, How do we find God there? Rabbi Nachman reminds us that somehow God is still "there" in the void ; for without some trace of the divine creative power to give it "life," even the Void could not exist. This, too, is a paradox unresolvable through human reason. For Rabbi Nachman, only the great *tzaddikim*, the most holy and righteous ones, can fully enter that Void and cross over without falling into confusion, doubt, and heresy. And so, Moses has to *come to Pharaoh, to the place* where God cannot be found, to ford the void, cross to the other side.

In the confusion of the Vacated space, there is silence, a level of thought that is beyond words. And this silence is the meaning of Moses' experience as related in the Talmud, *Menachot 29b*, in the story of Moses' anachronistically witnessing a vision of the death of Rabi Akiva and questioning God in anguish: "Is this the Torah and its reward?" The response: "Be silent, so it was conceived in thought." Moses, as he describes himself in Exodus 4:10, is *chvad peh u-chavad lashon*, "slow of speech and slow of tongue." In Rabbi Nachman's interpretation, this relates to the level of silence beyond speech. It is a kind of silence necessary to be able to "Come to Pharaoh," to come into the Vacated space. For he has to find in that space the traces, the signs, the letters, the fragments that will enable creation. And this, too, is the task and power of Israel, the *Ivri'im*, who through their *emunah*, their faith, cross the void. On this level, beyond speech, Moses comes to song, for every form of wisdom according to Rabbi Nachman has its own song and melody. And the song of *emunah* that crosses the Vacated space is the meaning of the Song Moses sings in Exodus 15 after the Jews crossed the Red Sea.

And here Rabbi Nachman gives an extraordinary interpretation of *machloket*—dispute, argument, rabbinic debate—which he says, enacts the same process of Creation. In the *tzimtzum*, God withdraws light to the sides and creates the Vacant space; only in this way can a finite creation occur without being absorbed and nullified by God's infinite light. Similarly, through dispute, the sages separate and "go to the sides," forming a Vacated space. The words of their disputes then enter this space and become part of the act of Creation. Rabbi Nachman's "prooftext" is a creative re-reading of Isaiah 51:16: "I have placed my words in your mouth . . . that I may plant the heavens and lay the foundations of the earth, and say to Zion you are my people *ami* [עמי]." The Zohar (introduction 5a) says, "Read the word not as *ami* "my people" but *imi* "with me," meaning to be a collaborator with Me; just as I can create heaven and earth through my Words, so can you."

WHERE DOES IT ALL LEAD

Rabbi Nachman's ideas on debate, language, song, silence, Vacated space take up all the themes I have been preoccupied with in my meditation. I look back and see that I have been arguing for the need for postmodern Jewish thought to reconstruct the shattered vessels of authority, *halakhah*, faith. It often happens that friends and readers of my academic work are surprised when they hear me speak in these terms. They assume that a person who wrote books about deconstruction and who is a contemporary Jewish woman would seek to "deconstruct *halakhah*," or practice the "hermeneutics of suspicion," and write critiques of modern Judaism in terms of gender, class, race, not quote Rabbi Nachman or argue that Chassidut is postmodern. The academic forms of postmodernism I encounter in contemporary literary and cultural theory generally value "transgression, subversion, interrogation"; these, too, are moves into the Vacated space, ways of clearing space, but they do not take that next step; they do not help me cross the Void, give me a song.

So how, I ask myself, is the way in which I quote and learn from Rabbi Nachman different from that of a "pre-modern" reader? In the end, I find all these labels ill-fitting and outmoded: "Orthodox/non-Orthodox; *Halakhah/Aggadah;* Heteronomy/Autonomy." The postmodern sensibility is skeptical of Grand Ideologies, and to use its jargon, "essentialist identities." "History" itself is no longer seen as a unitary, progressive, linear narrative, but a shifting constellation of relations between past and present, events and their interpretations. All the great totalizing systems of the nineteenth century have broken apart: Communism, Socialism, even Zionism. (I am amused to read that in China today, the weekly *Computer News* sells more copies than the *People's Daily*, the mouthpiece of the Communist Party.) Yet in contemporary culture, the dissolution of Grand Ideology has also engendered a severe backlash, a regression to the most primitive forms of ethnic and nationalist self-assertion, untouched by any postmodern ironic self-consciousness or epistemological skepticism.

So let me rephrase my question to myself: With what accent or intonation does a postmodern speak? What is the song? An accent is a certain pattern of stress in the sound of the voice. A sound that gives the voice a different melody, a different rhythm. The postmodern accent may place its stresses more on points of rupture and try to construct its melody out of fragments and pieces; it, too, is self-contracted. For Rabbi Nachman, only those of the stature of Moses, the paradigm of the great *tzaddik*, could safely enter the Void. But we ordinary postmodern Jews have already been thrust into it. Each of us is also called to "come to Pharaoh"; and each of us is also "slow of speech" like Moses. We stutter in the Vacated space, yet we do not seek prematurely to fill or negate it. Nevertheless, we need to remember that we are *Ivriim*, that we must cross and re-cross that void. We do so not only with the complex words of our academic debates and disputes, but also with our silence and our *emunah*. For there is something of the "pre-modern" in both of us, Gene: in the way we both understand that there is indeed a wisdom of faith in Israel, in a certain song and melody beyond words. How else can one articulate the *En Sof*, the endless Infinite One beyond all representation, ideology, who somehow yet surrounds the world, and can be traced in the Vacant space?

So I deeply respond to those moments in your book when you speak of your *emunah* in simple terms. And to the conditions in which it was sparked . . . a moment in a Manhattan fast food restaurant when the *halakhic* prescription to saying a blessing over a sandwich causes a flickering transfiguration of a mundane reality.[27] As you write:

> As an adult, I have been conscious of the Transcendent coming directly into my life. Sometimes it has been fairly clear and definite; mostly it has been general and unspecific; always, as I have reflected on it, it has been unspectacular and ordinary. Often my awareness has comes as a result of study, observance, prayer, or interaction with people; but mostly, my direct, personal exposure to Divinity has helped me grasp the spiritual depth of these somewhat indirect experiences rather than the other way around.[28]

And as you so eloquently say, an idea of God for Jews "must make a life with God possible . . . not just in their lives as members of corporate Israel but as individual Jews and persons as well. Life with God means a life of personal piety, in which we see all our experiences, our failures as well as our activism, in divine perspective. . . . It means a life of prayer in which we can speak to God out of the fullness of what we are and long for . . ."[29]

I also respond to the wish so poignantly expressed towards the end of your book: "High on my list of things I wish for in Jewish life today is the existence of Jews who regularly share ordinary intimacy with God. The simplicity of these encounters will refresh the appreciation of the genius of the prophets, psalmists, and other biblical authors whose spirituality could not borrow, as ours does, from the prior experience of millennia."[30] So now I ask myself, after all the time and energy I have spent writing this, how do all these issues, finally, relate to *amcha*? To the mass of our fellow Jews who have never read Cohen, Derrida, Levinas, Rosenzweig, Buber, or heard of Deconstruction, or post-Zionism or Shevirat Ha-Kelim? And to the mass of non-Jews, who as you rightly point out, also have the covenant of Noah with God?

I am struck forcefully by the great "spiritual thirst" in American culture. I see it in my students, the adults I teach in Jewish education classes, even in the bestseller lists. I see and hear it almost everywhere, in quite unexpected and startling everyday encounters. I go pick up a package at the front desk of my apartment building and engage the African-American woman who works there in a casual conversation. I know she lives with her ailing mother and ask how her mother's diabetes is, and somehow she begins talking to me about how throughout all her own hardships, she has "learned to trust God, that even in what seems to be the darkness, God is there." I go to my health club and see the soft-spoken fiftyish, carefully coifed and made up blonde woman with the Texas accent who has recently started working out. I have had a few casual conversations with her and I try to persuade her not to drive herself so hard in her workouts since she does not seem to be enjoying them. "You're a very determined person, I see. You don't give up." She responds, "That is the only way I've gotten through the hard times." She tells me of a husband who left after thirty-seven years of marriage and a son who died of brain cancer at the age of ten. Her face is pained; suddenly she says, "God got me through it. It's only in the desert that you find out what you are made of, not on the mountaintop." And she tells me how she begins her day reading the Bible, how much that helps her.

I have similar unexpected encounters with the hairdresser, the boutique manager, the taxicab driver, the secretary in my office. These are all non-Jews; their sense of God is strong and intimate, something many of my Jewish friends, even the learned ones, lack. I learn much from these people, as much as I learn from my academic colleagues who are engaged in talk about epistemological skepticism and bent on "demystifying" and "unmasking" oppressive ideologies. I do not consider the people I encounter in my daily rounds mystified, or oppressed. Each of them crosses their own void.

Today, people are looking desperately for God and for a communal and personal expression of that connection. We jostle against one another in this postmodern, multicultural world, which is secular only on the surface. This is what "fundamentalists" do not understand; they are still fighting a "modernity" that has already exhausted itself. But "postmodern" thinkers also need to be equally carefully not to negate the deep spiritual resources in what seems to be "pre-modern" but is only so on the surface. The Divine light is refracted through many prisms. And any postmodern Jewish thought must be able to address common human experiences of pain, loneliness, confusion, yearning, sorrow. A postmodern Judaism must be open to the voice of the other.

Two years ago, when I was on sabbatical in Jerusalem waiting at a bus stop in one of the more religious neighborhoods, a young boy of about eight, dressed in black, with peyot and yarmulke saw me reading an Israeli secular newspaper. "*Asur*" he said to me (Forbidden). He had been taught that the world "outside" was threatening, profane, forbidden. We take this to be a "pre-modern," fundamentalist attitude. At first, I was rather irritated; then I thought about it some more and remembered one of my favorite quotes from a famous writer whose life encompassed the breakdown of the traditional Eastern-European world of Jewish piety in the late nineteenth century, and lived long through its aftermath: "In our home," wrote I. B. Singer, "the 'world' itself was *treif*. Many years were to pass before I began to sense how much sense there was in this attitude."

CONCLUSION

R. Yohanan said: "Anyone who reads without a melody or repeats Mishnah without a song, of him Scripture says. 'And also I have given them bitter laws.'"[31] *Megillah 32a*

Hezekiah should have been the Messiah, but since he did not say *shira* after he had been miraculously saved, he was not worthy to be the Messiah. *Sanhedrin 94a*

A song for the Sabbath day.
It is good to thank God
and to sing praise to your Name, Most high
To proclaim Your kindness at daybreak,
and your faithfulness each night.
Upon a ten-stringed instrument and lute
in meditation *[higayyon]* upon the harp.32

But only in the Torah of God is his desire,
And in his Torah he meditates *[yehegeh]* day and night.33

Rava said that at the beginning of this verse, the Torah was called after the name of the Holy One Blessed be He [Torah of God]. But at the end of the verse, it is called "his Torah," that is, after the name of the student who has studied it.34

This, then, is my Torah. I wanted my *hagut*, my "meditation" to fully comprehend all the subtle senses and interconnections of the Hebrew word: to connect the head to the mouth, logic to liturgy, speech to song, thought to prayers. But how could I do all that in a written essay? I would have had to write a *midrash*, or a prayer, or like Rabbi Nachman compose a *niggun* or a tale.

For, finally, to write an essay is to have an audience. But an audience is not the same thing as a community. Jewish reading comes out of Jewish being together and that means so many things. Among them, the doing of *mitzvoth* together, and the singing of the *davenning* together, and the eating of the Sabbath and holiday meals together . . . the consolations of friends in times of trouble, and the exultation of friends in times of joy.

Universities call themselves "communities," but they are so only in a very superficial sense. Our academic discourse, even our sophisticated postmodern theories of discourse are so soundless, missing so many dimensions of language. Phillis Levin, a colleague and distinguished poet, once told my students that reading a poem out loud and hearing the rhythm are often what give you the understanding of the things you can't figure out. Perhaps this is also what Rosenzweig understood so well with his claim that the Song of Songs is the focal book of revelation. The "meanings" of a song cannot be gotten just from reading the lyrics on the page; they are often flat and senseless; one has to hear the song performed; meaning comes as much from the rhythms, the crying out of the singer, the *kriyah*.

The *halakhot* of writing *shira* (song) as part of a sacred text such as a *sefer Torah* require that the *shiroth* be written with large spaces between the phrases. Every phrase is distanced from another by a certain kind of space, "a space on top of a brick" as the Talmud describes it. For every phrase written, one leaves a blank space parallel to it. These blanks take me back to the *halal*, the Vacated space: the place where our frameworks, conceptions, ontologies, epistemologies, all our "isms" fail us. These are the gaps, the blanks, the fissures we live with in a postmodern world. We bridge them only with a certain kind of *emunah*, or we at least imagine what crossing and recrossing those spaces might be, if only in the sounds without words. The Hebrew root for *emunah, aleph, mem, nun* [אמן] signifies "confidence, trust," and in the verbal forms, can mean "to train or educate" "foster, nurse, bring up"; in the noun forms, *aman* means artist; *uman* "craftsman." This philology teaches us that *emunah*, faith, is also not "blind"; it is a craft, a skill and it needs to be educated, trained, nursed.

Academic systems of thought and theories of discourse come and go . . . and fairly quickly. There will, no doubt, soon be a "post-postmodernism," which will probably be called the "New . . . *X*." (The eminent literary and cultural theorist, Frederic Jameson, has already announced that we are beyond "postmodernism.") And the blindnesses of our own work will be incisively analyzed by those who will come later, in the same way that we at present critique the blindnesses of "modernist" thought. I think you sense this as much as I, Gene. Your own postmodernism, like mine, is provisional and instrumental; may we both continue to sanctify it in the service of renewing the Jewish people's Covenant with God.

The following story is told of the Rebbe of Mezritch: A stranger once came and knocked on his front door. The Rebbe asked, "Who is there?" The response was, "I." The Rebbe was shocked that a Jew could utter "I" so easily. "'I'? How can you say such a thing?" The Rebbe opened the door and invited the stranger inside. He asked if he had eaten yet and, upon receiving an answer in the negative, told the guest, "Go to such-and-such a place, a certain distance from here, and eat there." Since the Rebbe had instructed him thus, the Jew went on his way. The road was long and tiring, and he walked and walked, becoming covered with dust along the way. After a hard journey he arrived at the place, filthy and exhausted. A wedding was just about to begin in the village and, as was the custom, a festive meal was offered at the site for the poor. The man joined the poor guests and ate with them. At the end of the meal it was discovered that a silver spoon was missing. Immediately, all suspicion was focused on this Jew, since he was the only stranger, and everyone turned to him accusingly: "You stole !" The Jew replied, "Not I!" They continued to torment him and accuse him, and he steadfastly repeated, "Not I! Not I!" Eventually he managed to escape from them, and started his journey back towards the Rebbe, wondering all the way what the Rebbe's reason could have been for sending him to that place. He arrived at the Rebbe's house, knocked on the door, and once again the Rebbe asked, "Who is there?" The Jew was about to answer "I," as he had been accustomed to do, but suddenly he caught himself and answered, "Not I." Only through suffering and pain had the message penetrated his consciousness—now he knew that he was "not I." There is only one "I"—and that is . . .

NOTES

1. Eugene B. Borowitz, *Renewing the Covenant: A Theology for the Postmodern Jew* (Philadelphia: Jewish Publication Society), p. 301.
2. E.g.: Isa. 31; 33:18; 38:14; 90:9 ; Ps. 19:15; 37:30; 35:28; 63:5,7; 71:24; 77:13; 92:3,4; 115:7; see Rashi on Josh. 1:8–9;Ps.1:2; 63:7; 37:30.
3. *Berachot* 20b; *Eruvin* 54a; *Shulkhan Aruch* Ha-Rav,Orach Chayim 62:3.
4. Referring to P. Ochs, "Compassionate Postmodernism: An Introduction to Rabbinic Semiotics," *Soundings* 76.1 (Spring, 1993): 139–52.
5. Borowitz, *Renewing the Covenant*, p. 44.
6. Franz Rosenzweig, *The Star of Redemption*, 2nd ed. 1930, Trans. William Hallo (Indiana: Notre Dame University Press, 1985), p. 176.
7. Peter Pitzele, *Our Father's Wells: A Personal Encounter with the Myth of Genesis* (New York: Harper San Francisco, 1995), pp. 90–91.
8. Ex. 19:17.
9. Esth. 9:27.
10. Emmanuel Levinas, "The Temptation of Temptation," in *Nine Talmudic Readings*, trans. Annette Aronowicz (Bloomington and Indianapolis: Indiana University Press, 1990), pp. 30–50.

11. Ex. 24:7

12. Borowitz, *Renewing the Covenant*, p. 287.

13. Parker Palmer, *To Know as We Are Known: Education as a Spiritual Journey* (San Francisco: Harper San Francisco, 1930), pp. 67–68.

14. Ibid., p. 31.

15. Borowitz, *Renewing the Covenant*, pp. 273–74.

16. Ex. 24:7

17. Palmer, *To Know as We Are Known*, p. 69.

18. Ibid., p. 287.

19. Josh. 1:8

20. Levinas, "The Temptation of Temptation," pp. 46–47.

21. *Berachot* 7b.

22. Ibid.

23. Ibid., 62a.

24. Rav Avraham Isaac Kook, "The Moral Principles," in *Abraham Isaac Kook: The Lights of Penitence, The Moral Principles, Lights of Holiness, Essays, Letters, and Poems*, trans., Ben Zion Bokser (New York: Paulist Press, 1978), p. 148.

25. Edith Wyschogrod, "Hasidism, Hellenism, Holocaust," in *Interpreting Judaism in a Postmodern Age*, ed. S. Kepnes (New York: New York University Press, 1996), pp. 301, 318.

26. Borowitz, *Renewing the Covenant*, p. 168.

27. Ibid., pp. 111–12.

28. Ibid., p. 266.

29. Ibid., p. 60.

30. Ibid., p. 283.

31. Ez. 20:25.

32. Ps. 92:1–4.

33. Ps. 1:2.

34. *Avodah Zarah* 19a.

Bibliography

Baeck, Leo. *The Essence of Judaism.* Translated into English by V. Grubenwieser and L. Pearl. New York: Schocken Books, 1948.

Banon, David. *La Lecture Infinie, Les Voies de l'Interprétation Midrachique.* Paris: Éditions du Seuil, 1987.

Borowitz, Eugene B. *A Layman's Guide to Religious Existentialism.* Philadelphia: The Westminister Press, 1965.

———. *A New Jewish Theology in the Making.* Philadelphia: The Westminster Press, 1968.

———. *Choices in Modern Jewish Thought, A Partisan Guide.* New York: Behrman House, 1983.

———. *Choices in Modern Jewish Thought, A Partisan Guide.* 2d ed. West Orange, NJ: Behrman House, 1995.

———. *Choosing a Sex Ethic, a Jewish Inquiry.* New York: Schocken Books, 1968.

———. *Exploring Jewish Ethics, Papers on Covenant Responsibility.* Detroit: Wayne State University, 1990.

———. "How a Discipline Became Established," *CCAR Journal* (Spring 1997): 66.

———. *How Can a Jew Speak of Faith Today?* Philadelphia: The Westminster Press, 1969.

———. *Liberal Judaism.* New York: UAHC, 1984.

———. "Matters of Degree and Kind." *Conservative Judaism.* Vol. L, No. 1. (Fall 1997).

———. *Our Way to a Postmodern Judaism: Three Lectures.* San Francisco: University of San Francisco, Swig Dept. of Jewish Studies, 1992.

———. *Renewing the Covenant: A Theology for the Postmodern Jew.* Philadelphia: Jewish Publication Society, 1991.

———. "The Reform Judaism of Renewing the Covenant." *Conservative Judaism.* Vol. L, No. 1. (Fall 1997).

———. "What Is Reform Religious Zionism?" *Journal of Reform Zionism.* Vol. II. (March 1995): 24–30.

——. "Zionism and Reform Judaism: a Theological Reassessment." *Journal of Reform Zionism*. Vol. 1, No. 1. (March 1993): 44–50.

Boyarin, Daniel. *Intertexuality and the Reading of Midrash*. Bloomington: Indiana University Press, 1990.

Buber, Martin. *I and Thou*. Translated by W. Kaufmann. New York: Scribner, 1970.

Cohen, Hermann. *Religion of Reason Out of the Sources of Judaism*. Translated by S. Kaplan. New York: F. Ungar Pub. Co., 1972.

Dorf, Elliot. "Autonomy *vs.* Community, The Ongoing Reform/Conservative "Difference." *Conservative Judaism*, Vol. XLVIII, No. 2. (Winter 1996): 64–68.

Elazar, Daniel J. *Authority, Power and Leadership in the Jewish Polity*. Lanham: University Press of America, 1991.

——. *Federalism as Grand Design: Political Philosophers and the Federal Principle*. Lanham: University Press of America, 1987.

Elazar, Daniel J. and Stuart Cohen. *The Jewish Polity: Jewish Political Organization from Biblical Times to the Present*. Bloomington: Indiana University Press, 1985.

Ellenson, David. "Eugene B. Borowitz: A Tribute on the Occasion of His 70th Birthday." *Jewish Book Annual*, vol. 51 (1993–94): 125–136.

Fackenheim, Emil. *To Mend the World*. New York: Schocken Books, 1982.

——. *To Mend the World*. 2d ed. Bloomington: Indiana University Press, 1994.

Faur, Jose. "Sanchez' Critique of *Authoritas*: Converso Skepticism and the Emergence of Radical Hermeneutics." In *The Return to Scripture in Judaism and Christianity: Essays in Postcritical Scriptural Interpretation*. Edited by Peter Ochs. Mahwah, N.J.: Paulist Press, 1993.

——. *Golden Doves with Silver Dots, Semiotics and Textuality in Rabbinic Tradition*. Bloomington: Indiana University Press, 1986.

——. "Understanding the Covenant." *Tradition* 9 (1968): 42.

Fishbane, Michael. *The Garments of Torah, Essays in Biblical Hermeneutics*. Bloomington: Indiana University Press, 1989.

Fraade, Steven. *From Tradition to Commentary, Torah and Its Interpretation in the Midrash Sifre to Deuteronomy*. Albany: State University of New York Press, 1991.

Frei, Hans. "The 'Literal Reading' of Biblical Narrative in the Christian Tradition: Does It Stretch or Will It Break?" *The Bible and the Narrative Tradition*. Edited by Frank McConnell. New York: Oxford University Press, 1986.

Gibbs, Robert. *Correlations in Rosenzweig and Levinas*. Princeton: Princeton University Press, 1992.

Gillman, Neil. *Sacred Fragments: Recovering Theology for the Modern Jew*. Philadelphia: The Jewish Publication Society, 1990.

Greenberg, Simon. "Coherence and Change in the Rabbinic Universe of Discourse: Kadushin's Theory of the Value Concept." *Understanding the Rabbinic Mind, Essays on the Hermeneutic of Max Kadushin*. Edited by Peter Ochs. Atlanta: Scholars Press for South Florida Studies in the History of Judaism, 1990.

Griffin, David Ray, et al. *Founders of the Postmodern Vision*. Albany: State University of New York Press, 1993.

Griffin, David Ray, and Sandra Lubarsky. *Jewish Theology and Process Thought*. Albany: State University of New York Press, 1996.

Haas, Peter. "A Symposium on Borowitz' *Renewing the Covenant*." *Sh'ma* 22/426, 24 January 1992.

Habermas, Jürgen. "Modernity versus Postmodernity." *New German Critique* 22 (1981): 9.

———. *The Theory of Communicative Action 1*. Translated by T. McCarthy. Boston: Beacon Press, 1984.

Halivni, David Weiss. "On Man's Role in Revelation." *From Ancient Israel to Modern Judaism, Intellect in Quest of Understanding: Esssays in Honor of Marvin Fox*. Edited by Nahum Sarna. Atlanta: Scholars Press for Brown Judaica, 1990.

Handelman, Susan. *The Slayers of Moses, The Emergence of Rabbinic Interpretation in Modern Literary Theory*. Albany: State University of New York Press, 1982.

Hauerwas, Stanley. *A Community of Character: Toward a Constructive Christian Social Ethic*. Indiana: Notre Dame University Press, 1981.

———. *Christian Existence Today, Essays on Church, World, and Living In Between*. Durham, NC: The Labyrinth Press, 1988.

Heschel, Abraham Joshua. *The Prophets*. Philadelphia: Harper & Row, 1962.

———. *God in Search of Man*. Philadelphia: Jewish Publication Society, 1956.

Jabès, Edmond. *Le Livre des Questions*. Paris: Gallimard, 1963.

Kadushin, Max. *The Rabbinic Mind*. 3rd ed. New York: Bloch, 1972.

Kripke, Saul A. *Naming and Necessity*. Cambridge, Mass.: Harvard University Press, 1972.

Kristeva, Julia. "Revolution in Poetic Language." *The Kristeva Reader*. Edited by Toril Moi. New York: Columbia University Press, 1986.

Kushner, Lawrence. *Honey from the Rock*. San Francisco: Harper and Row, 1977.

———. *The River of Light*. Chappaqua: Rossel Books, 1981.

Lieberman, Saul. *Hellenism in Jewish Palestine*. 2nd imp. ed. New York: Jewish Theological Seminary of America, 1962.

Lindbeck, George. *The Nature of Doctrine, Religion and Theology in a Postliberal Age*. Philadelphia: Westminster Press, 1984.

Lyotard, Jean-François. *La Condition postmoderne, rapport sur le savoir*. Paris: Les Éditions de Minuit, 1979.

——. *Le Différend*. Paris: Les Éditions de Minuit, 1983.

——. *Le Différend: Phrases in Dispute*. Translated by Georges Van Den Abeele. Minneapolis: University of Minneapolis Press, 1988.

——. *The Postmodern Condition: A Report on Knowledge*. Translated by Geoff Bennington and Brian Massumi. Minneapolis: University of Minnesota Press, 1984.

Marshall, Bruce. *Theology and Dialogue*. Notre Dame, Ind.: University of Notre Dame Press, 1990.

Novak, David. *The Election of Israel: The Idea of the Chosen People*. Cambridge: Cambridge University Press, 1995.

——. *Jewish-Christian Dialogue: A Jewish Justification*. New York: Oxford University Press, 1989.

——. *Jewish Social Ethics*. New York: Oxford University Press, 1992.

——. "Review of Renewing the Covenant." *SH'MA* (February 1992).

——. *Halakhah in a Theological Dimension*. Chico, Calif.: Scholars Press, 1985.

Ochs, Peter. "A Rabbinic Pragmatism." Edited by B. Marshall. *Theology and Dialogue*. Notre Dame, Ind.: University of Notre Dame Press, 1990.

——. "A Rabbinic Text Process Theology." *The Journal of Jewish Thought and Philosophy*. 1.1 (1991):141–179.

——. "Max Kadushin as Rabbinic Pragmatist." *Understanding the Rabbinic Mind*. Edited by Peter Ochs. Atlanta: Scholars Press, 165–196.

——. *Peirce, Pragmatism, and the Logic of Scripture*. Cambridge, Eng. : Cambridge University Press, 1998.

——. "Postcritical Scriptural Interpretation." *Torah and Revelation*. Edited by Dan Cohn-Sherbok. New York, Toronto: Edwin Mellen Press, 1992.

——. *Understanding the Rabbinic Mind*. Atlanta: Scholars Press for the University of South Florida, 1990.

Ogletree, Thomas. *Hospitality to the Stranger: Dimensions of Moral Understanding*. Philadelphia: Fortress Press, 1985.

——. "The Public Witness of the Christian Churches: Reflections Based Upon Ernst Troeltsch's *Social Teaching of the Christian Churches*." *The Annual of the Society of Christian Ethics*. Washington D.C.: Georgetown University Press, 1992.

——. *The Use of the Bible in Christian Ethics*. Philadelphia: Fortress Press, 1983.

Ouaknin, Marc-Alain. *Concerto Pour Quatre Consonnes Sans Voyelles, Au-delà du Principe d'Identité*. Paris: Éditions Balland, 1991.

Peirce, Charles. *Collected Papers of Charles Sanders Peirce, Vol. 5*. Edited by Charles Harteshorne and Paul Weiss. Cambridge, Mass.: Harvard University Press, 1934.

Plaskow, Judith. *Standing Again at Sinai*. San Francisco: Harper and Row, 1990.

Putnam, Hilary. *Meaning and the Moral Sciences*. London: Routledge and Kegan Paul, 1978.

Reat, N. Ross and Edmund F. Perry. *A World Theology: The Central Spiritual Reality of Humankind.* Cambridge: Cambridge University Press, 1991.

Robbins, Jill. *Prodigal Son, Elder Brother: Interpretation and Alterity in Augustine, Petrarch, Kafka, Levinas.* Chicago: University of Chicago Press, 1991.

Roitman, Betty. "Sacred Language and Open Text." *Midrash and Literature.* Edited by Geoffrey Hartman and Sanford Budick. New Haven: Yale University Press, 1986.

Rosenzweig, Franz. *On Jewish Learning.* Translated by W. Wolf. New York: Schocken Books, 1965.

———. *The Star of Redemption.* Translated W. W. Hallo. New York: Holt, Rinehart, and Winston, 1970.

Rubenstein, Richard L. *After Auschwitz.* 2d ed. Baltimore: Johns Hopkins University Press, 1992.

Samuelson, Norbert. *Judaism and the Doctrine of Creation.* Cambridge, Eng.: Cambridge University Press, 1994.

Schwartz, Francie, and Eugene B. Borowitz. *The Jewish Moral Values.* New York and Philadelphia: The Jewish Publication Society, 1999.

Schwarzschild, Stephen. *The Pursuit of the Ideal.* Edited by Menachem Kellner. Albany: State University of New York Press, 1990.

Seeskin, Kenneth. *Jewish Philosophy in a Secular Age.* Albany: State University of New York Press, 1990.

Scott, Joan W. "The Evidence of Experience." *Critical Inquiry* 17 (1991): 773–797.

Umansky, Ellen. "Females, Feminists, and Feminism: A Review of the Recent Literature on Jewish Feminism and the Creation of a Feminist Judaism." *Feminist Studies* 14. No. 2. (Summer 1988).

Wittgenstein, Ludwig. *Philosophical Investigations.* 2nd ed. Translated by G. E. M. Anscombe. New York: Macmillan, 1958.

Wyschogrod, Edith. "Trends in Postmodern Judaism Philosophy," *Soundings* 76, No. 1 (Spring 1993): 129–138.

———. "Works That 'Faith': The Grammar of Ethics in Judaism." *Cross Currents.* 40.2 (1990): 176–193.

Wyschogrod, Michael. *The Body of Faith, God in the People Israel.* San Francisco: Harper and Row, 1983.

Index

différance, 124; différend, 67, 122
displacement, 123, 124
Dorff, Elliot, 93, 148, 169n
Durkheim, Emile, 86

Elazar, Daniel J., 101, 107n
Ellenson, David, viii, 32n, 34n
Emancipation, 13, 14, 15, 17, 23, 27, 62
Enlightenment, 14, 15, 18, 24, 25, 27, 51, 52,
    66, 67, 69, 71, 74, 75, 79, 83, 102, 112,
    113, 160, 178
ethic(s) 13, 15, 19, 24, 64, 65, 75, 168, 178ff
existentialism, ix, 4, 10, 17, 24, 25, 37, 52–
    55, 61, 62, 66, 72, 81, 82, 99, 121, 150, 177

Fackenheim, Emil, 56, 59, 63, 93, 103n,
    104n, 170n, 178
Faur, José, 33n, 88n, 141n
feminism/Feminist studies, 4, 19, 104n, 165
Feuerbach, Ludwig, 42, 86
Fonrobert, Charlotte, 34n
Foucault, Michel, 9, 10, 66, 177, 190
foundationalism, 7, 8, 11, 12, 38, 123, 127,
    129, 130, 131, 132; epistemological, 6, 102
Frei, Hans, 12, 127, 143n
Freud, 86, 89n
Freundel, Rabbi Barry, 182, 183
    fundamentalisms, fundamentalist, 37,
    41, 53, 73, 87, 127, 149, 188, 196; literal-
    ism, 87, 164

Geertz, Clifford, 12
Gibbs, Robert, 33n, 144n
Gillman, Neil, 92, 93, 103n
Green, Arthur E., 93, 189
Greenberg, Irving, 56, 93, 104n
Greenberg, Simon, 140n
Greenberg, Yudit, 31, 32, 34n, 114, 116–123,
    146, 152, 153, 159, 160, 163, 177
Griffin, David Ray, 143n, 144n

Haas, Peter, 34n, 113, 140n, 144n
Habermas, Jürgen, 15, 33n, 90n

halakhah/halakhic, 14, 16, 50, 51, 55, 59, 66,
    71, 77, 82, 86, 90n, 94, 115, 116, 120, 123,
    140n, 147, 154, 158, 165, 166, 168, 169,
    178, 181, 188, 193, 194
Harteshorne, Charles, 11
Hartman, David, 93
Halivni, David Weiss, 120, 140n
Handelman, Susan, 142n
Hauerwaus, Stanley, 75, 80n, 143n
Hegel, Georg, 24, 82, 93, 105n
Heschel, Abraham Joshua, 52, 53, 61, 62,
    63, 88n, 93, 104n, 105n, 114, 148, 151,
    169n, 177
hermeneutic(s), 25, 26, 140
Hobbes, 88n
Holocaust (*Shoah*), vii, 4, 7, 8, 19, 20, 31,
    41, 42, 44, 56, 58, 59, 62, 63, 74, 93,
    104n, 146, 160, 161, 177; Auschwitz, 64,
    67; Nazism, 42, 74; post-Holocaust, 22,
    31, 41, 56, 58, 62, 160; Treblinka, 64

imperialism, 9, 127
individualism, 6, 7, 11, 14, 17, 27, 40, 55,
    100, 126, 132; individual rights, 6
Irigaray, Luce, 10
Israel (people and place), 13, 15–17, 40, 43,
    51, 57–68, 77, 81–87, 99, 113, 123–125,
    136, 137, 146–150, 154–156, 160–163,
    175, 183, 188, 194; Israeli Six Day War,
    42, 56, 63; Israelites, 129, 180; State of
    Israel, 43, 55, 56, 58, 59, 161–163, 183

James, William, 10, 105n, 114
Jefferson, Thomas, 101
Judaism, Association of Jewish Studies, 92;
    Conservative: 21, 166, 169n; Hasidic, 25,
    189, 190; kabbalistic, 63, 190; liberal, vii,
    4, 5, 13, 16, 19, 22, 25, 49–51, 61, 62; 86–
    87, 99–102; modern, 13, 16, 17, 19, 27,
    28, 29, 30, 44; neo-Orthodox, 10, 21;
    non-Orthodox, 13, 23, 33n, 36, 41, 43,
    44, 70, 72, 94, 99, 115, 146, 148, 149, 155,
    157; Orthodox, 19, 21, 22, 41, 43, 44, 49–

Index of Biblical and Rabbinic Sources

RABBINIC SOURCES